Everyday People

Understanding the Rise of Trump Supporters

Robert Hartmann McNamara

ROWMAN & LITTLEFIELD
Lanham • Boulder • New York • London

Senior Acquisitions Editor: Alyssa Palazzo
Assistant Acquisitions Editor: Samantha Delwarte
Sales and Marketing Inquiries: textbooks@rowman.com
Credits and acknowledgments for material borrowed from other sources, and reproduced
with permission, appear on the appropriate pages within the text.
Published by Rowman & Littlefield
An imprint of The Rowman & Littlefield Publishing Group, Inc.
4501 Forbes Boulevard, Suite 200, Lanham, Maryland 20706
www.rowman.com

86-90 Paul Street, London EC2A 4NE United Kingdom

British Library Cataloguing in Publication Information Available

Library of Congress Cataloging-in-Publication Data

Names: McNamara, Robert Hartmann, author.
Title: Everyday people : understanding the rise of Trump supporters / Robert Hartmann
    McNamara.
Description: Lanham : Rowman & Littlefield, [2024] | Includes bibliographical
    references and index. | Summary: "Offers an empirical assessment of Trump followers
    and their links to extremist views and perspectives as well as a broader explanation of
    why such groups have become so popular"— Provided by publisher.
Identifiers: LCCN 2023003814 (print) | LCCN 2023003815 (ebook) | ISBN
    9781538180662 (cloth) | ISBN 9781538180679 (paperback) | ISBN
    9781538180686 (epub)
Subjects: LCSH: Right-wing extremists—United States. | Political Culture—United
    States. | Polarization (Social sciences)—United States. | United States—Social
    conditions—21st century. | Trump, Donald, 1946–
Classification: LCC HN90.R3 M39 2024 (print) | LCC HN90.R3 (ebook) | DDC
    320.53—dc23/eng/20230502
LC record available at https://lccn.loc.gov/2023003814
LC ebook record available at https://lccn.loc.gov/2023003815

This book is dedicated to my godchildren, Elsie and Jonah Newton. In a world that seems to have far too many people who are selfish, greedy, angry, and hateful, I am grateful for and have been inspired by Elsie and Jonah's example of generosity, love, and kindness.

Contents

Preface

The idea for this book really came from many of my thoughtful friends, family, and colleagues. There are so many people I think are reasonable, thoughtful, logical, and rational, yet when the discussion of Trump emerged, I was surprised to hear the dialogue of support that consistently overlooked much of the behavior Trump exhibited. Sure, some said he was a jerk, but then they would spend a considerable amount of time defending him and his policies. Many of these people were devout Christians, so I was surprised to listen to them support and defend Trump's actions. This happened so frequently that I began to wonder if perhaps I had misunderstood much of what Trump had said or done. And it went beyond the stereotypical supporter, who might proudly wear "Let's Go Brandon" tee shirts, MAGA hats, or have Confederate flag stickers on their pickup trucks. These were friends and family, highly educated professionals, who are thoughtful and kind people.

I tend to shy away from debates and discussions about politics and religion, so this exploration took me out of my comfort zone. As I began to learn more, I felt as though there was something missing from the discussions about Trump and the people who support him. While some friends and colleagues expressed concern that writing a book about Trump would invite a lot of negative attention, with a few even commenting on concerns for my safety (as they point out, of the many things we are lacking in this country, there does not seem to be a shortage of crazy), this book isn't about supporting or bashing Trump.

There are plenty of books on the market that do that. Instead, I don't see this as a book about Trump at all—if anything, he was remarkably consistent in presenting himself in a certain way as president. What I found was that Trump and Trumpism is really a symptom of a much larger set of forces that are operating, and this project is really about what causes us to suspend rational thinking and to develop misguided loyalties. Fear and complacency also prevent us from accepting some less than flattering things about ourselves and the way we see and relate to others.

In the end, my hope is that the fear, anger, and selfishness that seem to personify our culture these days has not "trumped" our ability to find and see the goodness in others and to have compassion for those who need help. While I do not believe there are any accidents or mistakes—only lessons, examples, and opportunities to grow—we as a country appear to be experiencing a very painful and disturbing one about ourselves and our nature. My hope is that we remind ourselves of the courage it takes to admit when we are wrong and the integrity found in taking responsibility for our mistakes. In the process, we may finally get the kinds of politicians, media, and leaders we can be proud of and who actually reflect what is good in the world.

Acknowledgments

As anyone who has done it can attest, writing can be a very lonely and isolating experience. There are hours spent reading, thinking, and wondering about the information collected, trying to formulate some sort of sense of disparate information, and sometimes talking to others only biases what one reads. My own experiences with many books over the years has confirmed that much of the work can be difficult for this reason. Fortunately, I have had the benefit of enormously talented people in the publishing industry who have been supportive of my work and who offer insight that makes my work far better than anything I could produce on my own. People like Katie Stevens and Betty Chen at McGraw-Hill or Sherith Pankratz, Meg Botteon, and Steve Helba at Oxford University Press. Others include Debbie Carlvalko, a freelance editor, who has been a steady source of encouragement for many book ideas and who has given me much of her valuable time and expertise to clarify my ideas. I am also grateful for the opportunity to work with my current editor at Rowman & Littlefield, Alyssa Palazzo, who is marvelously gifted and has helped to clarify many of the ideas in this book. I have been blessed beyond imagination to have worked with all of these extraordinarily talented and kind people over the years.

There are also several colleagues to whom I owe a debt of thanks for their insight and observations about this project. This includes Brad Collins at The Citadel; Maria Shelley, an amazing and insightful friend and colleague for nearly three decades; and Charles Crawford at the University of Western Michigan. Thanks also goes to Deb Lowry of the University of Monetvallo, for her help with this project. Many thanks also go to colleagues with whom I have discussed the many issues found in this book. I am so grateful for those who have patiently listened to my ideas and offered their insight, regardless of how far-fetched they may have been. To all of you, and for those I have inadvertently omitted, I could not have had so many academic adventures without you.

Chapter 1

Trump, Election Fraud, and the Attack on the Capitol

It should have been a relatively routine, if not elaborate procedure. On January 6, 2021, in a joint session located in the House chamber, members of Congress were meeting to certify the election of Joe Biden as the forty-sixth president of the United States. This process is outlined in the US Constitution and, historically, it is a rather routine affair, although in the past there have been issues that have arisen about the counting of votes. Because of its importance, and because it provides an essential context of understanding for the remaining chapters of this book, particularly how Trump and his supporters responded to the election and the attack at the Capitol, it is worth describing the certification process in more detail.

The president, some members of Congress, and many Trump supporters have claimed that the election was "stolen" through fraud, suggesting that Trump actually won the election in a landslide. The fallout from the attack on the Capitol has resulted in a detailed investigation that remains ongoing, but evidence continues to reveal that there are many unanswered questions about the role Trump played in the effort to decertify the election in 2020. As we examine the process of certifying votes as well as the aftermath of the violence that ensued, we begin to see a profile of Trump supporters and how much of the behavior by the president is routinely ignored, denied, minimized, or even endorsed by his loyalists.

THE CERTIFYING OF VOTES

The founding fathers to the US Constitution were concerned about voter fraud, particularly as it related to the election of the president of the United States. They were also concerned that claims of fraud or deliberate attempts to influence the election outcome could occur. Because free and honest

1

elections are critical to the creation and functioning of a democracy, the founding fathers spent considerable time and energy including it in the US Constitution. In keeping with the principle of checks and balances, Article 2 of the US Constitution provides that each state appoints electors for president and vice president by state legislatures. Congress has determined that the "electors of President and Vice President shall be appointed, in each State" on Election Day, that is, the "Tuesday next after the first Monday in November" every fourth year.[1]

Safe Harbor Provision

Since 1887, Congress has put the responsibility for resolving presidential election challenges on the states, known as the *Safe Harbor provision*. Under federal law, if a state has made a controversial or disputed determination regarding the presidential election, as long as the procedure used to determine the electors occurred at least six days before the electors are to meet, the process is valid.

In addition to the selection of electors, the governor of each state is required by federal law to send to the archivist of the United States, by registered mail and under state seal, "a certificate of such ascertainment of the electors appointed," including the names and numbers of votes for each candidate running for president and vice president. The governor is also required to do this within a specified period of time. This meeting is designated on the first Monday after the second Wednesday in December. It is in this meeting that the electors cast their votes for president and vice president of the United States. Once they have cast their votes, each elector signs certificates of their votes. A day after this meeting, the electors forward by registered mail two certificates to the archivist of the United States and one certificate to the federal judge in the district where the electors have met.[2]

At the first meeting of Congress, the archivist of the United States transmits every certificate received from the governors of each state to both houses of Congress. The date for counting the electoral votes is fixed by law as January 6 following each presidential election. Once received by Congress, a joint session of the Senate and the House of Representatives meets in the House chamber. The joint session convenes at 1:00 p.m. on that day. The president of the Senate is the presiding officer.[3]

Tellers and Counting of Votes

The president of the Senate opens and presents the certificates of the electoral votes of the states and the District of Columbia in alphabetical order.

The certificate from each state and the District of Columbia is read by *tellers* previously appointed from among the membership of the House and Senate. After the votes of each state and the District of Columbia have been read, the tellers record and count them. When this process has been completed, the presiding officer announces whether any candidates have received the required majority votes for president and vice president. If so, that "announcement shall be deemed a sufficient declaration of the persons, if any, elected President and Vice President of the United States."[4]

The Majority Required for Election

The Twelfth Amendment requires the winning candidate to receive "a majority of the whole number of Electors appointed." Section 15 establishes a procedure for making and acting on objections to the counting of one or more of the electoral votes from a state or the District of Columbia.[5]

Any such objection must be presented in writing and must be signed by at least one senator and one representative. The objection "shall state clearly and concisely, and without argument, the ground thereof." When a proper objection is received, each house of Congress is to meet and consider it separately. Both houses must vote separately to agree to the objection by simple majority. Otherwise, the objection fails.[6]

There are also procedures for each house of Congress to follow when debating and voting on an objection. These procedures limit debate on the objection to not more than two hours, during which each member may speak only once and for not more than five minutes. The general grounds for an objection to the counting of an electoral vote or votes are related to whether the vote was lawfully certified or done so in a timely manner. In the event that no candidate has received a majority of the electoral votes for president, the election is ultimately to be decided by the House of Representatives.

In that situation, the names of the three candidates receiving the most electoral votes for president are considered by the House, with each state having one vote. In the event that no candidate receives a majority of the electoral votes for vice president, the names of the two candidates receiving the highest number of electoral votes for that post are submitted to the Senate, which elects the vice president by majority vote of the senators.[7]

STOP THE STEAL: TRUMP AND ELECTION FRAUD

Even before the 2020 election, Trump had been making claims of rigged elections and primaries. He even made a claim in 2016, even though he won that contest. In 2020, in the last debate with candidate Joe Biden, Trump continued to claim that unless he won, the election had to be tainted. The justification for this perspective was because the 2020 election would make greater use of mail-in ballots as a result of the COVID-19 pandemic. Referring to the possibility of Biden winning the election, Trump said, "This is going to be a fraud like you've never seen."[8]

At the time, many experts and observers noted that Trump's comments were inaccurate—for instance, mail-in voting has proved to be safe and secure in the five states that already use it broadly. However, these types of statements were seen as foreshadowing from the White House if Trump did not win reelection. As it turns out, those predictions became an unfortunate reality. As we saw, there was not a smooth transition of power once Biden was declared the winner. Instead, Trump claimed he actually won in a landslide, and that, at the very least, the election should be postponed and completed again at a later date.

Trump's claims about the election being "rigged" were pitched at several levels. Because of the increased use of mail-in ballots as a result of COVID-19, Trump claimed that the election would be compromised because of:

1. Fraudulent ballots being submitted.
2. Governments creating counterfeit ballots.
3. "Ballot dumping," or dramatic shifts in voting polls later in the election.
4. Voting machines used to tabulate or count the votes were corrupted to count more votes for his opponent, even votes that Trump supporters cast for him.
5. Dead people casting votes.
6. Unsolicited ballots were sent to 80 million people.
7. Unverified ballots were counted. Trump claimed that many mail-in ballots did not have the proper signatures or were not submitted by Election Day—which should invalidate them.
8. Poll watchers were denied the chance to observe the counting of ballots.

Was there any empirical or legitimate basis to any or all of these claims? The following provides an evaluation of these claims, based on the actual evidence and facts related to the topic, as well as reports by various federal and state agencies, including the US Department of Justice (DOJ), the Department of Homeland Security (DHS), various fact-checking agencies, and state and federal court decisions. Trump's allegations of massive voting fraud have also been refuted by a variety of judges, state election officials, and members of his own cabinet.[9]

Poll Watchers

During the election, Trump tweeted that many mail-in and absentee ballots were processed without proper oversight by poll watchers. He even went on to claim that Trump observers were not allowed to be present during the count. The implication, of course, is that Democrats tried to prevent Republicans from observing the process of counting the ballots. In reality, the main issue was not the presence of poll watchers, but how close observers could get to the election workers attempting to count the ballots. Additionally, the counting that occurred in Pennsylvania, a key swing state in the election, was live streamed, making the claim that they were not allowed to observe a non-starter, particularly since observers have no role to play in the counting of ballots.[10]

Ballot Dumping

Trump, famous for his heavy stream of Twitter posts, offered numerous tweets about the shift in trends during the election. That is, he claimed that he had a lead early in the voting only to discover later that Biden had won. This, he claims, occurred because so many people had fraudulently submitted mail-in ballots. He said, "I go from winning by a lot to losing a tight race. It's corrupt." In another tweet, Trump states: "It's about big leads on election night, tremendous leads, leads where I was being congratulated for a decisive, easy victory, and all of a sudden by morning or a couple of days later, those leads rapidly evaporated."[11]

It's fair to wonder how and in what ways the trends shifted. As experts and election officials noted, however, it's the nature of voting, particularly in the counting of votes, that it does not all occur at the same time. In-person votes tend to be counted more quickly, particularly since Trump had been reminding supporters to avoid mail-in ballots and vote in person. In comparison, mail-in ballots take longer to count—think of the logistics involved—envelopes must be opened and ballots must be verified before being counted.

As a result of the pandemic and concerns about social distancing, many people who used mail-in ballots tended to vote for Biden. Adding to the problem is that many states prevented election officials from counting mail-in ballots before they arrived on Election Day. Additionally, larger cities are often slow to report their voting numbers and, according to election experts, people in large cities tend to be more likely to vote as Democrats. These factors then delayed the counts and resulted in the shifting trends in the voting.

As an illustration of state laws regarding the counting of ballots, Trump pointed to Wisconsin, where he led early, but by 3:00 a.m. the next morning, the vote count shifted to Biden. As Trump tweeted: "In Wisconsin, as an example, where we were way up on election night, they ultimately had us miraculously losing by 20,000 votes. And I can show you right here that Wisconsin, we're leading by a lot, and then at 3:42 in the morning, there was this. It was a massive dump of votes. Mostly Biden."[12]

In reality, the change occurred because Wisconsin law requires the results of absentee ballots to be reported all at once. In Milwaukee, there were 169,000 absentee ballots that had to be counted, which took until about 3:00 a.m. Additionally, the counting of those ballots was live streamed on YouTube. At the end of the count, police officers escorted the city's elections director to the county courthouse to deliver the ballot data.[13]

Corrupt Voting Machines

In addition to claims about ballot dumping, Trump also took issue with the voting machines that tabulated votes. He claimed there were questions about whether or not the machines failed to count all votes, lost or deleted some votes, or the software actually altered votes (ostensibly from Trump to Biden). According to the Cybersecurity Agency and Infrastructure Security Agency, there was no evidence that any voting machine was in any way compromised, including deleting, losing, or changing votes.[14]

Trump typically pointed to an instance in Michigan where he claimed that nearly six thousand votes had been switched from Trump to Biden. According to the Michigan Department of State, a few thousand votes were discovered to be the result of human error, not the company responsible for the voting machines. This was later verified by an independent research firm on voting technology and the error was corrected. However, it did not have an impact on the outcome of the election in that state.[15]

Dead Voters

To demonstrate more evidence of voter fraud, Trump repeatedly made the claim that, particularly in Pennsylvania and Michigan, deceased people filled out ballots and voted. According to voting experts, dead people casting ballots is a relatively common complaint made by some politicians, but it lacks empirical substance. In Trump's case, officials in both states say there is no evidence or support for Trump's claim. What some experts do note, however, is that it is common for state voter rolls to include voters with birth certificates that make them seem extraordinarily old, but this is often a result of data entry mistakes made by people or software glitches. But having inaccuracies in voter registration rolls is different from dead people voting.[16]

Mail-in Ballots

Trump also repeatedly claimed that mail-in ballots were a deliberate attempt to steal the election from him. He stated, "The ballots are out of control. You know it. And you know who knows it better than anybody else? The Democrats know it better than anybody else."[17]

Trump cited a case of military ballots marked for him being thrown in the trash as evidence of a possible plot to steal the election. In reality, election officials in one state reported that a contract worker accidentally placed seven ballots and two unopened ones in an election office in a Republican-controlled county. According to various reports, the problem was immediately addressed and remedied.[18]

Trump also claimed a West Virginia mail worker was "selling ballots." In response to that allegation, the investigation revealed that a postal worker altered eight absentee ballot applications during the state's primary election, where five ballot requests were changed from Democrat to Republican. In three other ballots, the postal worker changed the affiliation to Republican. The worker pled guilty to the charges of election fraud and tampering with the mail.[19]

During the election, the president repeatedly attacked the idea of mail-in ballots, despite the fact that an intelligence report in September warned that Russia would likely attempt to undermine the public's trust in the election process by raising the question of the legitimacy of mail-in ballots.[20] Such a claim is furthered by Trump's argument that foreign governments were attempting to derail the election by manufacturing ballots.

Foreign Governments and Mail-in Ballots

In the summer of 2020, in the absence of any evidence or proof, Trump also claimed that foreign countries would produce counterfeit ballots in an attempt to alter the outcome of the election. At the time, experts noted that producing counterfeit ballots is extraordinarily difficult given the security safeguards such as bar codes and signature checks, which make it quite difficult for a foreign government to influence the ballot count. Moreover, US intelligence officials, along with the US Attorney General's Office, stated there was no evidence of this type of activity. Regardless, the president continued to repeat unfounded claims about millions of foreign-made counterfeit ballots.[21]

Unsolicited Ballots

President Trump also claimed that the government sent out 80 million unsolicited ballots, thereby creating a threat to fraudulently alter the election. In an interview with Fox News, Trump stated, "In the country they're going to send out 80 million unsolicited, in other words people that don't even know what a ballot is, all of a sudden here comes the ballot. . . . A lot of people use the word absentee. Get an absentee ballot where you request it, it comes to you, you vote and you send it back. That's different. But they're just sending out—all over they're sending out 80 million ballots."[22]

As part of the election process and in light of the challenges presented by the COVID-19 pandemic, mail-in ballots were sent automatically to eligible registered voters in nine states and the District of Columbia, comprising about 44 million ballots—not 80 million, as the president claimed—and they went to all types of registered voters—Republicans, Democrats, and Independent voters. More importantly, of the nine states in question, five of them had followed this protocol or something like it in previous elections.[23]

The president continued to push the baseless claim that Democrats engaged in voter fraud by sending out millions of unsolicited ballots in an attempt to change the outcome of the election. This is true despite any evidence of widespread voter fraud. Even the Federal Bureau of Investigation (FBI) director dismissed the notion that there had been any kind of coordinated national voter fraud in a major election.[24]

Trump and Nevada's Rigged Election

In the months prior to the 2020 presidential election, the governor of Nevada signed a bill passed by the state legislature that sent mail-in ballots to all active registered voters during a state of emergency or a declaration of a disaster, such as the COVID-19 pandemic. Those voters automatically received ballots for the 2020 November election. The bill was passed due to concern about limited polling places and long lines that occurred during Nevada's primary in June 2020 because of the pandemic.[25]

In a few months prior to the November 2020 election, Trump made baseless claims that Nevada had contributed to the rigging of the election in two ways: by accusing Governor Steve Sisolak, a Democrat, of hiding votes, and by allowing ballots that did not have the proper signatures or submission dates. In the first instance, Trump argued:

> He's [Sisolak] a, he's a political hack. Let me just tell you. He's in charge of ballots. There's no way he's gonna be honest about it. It, it's a rig. It's a rig. 100% rigged. I have no doubt about it in my mind. . . . The governor totally controls it. The governor's the one who made it very difficult, and he controls it, and that's okay. He wants to play that game, we'll play the game. You know what the game is? The game is he's also controlling ballots, and it's a crooked operation. As far as I'm concerned, this is a rigged election.[26]

In actuality, under Nevada state law, elections are supervised by the Nevada secretary of state, who does not work for the governor. Trump also falsely charged that Nevada doesn't require mail-in ballots to be signed and doesn't require verification of the ballots that are signed. He said in an interview on Fox News: "Now they have a new thing where they don't want to verify signatures because that makes it easier to—so you don't have to verify a signature. You see that one in Nevada."[27] Actually, the new law requires mail-in ballots to include valid voter signatures, which must be verified by election officials. It also articulated, in more detail than in the past, the procedures for dealing with suspect signatures and provisions for allowing voters to verify them. But it did not change the signature requirement.

THE TRUMP RESPONSE TO THE "RIGGED" ELECTION

Lawsuits

All of the allegations made by Trump about the election were found to be without merit. In fact, the Department of Justice and the Department of Homeland Security concluded that no serious fraud occurred and the claims referenced above are inaccurate, distortions, or have no factual basis to them. Despite this, President Trump and his allies filed lawsuits; made repeated allegations of election fraud in news and social media; organized protests; tried to convince state legislatures to act; and held hearings in various locations to argue that the election was rigged.[28]

Remarkably, Trump elicited the support of some members of Congress: prior to the attack on the US Capitol, thirteen senators and more than one hundred Republican lawmakers planned to object to the certification of Biden's win when Congress met in a joint session on January 6, 2021.[29] Little did anyone realize at the time what would happen on that day, and the ongoing investigation continues to reveal the extent of the damage.

A primary strategy for Trump has been to use the legal system to validate his claims. The president and his allies filed sixty-two lawsuits in state and federal courts, including two direct appeals to the US Supreme Court, seeking to overturn election results in states the president lost. Of the total number of lawsuits filed, sixty-one have failed; the only win was a minor procedural matter that had no bearing on the election's outcome.[30] Some of these lawsuits were dismissed for lack of legal standing and others were denied consideration based on the lack of merits about the claims of voter fraud. The decisions came from both Democratic-appointed and Republican-appointed judges—including federal judges appointed by Trump.[31] However, the range of objections in these lawsuits by Trump is considerable.

For instance, a lawsuit filed by Republican Louie Gohmert argued Vice President Pence had the authority to decide which states' Electoral College votes could count. That case was dismissed. In other instances, the US Supreme Court rejected a request from Pennsylvania Republicans that claimed the Republican-led state legislature's expansion of absentee voting violated the state's constitution. Others took issue with the timeline of when the state legislatures met to certify the votes. A federal judge dismissed a lawsuit filed by voters in Wisconsin, Pennsylvania, Georgia, Michigan, and Arizona, which argued that those officials charged with certifying votes for their particular state should have met sooner, which invalidated those votes.[32]

In addition to the legal challenges, as well as Trump's repeated insistence that he actually won the election in a "landslide," and spurred on by supporters and others who stood to gain from the controversy, the public was subjected to a nearly constant barrage of social media about the legitimacy of the election. A catchphrase, "Stop the Steal," became the moniker to describe Trump's claim—that people needed to prevent such an obvious miscarriage of justice. But Trump did not stop at using the legal system to his advantage. He also attempted to sway election officials to either stop the counting of ballots or change the recording of votes.

Trump's Attempt to Intimidate Officials

In some cases, largely as a result of political pressure, media attention, and in part to prove that no illegal activity occurred, several key states undertook a recount of votes in their state. In fact, in an extraordinary moment, President Trump actually contacted the Georgia secretary of state, Brad Raffensperger, a Republican, in an effort to convince him to "find" a sufficient number of votes that would swing the state in his favor. This occurred after an initial recount showed no impropriety and that the election was valid.[33]

Trump even went so far as to allude to the fact that Raffensperger could be criminally prosecuted for failing to do so. In a recorded conversation, Trump said to Raffensperger, "I just want to find 11,780 votes, which is one more than we have. You know what they did and you're not reporting it. . . . You know, that's a criminal—that's a criminal offense. And you know, you can't let that happen. That's a big risk to you and to Ryan, your lawyer. That's a big risk."[34]

Mr. Raffensperger politely but firmly rejected the president's requests, standing by the election results in his state and repeatedly insisting that Mr. Trump and his allies had been given false information about voter fraud. Mr. Raffensberger said, "Well, Mr. President, the challenge that you have is the data you have is wrong." Legal experts said Mr. Trump may have himself actually violated Georgia state law against solicitation of voter fraud and extortion by seeking to exert pressure on Mr. Raffensperger.[35]

This was an extraordinary moment—President Trump wielded considerable political influence in the Republican Party and his request arguably constituted an attempt to subvert a legitimate election. Georgia actually held two recounts of its presidential election results, both reaffirming Biden's win in the state. Wisconsin had one recount that confirmed Biden's victory there. The initial recount in Georgia was a manual one, and local election officials identified 1,912 ballots in four counties that were uncounted as a result of human error. This recount found that Biden won by 12,284 votes instead of the initial 14,196. A second recount, requested by the Trump campaign, found an additional 505 votes, resulting in Biden receiving 11,779 more votes than Trump in that state.[36]

The Evidence Against Voter Fraud and Trump's Claims

This is not the first time Trump has declared an election had been rigged or stolen. In 2012, Trump tweeted that there were voting machines switching Romney votes to Obama. Trump also claimed that the 2016 Democratic primary was rigged against Bernie Sanders, a claim he made again in 2020. In fact, so frequent are Trump's claims of election fraud that he actually argued that there were 3 million votes made against him in 2016, when he won the election.[37]

Additionally, a White House commission that Trump created to investigate election fraud disbanded without finding any evidence to support the president's claims. Despite all the allegations, the Electoral College elected Biden the next president. Biden finished with a record 81,281,502 votes nationally, defeating Trump in the popular vote by 7 million votes. With 51.3 percent of the national popular vote, Biden won with the highest share of the vote for a challenger of an incumbent president since Franklin D. Roosevelt in 1932. Trump won 46.8 percent of the vote nationally.[38]

One would think that this should have ended the debate and, while the controversy might continue, surely the issue was put to rest. All but one of the lawsuits were rejected by the courts; independent verification of the election in every state could not find any substantial evidence of voter fraud; even the US attorney general, Bill Barr, declared that there was no voter fraud and that the election was a valid one.[39] In fact, in an interview, Barr stated that he thought Trump's claims of election fraud were without merit from the start. Barr said, "If there was evidence of fraud, I had no motive to suppress it. But my suspicion all the way along was that there was nothing there. It was all bullshit."[40]

THE ATTACK ON THE US CAPITOL

It is important to remember that the months, weeks, and days leading up to the attack on the US Capitol were filled with unsubstantiated claims by Trump and his supporters about the election being stolen. It is also important to note that protests, some of which turned violent, occurred in other states outside of Washington, DC. Thus, the attack on the US Capitol was not a spontaneous reaction to the outcome of the election; it was a more orchestrated event designed to delay the constitutional requirements regarding the election, and/or overthrow the process altogether, and keep President Trump in office.

Since the tragic events of that day, there have been numerous reports that offered a timeline of events, and new information continues to unfold about the role President Trump played in what many experts and observers are calling an insurrection. Thus, while it is tempting to consider the attack on the US Capitol episodically, one that did not last very long, although it did last for more than five hours, the reality is that much of the rhetoric and arguments about the rigging of the election are a part of this almost inevitable outcome.

While it is also tempting to offer assessments of the level of desperation Trump may have felt as these baseless claims about fraud were discarded, it is important to understand what took place and how the country has responded to these events. It is also essential to include statements made by Trump, which will provide readers an understanding of the context within which so many protestors claimed, as many stated publicly, they were doing what their president told them to do. While legal experts can always debate whether Trump's intent was to incite people to violence or to overthrow the election itself, or whether his words were protected under the First Amendment to the US Constitution, it is worth noting what he said, when he said it, and how a reasonable person might connect his words to the behavior of those involved in the riots.

On January 6, 2021, crowds began forming early in the morning on the White House Ellipse for Trump's "Save America" rally. During his speech, Trump continued to make inaccurate statements, such as claiming the election was rigged and that Democrats had committed voter fraud. By midday, the Capitol was buzzing as Congress convened in a joint session and pro-Trump protesters began to gather around the building's perimeter.[41] Trump tweeted: "States want to correct their votes, which they now know were based on irregularities and fraud, plus corrupt process never received legislative approval. All Mike Pence has to do is send them back to the States, AND WE WIN. Do it Mike, this is a time for extreme courage!"[42]

At noon, Trump began his speech, which lasted more than an hour, repeating false claims about a stolen election and telling the crowd to "never give up" and "never concede." Trump ended his speech by urging his followers to march down Pennsylvania Avenue. "We're going to the Capitol," he said. "We're going to try and give them [Republicans] the kind of pride and boldness that they need to take back our country."[43]

Crowds from the pro-Trump rally gathered outside the US Capitol building, and by 1:00 p.m., an initial wave of protesters stormed the outer barricade west of the Capitol building as senators and Vice President Pence walked to the House chamber. Soon after Trump ended his speech, violence broke out as a mob forced its way into the Capitol building. They broke down doors and shattered windows, forcing Congress to adjourn and take shelter. Ashli Babbitt, an Air Force veteran and avid Trump supporter, was shot by Capitol Police while trying to get into the Speaker's Lobby.[44] Rioters rampaged through the Capitol building searching for Vice President Pence, chanting "Where's Mike Pence?" whom they wanted to hang from a tree as a traitor. Other references were made of comments by rioters about "heads on spikes," alluding to Pence as well as Speaker of the House Nancy Pelosi, who was a potential target for execution, and Senator Chuck Schumer, the Senate majority leader. The implication, of course, was to kill them and thereby invalidate the certification process.[45]

To illustrate the intensity and impact of the riots, consider how many police officers were injured as well as the extent of their injuries. Many officers characterized the event as "medieval," because they engaged with rioters in hand-to-hand combat while others used blunt instruments as weapons as they invaded the building. Other rioters had stun guns, bear spray, and plastic handcuffs. Officers were hit in the head with baseball bats, flagpoles, and pipes. One officer lost consciousness after rioters used a metal barrier to push past her as they tried to reach the Capitol steps.[46] Estimates vary on the number of rioters who surrounded or entered the Capitol on January 6, but a review of footage shows that thousands swarmed the building.[47]

The Capitol assault resulted in one of the worst days of injuries for law enforcement in the United States. Approximately 140 officers—about an equal number from the Capitol Police and the Metropolitan Police Department in Washington, DC—sustained a host of injuries including concussions, fractures, and burns; one officer even had a mild heart attack during the riot. Tragically, in the aftermath, a few officers involved in the response committed suicide.[48]

The number of those injured does not account for the dozens of officers who will likely suffer with post-traumatic stress disorder or the officers who contracted COVID-19 from unmasked Trump supporters who overran the Capitol.[49] For instance, at least thirty-eight Capitol Police officers tested positive for the coronavirus or were exposed to it, while nearly two hundred

National Guard personnel who were deployed to protect the Capitol in the weeks after the siege also tested positive.[50]

The significance of the length of the riot is also an important consideration, particularly since most police officers who encounter violent situations do not usually experience them for a long period of time. As Chuck Wexler, executive director of the Police Executive Research Forum points out, "If you're a cop and get into a fight, it may last five minutes, but these guys were in battle for four to five hours."[51]

Adding to the problem was that many officers were not provided sufficient equipment nor given adequate training to handle a situation like the one that unfolded. For example, according to one account, only about 170 of the roughly 1,200 Capitol Police officers on duty at the time of the attack were equipped with riot gear. The lack of equipment clearly played a role in the extent and type of injuries officers sustained. Some officers without helmets sustained brain injuries, one officer suffered two shattered spinal discs, and another was stabbed with a metal fence stake, said Gus Papathanasiou, the chairman of the Capitol Police Union. Out of the roughly two thousand officers on the Capitol Police force, fewer than two hundred had received recent training in dealing with protests.[52]

There continues to be some debate about the role of the Capitol Police leadership during the time leading up to and during the riot. A report by the US Inspector General's Office, titled *Review of the Events Surrounding the January 6, 2021 Takeover of the US Capitol*, found that three days before the mob attack Capitol Police officials were warned in an intelligence assessment of the potential for violence, with Congress being the target. The report indicates that the Capitol Police wrote in a plan for the responses to the pro-Trump rallies on January 6 that there were no specific known threats related to the joint session of Congress. The report also indicated that the Capitol Police Civil Disturbance Unit, which is responsible for handling large protests, was ordered by supervisors not to use "heavier, less lethal weapons," such as stun grenades, which would have been effective in repelling rioters. The report concluded that the Capitol Police were operating at a decreased level of readiness as a result of a lack of adequate equipment and training.[53]

There are also questions about whether the FBI knew of the potential for violence but did not inform the Capitol Police of this possibility before the event.[54] While conflicting reports exist, some contend that the New York Police Department (NYPD) as well as the FBI made Capitol Police aware of a potential threat of violence prior to the event, with the Capitol Police assuring officials they could handle the threat. Others argued that there were no indications from the start that the protests would turn violent. In either scenario, it became quite apparent that the Capitol Police were ill-equipped to handle the number of people and the level of violence that ensued.[55]

What many experts note is the fact that President Trump's urging of people to march on the Capitol likely resulted in many more people attending than would have otherwise. Experts also note that, beyond law enforcement agencies, outside organizations that monitor white supremacist activities urged officials to anticipate a high level of violence at the rallies. Either all of this information was ignored, considered insufficient, or the Capitol Police, perhaps, underestimated the size of the crowd and thought they were able to handle the protestors.[56]

As these attacks were occurring, Congress met in a joint session to confirm Joe Biden's win, over the objections of some Republicans. Representative Paul A. Gosar (R-AZ) and Senator Ted Cruz (R-TX) objected to certifying Arizona's electoral college votes. Shortly before he opened the session, in response to Trump's demands, Vice President Mike Pence released a letter, saying he would not intervene in Congress's electoral count. He stated: "My oath to support and defend the Constitution constrains me from claiming unilateral authority."[57] As per the protocol governing such objections, the joint session then separated into House and Senate chambers to debate the issue. Shortly after 1:30 p.m., suspicious packages, later confirmed to be pipe bombs, were found at Republican National Committee headquarters and Democratic National Committee headquarters in Washington.[58]

By 2:20 p.m., both houses of Congress adjourned and began to evacuate as rioters forced their way into the Capitol. Around this time, Trump tweeted: "Mike Pence didn't have the courage to do what should have been done to protect our Country and our Constitution, giving States a chance to certify a corrected set of facts, not the fraudulent or inaccurate ones which they were asked to previously certify. USA demands the truth!"[59] By 3:30 p.m., White House press secretary Kayleigh McEnany tweets that the National Guard and federal forces were on their way to the US Capitol. Trump remained quiet, even as the country called on him to make a statement that could end the chaos. By 4:00 p.m., Biden called on Trump to "demand an end to this siege."[60]

Around 6:00 p.m., Trump tweeted, "These are the things and events that happen when a sacred landslide election victory is so unceremoniously and viciously stripped away from great patriots who have been badly and unfairly treated for so long. Go home with love and in peace. Remember this day forever!" An hour later, Facebook removed Trump's posts and Twitter removed Trump's tweets and shut down his account for the repeated and severe violation of its civic integrity policy. Later, Twitter permanently banned Trump for the incitement of violence.[61] After more than five hours of violence, the police were able to restore order and secure the area, and Congress reconvened to certify the electoral-vote tally. At approximately 3:00 a.m., more than thirteen hours after the Capitol was breached, Vice President Pence officially affirmed the election results, declaring Biden the winner.[62]

The projected cost of the damage done during the riots is estimated to be up to $10 million, as windows, doors, and walls were broken, and historic statues, murals, furniture, and other items were damaged or destroyed. Additionally, according to the architect of the Capitol, J. Brett Blanton, Capitol workers sheltered congressional staff members in their shops to protect them from rioters, while other members ran to the roof to reverse the airflow to clear the air of chemical irritants. Still others rendered aid by providing bottles of water and eyewash stations to Capitol officers and staffers in need of assistance.[63]

THE AFTERMATH OF THE INSURRECTION: CONGRESSIONAL RESPONSE

In the days after the riot, many members of Congress demanded that Trump take responsibility for inciting violence. Democrats, including House Speaker Nancy Pelosi and Senate Minority Leader Charles E. Schumer, called for Trump's removal from office, either through impeachment or by using the Twenty-Fifth Amendment to the US Constitution, which outlines the protocol when a president has become incapable of remaining in office. Eventually, Trump was impeached by the House, with some Republicans voting in concert with Democrats, but Trump was acquitted in the Republican-controlled Senate. However, seven Republican senators voted to impeach Trump for his role in inciting the protestors to commit violence.[64] Since January 2021, many rioters have been identified and prosecuted, with many more cases waiting to be resolved. In addition, a congressional committee was formed to investigate the details of the riot as well as what role Trump, and other congressional leaders, played in the event.

Trump's Second Impeachment

In response to Trump's role in the riot at the Capitol building, on January 11, 2021, the House introduced a single article of impeachment against the president. The next day, the House also passed a resolution that asked Vice President Mike Pence to invoke the Twenty-Fifth Amendment to the Constitution that would remove Trump from office. Pence refused. A day later, on January 13, the House passed the article of impeachment to the Senate, which included ten votes in favor of impeachment from Republican representatives—more than any other of a previous president charged with impeachment.[65]

On January 20, 2021, Trump's term as president ended. This is important since the House managers did not deliver the article of impeachment to the Senate until January 25. This led to a debate about whether a former president could be impeached. In a vote of 55–45, the Senate voted to hold a trial even though Trump was no longer in office. On February 13, after the trial, the Senate voted 57–43 against impeachment, ten less of the threshold needed to impeach the president. This vote included seven Republican senators: Richard Burr, Bill Cassidy, Susan Collins, Lisa Murkowski, Mitt Romney, Ben Sasse, and Pat Toomey.[66] Republican senator Susan Collins made the following statement regarding her vote as well as Trump's role in the riot. She said the following:

> Rather than facilitating the peaceful transfer of power, President Trump was telling Vice President Pence to ignore the Constitution and to refuse to count the certified votes. He was also further agitating the crowd, directing them to march to the Capitol. In this situation, context was everything, tossing a lit match into a pile of dry leaves is very different from tossing it into a pool of water, and on January 6th the atmosphere among the crowd outside the White House was highly combustible, largely the result of an ill wind blowing from Washington for the past two months. President Trump had stoked discontent with a steady barrage of false claims that the election had been stolen from him. The allegedly responsible officials were denigrated, scorned and ridiculed by the President with the predictable result that his supporters viewed any official that they perceived to be an obstacle to President Trump's re-election as an enemy of their cause. That set the stage for the storming of the Capitol for the first time in more than 200 years.[67]

Although he ultimately voted to acquit Trump of the charges, arguing that Trump was no longer a sitting president, Mitch McConnell, the Senate majority leader, stated that Trump was responsible for the violence that occurred at the US Capitol. He said:

> There's no question—none—that President Trump is practically and morally responsible for provoking the events of the day. No question about it. The people who stormed this building believed they were acting on the wishes and instructions of their President. . . . As I stood up and said clearly at that time, the election was settled. It was over. But that just really opened a new chapter of even wilder, wilder and more unfounded claims. The leader of the free world cannot spend weeks thundering that shadowy forces are stealing our country and then feign surprise when people believe him and do reckless things.[68]

Thus, even members of Trump's own party, including senior leadership within the Senate, believed he incited the violence that occurred on January

6, and many people who have been charged for the violence that day believe they were following the instructions and orders of their president. And yet, many still supported Trump in his claims of a rigged election and insisted that he had no role to play in the ensuing violence.

Congressional Committee to Investigate Capitol Violence

The logic behind the need for a commission to investigate the January 6 events should not be in dispute. As Jenkins (2021) notes, in the past, such bodies were instrumental in learning exactly what occurred, devoid of politics, as well as how to prevent such events in the future. As he notes, the Warren Commission investigated the Kennedy assassination; the Kerner Commission examined the riots in cities around the country in the 1960s; and the 9/11 Commission helped the country to understand the terrorist threats facing the United States.

Experts also agree that such bodies provide the most accurate historical record of events—the proposed commission investigating the events at the US Capitol would provide a context to understand the events that led up to and explained how the riots occurred. It would also give an account of the participants in the riot—were they simply citizens caught up in the emotions of the day or was the attack part of a coordinated mob following some type of plan? Similarly, were the events on January 6 a disruption, a demonstration, an attempted coup, or an act of terrorism? These and other critical questions could only be answered by an independent, bipartisan commission.[69]

It is with all this in mind that a bill was introduced to create a bipartisan commission to investigate one of the most extraordinary events in American history.[70] While investigations had been started by other federal agencies, such as the DHS and FBI, such a commission would focus on accountability—not just for participants involved in the riot but also to address the questions surrounding the lack of adequate security at the Capitol and the gaps in intelligence on the days leading up to the attack.

While the House passed the bill, 252–175, with thirty-five Republicans joining all Democrats to approve the measure, when it reached the Senate, only six Republicans voted with Democrats and several other senators did not vote at all. As a result, the vote count was 54–35, six less than the sixty needed to approve the bill.[71]

When the idea of a January 6 commission failed in the Senate, perhaps in part because many Republicans feared what the commission would discover, House Democrats elected to form their own committee. Democrats remained committed to a bipartisan effort, and Speaker Pelosi attempted to collaborate with the House minority leader, Kevin McCarthy, to create one.

McCarthy nominated several prominent Republicans—two in particular, Representatives Jim Jordan of Ohio and Jim Banks of Indiana, who were known to be Trump sympathizers and who had objected to the certification of the election.[72]

After rejecting these two representatives, Pelosi asked McCarthy to identify replacements. In response, McCarthy then pulled all of his nominees from the committee, claiming that Speaker Pelosi was attempting to manipulate the process and the committee members. Pelosi then nominated two House Republicans, Wyoming's Liz Cheney and Illinois's Adam Kinzinger, both of whom voted to impeach Trump and who stated they were committed to finding out what exactly happened on that day and promised to hold those involved accountable for their actions.[73]

The FBI and the Capitol Riot Investigation

In August 2021, the FBI completed its investigation into Trump's role in the insurrection at the Capitol and concluded that it was not an organized plot including Trump. The findings indicate that there was no grand scheme designed to storm the Capitol or take hostages and execute congressional leaders. At the time the report was issued, more than 570 participants had been arrested by federal officials, and while investigators did find that groups such as the Oath Keepers and Proud Boys made plans to break into the Capitol, little else was organized beyond that.[74] It is also noted that prosecutors have not generally charged defendants with conspiracy or even racketeering, which are commonly used against organized criminal gangs. In fact, only about forty defendants of the 570 arrested were charged with conspiracy.[75]

This report, which found no direct involvement by Trump, doesn't absolve him of any responsibility in instigating the violence during the riot. As many rioters who have been arrested have claimed, they were simply following the instructions they believed were given by their president. While that by itself doesn't necessarily implicate Trump, his words and actions on and before January 6, including urging supporters to march on the Capitol, may ultimately result in Trump being assigned responsibility for what occurred.

Rioters Arrested, Charged, and Prosecuted

Despite the extensive damage to the building and the injuries to law enforcement officers, because many rioters were allowed to leave the Capitol after the area had been secured, the arrest and prosecution of those responsible for the violence has been time-consuming. While the events at the Capitol are perhaps the most documented crimes in US history, as evidenced by the extensive video footage and photographs taken by the participants and often posted on social media, the FBI has painstakingly attempted to identify each offender through video footage, media posts, phone location data, and other sources in an effort to make arrests. Nearly nine months after the events on January 6, the FBI continued to solicit the help of the general public to identify the many individuals who took part in what some observers are calling an insurrection or attempted coup. As of August 2021, 615 people had been arrested, with twenty-eight offenders submitting guilty pleas as a result of plea bargain agreements with the federal government.[76]

Despite the bravado of some participants before, during, and after the attacks, with many participants taking photos or videos of themselves, some offenders have expressed remorse for their actions. For instance, Jacob Chansley, the self-described QAnon Shaman who posed for photos on the Senate dais while sporting face paint and a furry hat with horns, wrote an apology from jail, asking for understanding as he was coming to grips with his actions.[77] Similarly, Dominic Pezzola, a member of the extremist group Proud Boys who posted a video of himself giving a speech inside the Capitol while smoking a "victory" cigar, has argued that he now realizes he was duped into the mistaken belief that the election was stolen from President Donald Trump. He also claims that his incarceration puts his family in financial jeopardy.[78]

Interestingly, other rioters, even those charged with serious and violent offenses, claim they were following Trump's instructions.[79] For instance, Garret Miller, a person who participated in the attack, who threatened to assassinate Democratic Representative Alexandria Ocasio-Cortez, said: "I believed I was following the instructions of former president Trump. I also left Washington and started back to Texas immediately after President Trump asked us to go home."[80]

Robert Bauer, another rioter charged in the attacks, told federal law enforcement officials that he "marched to the US Capitol because President Trump said to do so." Similarly, Jacob Chansley's attorney said his client "heard the words of the president. He believed them. He genuinely believed him. He thought the president was walking with him."[81] Parenthetically, during his speech at the "Stop the Steal" rally before the riot, Trump had urged his supporters to "walk down to the Capitol" alongside him to protest the certification of the election. Trump stated, "You'll never take back our country with weakness. You have to show strength, and you have to be strong." While Trump never actually walked with protestors to the Capitol building, many supporters took his words as a call to action.[82]

Police Officers File Suit Against Trump for Attacks

In August 2021, eight months after the January 6 attack on the US Capitol, seven Capitol Police officers who were injured filed a lawsuit in federal court against President Trump, Roger Stone, a Trump ally, and members of the far-right extremist groups Proud Boys and Oath Keepers, accusing them of collaborating to commit acts of domestic terrorism in an effort to remain in power. The lawsuit provides a detailed account of the injuries that officers sustained while trying to protect members of Congress as well as holds those who were responsible for instigating the violence accountable.

"We joined the Capitol Police to uphold the law and protect the Capitol community," the group of officers said in a statement released by their lawyers. "On January 6, we tried to stop people from breaking the law and destroying our democracy. Since then, our jobs and those of our colleagues have become infinitely more dangerous. We want to do what we can to make sure the people who did this are held accountable and that no one can do this again."[83]

WHAT DOES IT ALL MEAN AND WHY DOES IT MATTER?

The claims of election fraud and the events surrounding the attack on the US Capitol building are two of the most defining features of the Trump presidency. And while the investigations into one are complete, federal officials continue to uncover more information about the attacks on January 6. The congressional committee has recently requested numerous documents from federal agencies as well as telecommunications companies in an effort to know more about who was involved and what they knew in advance of the attack, and they are continuing to review video footage of the events of that day.[84] While the FBI report mentioned earlier indicated that there was no evidence that President Trump was directly involved in the planning of the violence, questions remain about whether or not his actions or inactions constitute an incitement of the mob or whether he attempted to interfere in the election process.

What is most fascinating about the Trump presidency, in general, and his actions, in particular, is that despite all the mounting evidence of false claims, questionable ethics, or even potentially outright criminal actions, some by Trump's own words and deeds, Trump's base, including the vast majority of the Republican Party, continue to support him. While party politics suggests that one group will almost always continue to support a controversial political leader, particularly the president of the United States, in many ways Trump is unlike any president before him. And one has to wonder if the base of support would remain as strong if this were a different political leader.

What is it about Trump that garners such loyalty? Is it fear? Is his ideology so appealing? Is it that Trump does not play by the rules and such a maverick approach is endearing? Or is it that his supporters gain more than they lose by his presence and are willing to endorse his behavior and positions or ignore or minimize them? Or is it the case that his followers are misguided, have been misled, or are blindly following Trump's ideas because they have done so for the past several years? Is there no limit to what Trump can do without making his base of followers pause and reconsider their position? In chapter 2, we will discuss how Trump came to power, define what Trump stands for— sometimes called *Trumpism*—and offer a description of the various types of Trump supporters—what we will call *Trumpsters*.

In fairness, while there are some defining features of Trumpsters, this is not a homogeneous group of people. That is, simply voting for Trump doesn't automatically make one a Trumpster. But for those who are in that category, many questions remain about what it means to be a Trumpster, such as whether they are deluded in their thinking or have become part of a cult. In addition, there are lingering questions about Trump supporters who are Christians, and how they resolve the incongruence between much of Trump's behavior and positions that appear to be at odds with a Christian ideology. Still other questions focus on extremist supporters, such as white supremacist groups, who have been given a higher profile as a result of Trump's election to the presidency. Finally, many comparisons have been made between Trump and Trumpsters and Nazi ruler Adolf Hitler and the Nazi Party. These and other issues will be addressed in subsequent chapters.

While it might be tempting to consider the behavior of Trump and his loyal base of extremist followers as an aberration or a new phenomenon, such a perspective would be inaccurate. Whether we consider the treatment of Chinese immigrants in the nineteenth century, the internment of Japanese Americans, many of whom were US citizens, the exploitation and efforts to exterminate Native American tribes, or the long history of mistreating Black and Brown people in this country, the tendency to see weaker groups as some type of threat is a common feature of American society. What has occurred in this latest version of this process, however, is an escalation of hostilities to include other Whites who disagree with Trump's views as eligible targets for mistreatment, violence, and criticism.

It is also worth considering the idea that Trumpism and Trumpsters can be understood as a type of social movement in the United States. While social movements of various types are generally understood as groups of people who act outside the system to effect some type of social, economic, or political change, there is an argument to be made that segments of the Trumpster population go beyond routine activities normally associated with most social movements (e.g., supporting one political candidate over another, or engaging in demonstrations for or against a particular cause) and into the realm of justification and use of violence to promote a climate of fear, hostility, and intolerance. This is seen in the extremist behavior of white supremacists and right-wing Christian groups who believe the use of violence and other acts of intolerance and discrimination are appropriate, acceptable, and demonstrative of loyalty to a cause or ideology.

Thus, what we are seeing in the evolution of Trump supporters is not only an extension of a well-documented pattern of the mistreatment of others over the sweep of US history but it also has a population size large enough to make Trumpism worthy of consideration as a social movement. Moreover, as we will discuss in chapter 2, the rise in popularity of what some observers are calling Trumpism, populism, or right-wing extremism is not unique to the United States. As we will see, several other countries have embraced this form of political thought and governance.

Trump Supporters as a Social Movement

Most sociology textbooks on social movements generally define them as organized efforts by a large group of people who either want to bring about some social change that they believe will improve society or want to remedy a problem or trend that adversely affects it.[85] Clearly the United States has had its share of significant social movements over time, including the abolitionist movement to end slavery, the civil rights movement of the 1950s and 1960s, the feminist movement, and the efforts to end the Vietnam War in the 1960s and 1970s.

While there are many different types of social movements, it is important to note that there can be a significant amount of overlap between different types of movements and some of them, including conceptualizing Trump supporters as a type of social movement, fit into multiple categories. For example, an *innovative* (or liberal) *social movement* attempts to enhance society by attempting to effect a new change to society. A recent example of this type of movement in the United States has been the efforts to legalize marijuana in many states.[86] In contrast, a *conservative social movement* attempts to resist new or dramatic changes to society and to actually attempt to preserve trends and issues as they currently exist. To use the same example, a conservative social movement would attempt to keep marijuana as an illegal drug and limit its access for people.

Related to maintaining the status quo are *reactionary social movements*, which attempt to see the past in a romantic way and seek to return to "the good old days" of the past as it relates to a given issue. This includes attempts to eliminate new laws and policies that have caused significant departures from a previous way of life.[87] In the case of Trump supporters, for example, one could argue that an important issue for this group of people is the rejection of same-sex marriage, liberal policies that promote diversity, access to abortion, and feminism, which they believe to have caused traditional family values to be eroded. More generally, liberal policies have created the need to "make America great again" by returning to a previous era when white culture was preserved and celebrated.

Sometimes social movements focus on specific actions, such as creating or eliminating certain policies on a given topic or addressing specific groups or topics, while other movements are more global in their approach and attempt to fundamentally change the configuration and structure of society. This is important because another type of social movement, called a *reform movement*, attempts to change people's behavior or to modify a particular social policy, but it does not attempt to eliminate or replace an entire social institution.[88]

Reform movement members may focus on seeking the creation of new laws, repealing existing ones from politicians, or perhaps helping specific politicians with similar views to get elected to office. They may also seek redress from the courts to protect their interests, but they work within the existing system to effect change. This is different from what is called a *revolutionary movement*, which aims to make more fundamental and structural changes to society by replacing or eliminating entire social institutions or the type of governance.[89] Examples here would include that segment of Trump supporters who wish to eliminate democracy and institute a more authoritarian form of government in the United States.

An *identity movement*, as the name implies, attempts to construct a new social identity for groups that have been stigmatized by society in some way, either by race, religion, sexual orientation, or political views. The goal, of course, is to provide a sense of empowerment and pride for members of these groups as well as to achieve some level of equality.[90] One could argue that Trump supporters feel a similar sense of oppression, as they feel the efforts to enhance diversity in the United States, as seen by many liberal policies that elevate the status of historically oppressed groups, have actually resulted in the oppression of White rights and the stigmatization of white culture. In response, many Whites have embraced a form of populism and white nationalism designed to preserve or restore white culture.

While this is not a complete list of all the different types of social movements, these serve as good illustrations of how to conceptualize Trump supporters not simply as an extreme group of radicals, hell-bent on blind loyalty to a charismatic leader, but rather as a heterogeneous and wide-ranging group of people rallying around a larger set of important social trends and issues in the United States. As we will outline in the forthcoming chapters, there are some unique aspects to this large segment of the population that are worthy of discussion; in part because they have reshaped social life in the United States.

Chapter 2

Republicans, Trumpism, and Trumpsters

In chapter 1, we examined two of the most extraordinary events in American history: President Trump's claims of a stolen presidential election and what some observers are referring to as an insurrection at the US Capitol, where rioters attempted to prevent the certification of Joe Biden as the winner of the 2020 election. As the investigation into the violence at the Capitol continues, and while there is overwhelming evidence to support the idea that the election was fair and appropriate, there remain many in the Trump camp, including Republican members of Congress, who continue to make claims that the election was stolen from Trump.

What has also occurred in many states has been the tendency for Republican-controlled state legislatures and governors to pass laws that make the process of casting votes more difficult, particularly for minorities and people of color, who tend to lean Democratic in their voting preferences. These laws are being passed under the rationale of preventing voter fraud in the future and many will likely be challenged in court. But as we begin to examine *Trumpism* and *Trumpsters*, an important part of that discussion begins with understanding how and why many congressional members of the Republican Party remain so loyal to Trump. As was mentioned in the previous chapter, it is critical to provide context to understand the events and the behavior of Trump's loyalists. In the case of Congress, part of the answer to this question stems from the history of the Republican Party.

CONTEXT TO TRUMPISM: THE HISTORY OF THE REPUBLICAN PARTY

It might seem that the latest version of extremism in the Republican Party is unusual. However, the history of both the Democratic and Republican Parties demonstrate a consistent tendency for splintering and realignment. What we may be seeing in the latest version of the Republican Party, which appears to be based on an interest in the acquisition of power more than shaping social policy, is not a new phenomenon. The Republican Party, sometimes called the Grand Old Party (GOP), was formed in 1854 by anti-slavery activists like Abraham Lincoln. The ideology behind the party was based on the notion of freedom—particularly as it related to slavery, where men, their land, and their labor should be free.[1]

It is important to note that a pivotal, if not often overlooked, event in American history was the signing of the Treaty of Guadalupe Hidalgo with Mexico, which meant economic and geographic expansion opportunities for the United States. Several states disagreed on whether the system of slavery should extend to this new region. Some experts noted that free workers would be hampered in their efforts to secure employment if slavery were expanded. From a moral perspective, Northern states opposed slavery, and many members felt that the American experience was really about the equal opportunity for people to succeed in life. As a result of this disagreement, the Republican Party was formed.[2]

At the time, the country was split between free and slave labor. Republicans, primarily in the Northern states, were in favor of free labor. Based largely on the egalitarian idea that anyone can succeed in America if they work hard, the goal for Republicans was not to abolish slavery right away, but the country's economy would be more successful if it instead relied on a free market system. This was at odds with Democrats, who were primarily in Southern states where the economy largely relied on slavery. In the mid-1800s, Republicans didn't want to admit additional slave states to the Union. That conflict led to the Civil War.[3]

The rationale behind this thinking was in part economic: many members of Congress opposed the Kansas–Nebraska Act, which opened the areas outside the Mason-Dixon line to slavery as the west expanded. The founding members of the Republican Party also felt that there were better and more equitable means of economic growth, including an openness to new immigrants and giving free western land to farmers.[4]

After Lincoln was elected president, eleven Confederate states in the South seceded from the Union, and the American Civil War broke out. The war devastated the South, economically and socially. Lincoln, who was very popular in the North, was able to bring the country together during Reconstruction, but Southerners resented the government's intrusion into their way of life. The Republican Party soon became split between moderates, who felt that Reconstruction should not be punitive against the Southern states, and radical Republicans, who wanted strict laws against Confederate states.[5]

Although Lincoln was successful in brokering the tensions between the two groups, his assassination resulted in Vice President Andrew Johnson being appointed president. While radical Republicans thought they had an ally in Johnson, he actually attempted to foster a coalition between moderate Republicans and Democrats. However, in the next election, Republican radicals took control of Congress in 1866 and passed many Reconstruction laws over Johnson's veto.[6]

After the Civil War, Democrats continued to exert considerable economic and political control over the South. Meanwhile, as the North industrialized, the GOP quickly became synonymous with the business world and in turn, developed a reputation as the party of the elite. That reputation became especially clear at the turn of the twentieth century.[7] The country's rapid industrialization sparked the Progressive era, where working Americans called for more business regulation and safer working conditions. But Republican administrations in the 1920s were worried that policing the business world would hurt the massive economic growth that was taking place at the time. The stock market crash signaled the end of the "roaring 20s" era and raised numerous questions about the role of the government. Until that time, President Hoover and Republicans felt that the only role of government was to protect big business interests. The Great Depression, which caused millions of people to lose their jobs, changed that way of thinking.[8]

As a Republican, President Herbert Hoover was criticized for his efforts at addressing the problem, which were seen as wasteful government spending or not going far enough to help people who were unemployed. He believed in a small federal government and that assistance would result in Americans becoming too reliant on the government and stop working, which would slow down the economic recovery and stunt its long-term growth.[9]

The Great Depression and Hoover's response cost him the presidency in 1932. The election of Franklin D. Roosevelt allowed the Democrats to gain a substantial congressional majority for the first time since the 1850s. Additionally, President Roosevelt sought to gain the support of voter groups that typically voted Republican, such as African Americans, ethnic minorities, and rural farmers.[10] Within FDR's first one hundred days in office, he expanded the federal government by signing and implementing a variety of relief and recovery programs to help Americans experiencing the economic crisis.[11]

In response to Roosevelt's New Deal and the policies of the Democratic Party, the Republicans split into two factions. The first wing was the liberal faction, which favored expanding the New Deal social programs, but felt that such programs would be managed better by Republican administrations. This group favored civil rights for minorities and worked with Democrats to push forward legislative changes.[12] The other group, the conservative faction, advocated a return to laissez-faire economics and fiscal conservatism. Even though the conservative faction of the Republican Party also supported civil rights reforms, they started to form alliances with conservative Southern Democrats in the late 1930s as a way to prevent progressive laws from passing. After the 1938 midterm election, the "Conservative Coalition" formed a majority in Congress and prevented Democratic administrations from expanding the New Deal and other associated social programs.[13]

The Democratic Party also saw shifts in the 1960s, largely due to the challenges for civil rights. The liberal faction of the party favored civil rights legislation while the Southern faction adamantly opposed it. These tensions came to a head when Lyndon Johnson became president after John F. Kennedy was assassinated in 1963. Despite being a Southerner, Johnson had a strong record in supporting civil rights and was successful in getting meaningful civil rights legislation through Congress. In response to these changes, the Republican Party began to appeal to White Southerners opposed to the changes to their way of life.[14]

Until the 1960s, Southern states had overwhelmingly voted for the Democrats, but as White Southerners looked to block the tide of civil rights, they found a champion in Barry Goldwater and the Republican Party. Goldwater was defeated by Lyndon Johnson in the 1964 election but still won five states. Over the next fifty years, the GOP became the dominant party in the South, and Goldwater became the ideological benchmark for conservatives.[15]

Nixon, Reagan, and the Party of Law and Order

By the mid-1960s, a host of cities across the United States experienced riots and violence, ostensibly based on racial injustice and discrimination. In 1967, a presidential commission, called the Kerner Commission, was appointed to investigate the unrest. The reasons for the riots stemmed from the long-standing mistreatment of Blacks by Whites, as well as their lack of equality of opportunity in American society. The Kerner Commission concluded that there were in fact separate and unequal standards for Blacks and Whites, and these challenges posed serious threats to the country.[16]

When Richard Nixon campaigned for the presidency in 1968, a central piece of his platform focused on responding to the violence many cities experienced. His appeal to voters was to restore law and order, largely in reaction to the Black Power movement. Years later, President Trump had a similar response to the Black Lives Matter movement, which was seen by many Black Americans as a form of repression. Nixon's stance at the time created a schism within the Republican Party that allowed more conservatives to take over the party, ultimately resulting in the election of Ronald Reagan in the 1980s.[17]

When Ronald Reagan ran for president, he represented a departure from moderate Republicans like Gerald Ford, arguing that a "real" conservative was needed to guide the country into the future. Initially, the general public viewed this form of conservatism as an extreme version of the Republican Party. However, after a shrewd campaign, which changed a narrative based on race to one of economic development, Reaganism began to appeal to White voters, particularly from the working and middle class.[18]

Reagan was elected in 1980 by campaigning as a non-politician and an outsider to DC politics. His platform was to approach the struggling economy from a fiscally conservative perspective that included cutting taxes and eliminating many social programs that created a dependency on the government by many citizens. That prompted some voters who were hurt by the recession to vote for Reagan. His popularity helped him win reelection, and this new form of conservatism became popular.[19]

By the 1990s, the GOP's main platform was government deregulation, lower taxes, and national security. It was also known as a party of conservative family values—opposing gay marriage and abortion. In the early 2000s, particularly with the development of the Tea Party, Republicans started to embrace more extreme candidates, culminating in the endorsement and election of Donald Trump in 2016.[20]

Since 1980, moderate and liberal Republicans have increasingly found themselves on the outskirts of the party. As Rigueur (2016) explains, clear divisions have formed, leading to the rise of the Tea Party, which developed out of frustration with both the Democratic and the Republican Party under George W. Bush. As Rigueur (2016) has noted, the election of Barack Obama in 2012 was an indication that the Republican Party needed to come closer to the center of the spectrum and to cultivate more non-White voters.[21]

Instead, the party doubled down on catering to Whites despite the fact that this demographic segment of the voter population is shrinking. What has emerged, then, is a smaller, more vocal party that often endorses extremist views on a host of topics and embraces its Whiteness and disdain for minorities and their issues. Such an approach is seen by many experts as a losing strategy for the party as the diversity of the United States continues to grow and the size of the White population continues to shrink.

Modern-Day Republicans: The Tea Party

The Tea Party movement began in 2009 and was made up of conservative Republicans who were frustrated with the country's economic situation, calling for lower taxes and government spending. Tea Party lawmakers also had more extreme views on issues like abortion and immigration, and would soon help cause the 2013 government shutdown—the first in nearly two decades—to prevent funding for the Affordable Care Act. The growing influence of the Tea Party resulted in Republicans taking control of the House of Representatives in 2010.[22]

While many Republicans and conservative thinkers argue that the Republican Party is about smaller government, states' rights, and greater autonomy for individuals, not everyone agrees that this is really what the party represents. For instance, Balakian (2020) points out that the Republican Party tends to be rather selective in invoking these principles. As he notes, the "idea of 'pulling yourself up by the bootstraps,' may be fine for private life, but when applied to solving complex social problems it is absurd and destructive."[23]

For instance, Balakian (2020) points out that Republicans tend to ignore the importance of large-scale government when it comes to helping people, ending segregation, creating voter rights protections, or providing health care to people who need it. However, when it comes to funding corporations, especially bailouts when companies act irresponsibly, subsidizing farmers, and maintaining a strong military, Republicans actually endorse big government. Further evidence of the inconsistency in applying a conservative ideology is seen in the willingness of Republican administrations to ignore fiscal responsibility when it comes to the national debt. In fact, by one estimate, Republican administrations have increased the national debt more often and at far greater levels than Democrats over the past fifty years.[24]

Trump's election as president in 2016 is seen by many experts to be the start of a new era for the Republican Party—one that is characterized by extreme populist views and marked by an almost total and blind loyalty to Trump on any issue. Trump's popularity has been driven primarily by White voters, who have become disenchanted with the existing political process in American society. Another reason for Trump's popularity had to do with the economy. The 2008 financial crisis, which was created by changing regulations that allowed banks and insurance companies to maximize profits, driven by legislation and deregulation from a Republican-controlled Congress, caused millions of people to lose their jobs and homes, problems that many Americans still experienced in 2016. This is particularly true of lower-income Americans.[25] Yet, for some reason, Republicans are rarely assigned responsibility for creating the problem in the first place.

Deindustrialization, along with trade deals and relaxed immigration policies (necessary given the shortage of workers), coupled with both automation and a rise in outsourcing manufacturing to foreign countries, led to the loss of millions of jobs in the United States. As workers were losing jobs, many became convinced that their problems were not the result of greedy corporations or politicians that created these policies in the first place but instead were the result of liberal thinking that was illustrated by the influx of immigrants and programs dedicated to providing opportunities for minorities.[26]

THE RISE OF TRUMP AND TRUMPISM

Similar to Reagan, Trump resonated with the middle and working classes by pitching himself as a DC outsider who could fix their financial situations. He vowed to "drain the swamp," disrupt the status quo, bring jobs back to the United States, and implement zero tolerance immigration policies.[27] A strong economy and low unemployment rates at the time also helped to convince voters that Trump was ideally suited to serve as president.

Most Americans, both Democrat and Republican, think Trump's policies are controversial. Critics say his trade policies hurt Americans by raising prices on consumers. Others argue that some of his immigration policies were xenophobic and went against the United States' moral responsibility to welcome immigrants. They also point to policies that have made the United States more isolated from the rest of the world. His critics also say his behavior showed a disregard for the rule of law.[28]

Trump knows Republican allies will not push back against his divisive language and behavior. Those who have tried to push back have found that he endorses their opponents, often resulting in failed reelection attempts. Other conservative critics have either retired from politics altogether or have left the Republican Party.[29]

TRUMPISM DEFINED

What, exactly, is Trumpism and why are there so many people in support of the things Trump says and does? Is it an actual ideology, or is it simply a position that reflects Trump's personality more than an actual platform? To begin, a political ideology can be understood as a set of ideals, principles, and doctrines that provide a roadmap or framework to achieve some type of social order in society. Not only should a political ideology identify the goals of how a society should work, it also outlines the means by which those goals are achieved.[30] This would include things like the economy, education, religious freedom, and gender issues. While this is a rather simple definition, it gives us a starting point for understanding Trumpism.

However, there is considerable disagreement about whether Trumpism is really a political ideology at all. In fact, since 2016, experts, social observers, and others have consistently disagreed as to what constitutes Trumpism. On one hand, some experts argue Trumpism has no ideological foundation—that Trumpism denotes a feeling about society rather than abstract principles that guide action. In this way, Trumpism appeals to certain groups because it is based on the idea that traditional government continues to exploit them and prevents any meaningful progress. This approach is what sociologist Michael Kimmel refers to as *aggrieved entitlement*.[31] Similarly, former National Security advisor John Bolton argues that Trumpism has no philosophical foundation but rather is the culmination of the whims and biases of Trump himself.[32]

Others refer to Trumpism as an American version of illiberalism.[33] According to Main (2021), illiberalism is a political ideology that is anti-democratic, anti–human rights, anti–rule of law and anti-diversity.[34] Other experts note that Trumpism is either outright fascism, or some version of it.[35] These observers note that whatever form it takes, Trumpism represents a danger to democracy despite the fact that many supporters endorse it.

One way to begin defining Trumpism is to solicit the source—in other words, to ask Trump what Trumpism means. In 2021, at a Conservative Political Action Conference, Trump stated that Trumpism means "great trade deals . . . not deals where we give away everything, our jobs, our money. It means low taxes and eliminating job-killing regulations. It means strong borders, but people coming into our country based on a system of merit." He continued, "It means no riots in the streets. It means law enforcement. It means very strong protection for the Second Amendment and the right to keep and bear arms. It means support for the forgotten men and women who have been taken advantage of for so many years."[36] Clearly this definition lacks the philosophical framework that is reflective of conventional philosophical ideologies. Arguably, what Trump offered was little more than policy agendas and even those lacked specificity.

Mounk (2019) points out one way to define Trumpism is by identifying it as a form of populism.[37] According to the Center for Research on Extremism, populism refers to an ideology that considers society to be ultimately separated into two antagonistic groups, "the pure people" and "the corrupt elite." The opposition between "the people" and "the elite" in populism is not because the two groups have different socioeconomic positions but because they have different moral statuses; "the people" are supposedly pure and authentic, whereas "the elite" are not. Many experts argue that populism is a rather simple explanation and does not even qualify as an ideology.[38]

The development and popularity of populism stems from three primary factors: (1) the perception that the standard of living for the working and middle class is decreasing; (2) dramatic demographic changes resulting in a shrinking White population, which generates fear and anxiety about the position of Whites in the future; and (3) the rise of social media, where extremist views and perceptions of minorities and others is presented to the population without much filtering, verification, or accountability.

Populists argue that the political system does not represent working- and middle-class people and the elites who control the social institutions are the cause of the problem. Populists take advantage of people's disenchantment with the existing political system and attempt to capitalize on a promise to give the power back to the people. However, as most experts note, in reality what occurs is a form of democracy that does exactly the opposite.[39]

It is what Mounk (2019) calls a "democracy without rights." In this way, a populist approach begins to resemble a form of authoritarianism or even a dictatorship. A populist leader convinces his followers that he alone is their champion, and he is the only one who can remedy the situation for the betterment of society.[40] It also explains why Trump has continued to ignore or minimize the democratic institutions created to prevent a dictator from assuming power over the country. In Trump's case, he continued to defy laws, regulations, institutions, and the rule of law since, in his mind, "I alone can fix this."[41]

It also explains the incitement of supporters on January 6 to storm the Capitol, because, after all, Trump was the only person who spoke for the country and he could not accept the fact that millions of people voted him out of office. If one believes in Trumpism, and millions of Americans do, the only way Trump could have lost the election was by having it stolen from him. Thus, Trumpism is based on a platform of populism; but the danger in such a position is that it gives an enormous amount of power and control to an individual rather than to institutions designed to keep the process fair and equitable.[42]

A more extreme view of Trumpism is that it is a form of fascism. Stanley (2020) offers insight into the nature of political fascism and applies many of its defining features to the Trump administration. Stanley argues that fascist politics do not necessarily lead to a fascist state, but, in the end, it is a means of obtaining and keeping power.[43] For example, Stanley (2020) argues that critical elements of fascist politics include: (1) a description of a mythical past; (2) extensive use of propaganda; (3) a focus on anti-intellectualism; (4) unreality, hierarchy, and victimhood; (5) an emphasis on law and order; (6) concerns about sexual anxiety; (7) appeals to the heartland; and (8) a dismantling of public welfare and unity. What makes fascist politics so dangerous, he says, is that there is a particular emphasis on dehumanizing segments of the population, which ultimately justifies inhumane treatment of people, even their extermination, and the repression of freedoms. But the most telling symptom of fascist politics is division—the concerted effort to separate the population into ingroups and outgroups.[44]

Stanley (2020) argues that fascist politicians confirm their "us versus them" distinction by a revisionist version of what he calls *a mythical past*, where they rewrite the population's understanding of its past by twisting events and trends through the use of propaganda promoting anti-intellectualism and attacking universities and education systems that challenge their ideas. There really is only one role for the university under fascism—to support the dominant view and the mythical nation; otherwise it is seen as a threat that must be extinguished.[45] One can easily see this in the latest discussions about critical race theory and the teaching of American history in public schools.

Stanley (2020) points out that, essentially, the goal of education becomes creating obedient citizens, not critical thinkers who might question the existing narrative. In fact, under fascist politics, research and university life is dominated by revisionist history and the control of research to promote the fabricated narrative. In those instances, when fascist politicians cannot invent a nostalgic version of the past, or if they cannot control scholars who might criticize the inaccuracies of the claims being made, they are either attacked professionally, as in the case of some states threatening to eliminate tenure for professors, or sometimes physically. An alternative approach is to selectively identify events that promote a positive view of society. As Stanley points out, there are a host of examples of this feature of fascist politics all over the world. In the end, anti-intellectualism attempts to create conflict between certain groups, which teaches people to hate each other rather than tolerate and explore difference of opinion.[46]

Ultimately, fascist politics create a sense of unreality in which conspiracy theories and fake news dominate discussions and replace actual facts and meaningful debate.[47] Recent examples in the United States include the allegations of voter fraud and "Stop the Steal" claims by Trump about the election or the characterization of immigrants as criminals, terrorists, and job stealers. Fascists also attack the "liberal media" for censoring discussions about the promotion of conspiracy theories. Similarly, the wave of legislation against teaching critical race theory or LGBTQ topics in schools is framed as an issue of parental rights.

All of this is designed to create a sense of what Stanley (2020) calls an "unreality" that departs significantly from what is actually occurring. Conspiracy theories are particularly dangerous because they provide simple explanations for irrational emotions such as xenophobia and the resentment, hatred, and vilification of others. Conspiracy theories also create a sense of general suspicion and mistrust—of institutions as well as toward one another. And this is the ultimate goal of fascist politics—to destroy the relations of mutual respect between citizens and replace it with the trust in one leader—whom followers regard as the only person worthy of their respect, loyalty, and trust.[48]

This unreality is extended to include a distorted victimization of Whites. For example, members of the Republican Party in the United States are attempting to promote a narrative that denies the way slaves were treated, claiming it victimizes White Americans, especially from the South.[49] Similarly, criticism of critical race theory is an effort to minimize the long-standing discriminatory treatment of Blacks, which questions the framework and structure of the entire system. Instead, many conservatives want to attribute the problem to a rotten apples theory, where the discrimination is seen as being committed by select individuals rather than a system-wide problem.[50] This tendency to ignore events or minimize their impact is also seen in Trump supporters and even members of Congress recasting the events of January 6 as a mild protest by patriotic demonstrators.[51]

In the construction of an unreality narrative, many conservatives cast the problem as minorities, immigrants, and other outgroups taking jobs away from "real" citizens, and diversity is a threat to the acceptable ways of life Whites have enjoyed and come to appreciate. Additionally, since minorities challenge existing laws or even engage in lawbreaking behavior, a tough law and order approach is needed to protect the dominant group's way of life. In other words, fascists attempt to turn arguments about equality into a type of victimization of Whites. And given that fascists play into the idea that loyalty to one's tribe is a core requirement, any perceived threats to the group are seen as threats to the entire nation. Constructing fear of certain groups makes it easier to "sell" the idea of nationalism or a national identity.[52]

Questions regarding sexual activity are also raised since the dominant view of society is patriarchal—there is no real place for a growing sense of gender equity. Fascist propaganda promotes fear of race mixing, of interbreeding, and a panic about a departure from the patriarchal family structure. Transgendered people, or any member of the LGBTQIA community, are seen as a threat to traditional gender roles.

Finally, consistent with this fear narrative, many conservatives view certain groups as lazy and surviving off the hard work of others. The welfare state, then, produces a form of chronic dependency and entitlement. All of these arguments serve as illustrations of the division between "us" and "them."[53]

Some experts argue that while Trump's language and policies are offensive at a number of levels and potentially threaten democracy in America, they fail to meet the threshold of a true definition of fascism.[54] For example, at its core, fascism reflects the breakdown of social order due to an economic crisis and the ensuing confrontation between different social classes and ideological groups, all vying for political control. As a practical matter, fascism strips away individual rights and glorifies the state. Under a fascist regime, the state has complete control over every aspect of national life.

Fascism bans political opposition, ends constitutional rule, enforces cen-
sorship, and imprisons political opponents. Totalitarianism and state terrorism
are defining attributes of fascism. Fascists do not oppose private property but
control all aspects of the economy, sometimes referred to as *state capitalism*.
Fascism also controls the monetary system, sets prices, and promotes large
government projects and all sorts of public works as part of the pursuit of its
alleged "full-employment" economy.[55]

Obviously, there are different examples of fascism, as seen in Italy under
Mussolini as well as in Germany under Adolf Hitler. These two examples
are sometimes seen as a form of classical and extreme versions of fascism.
Under this form of government, fascism's goal is to create fear and identify
all manner of enemies of the state. To counter this, Mussolini made use of
paramilitary squads, known as the *Blackshirts*, whose activities were instrumental in the pursuit and collection of political power and the creation of a
dictatorship in Italy. Similarly, in describing the Nazi rise to power in the
1920s, Hitler formed the paramilitary organization known as the *Brownshirts*,
with a similar set of responsibilities as Mussolini's Blackshirts. Under Hitler,
the goal was the extermination of Jews and the promotion of Whites as the
superior race.[56]

In comparing this form of fascism to the efforts and activities of the Trump
administration, the similarities are fewer and less compelling. While there is
disdain for non-Whites and a rhetoric and platform of ignoring the existing
rule of law, coupled with a dismantling of the existing protocols that allow a
dictatorship to flourish, Trump's economic policies can be defined as extreme
neoliberalism that is driven by free market principles, not governmental
control. As far as his opposition to "free trade" is concerned, it was initiated by his belief that other countries were bending the rules at the expense
of the United States, not because he was, in principle, against the idea of
"free trade."[57]

What some observers note is that the Trump presidency and its policies
were ultimately seeking plutocratic control of the country, not fascism. What
Trump did was use a wide range of what is sometimes called *proto-fascist*
rhetoric and challenged the existing democratic rule, based on his campaign against corporate elites who continued to further their own interests.
The irony, of course, is that Trump's words and actions reflected a similar
approach and catered to the very elite group that he chafed against on the
campaign trail. Despite efforts to "drain the swamp," Trump actually took
great personal and political advantage of the existing system and made
numerous efforts to undermine the rules. But Trump's efforts have been
used by many other authoritarian political figures around the world, who use
similar disparaging and condescending language and tactics, all designed to
portray him as a benevolent leader and champion of the working class.[58]

Still others have recently pointed out that the version of Trumpism that began in 2016, what is sometimes referred to as *pre-presidential Trumpism*, evolved over time. By 2020, with Trump's attempt to overthrow the election results and his actions surrounding the January 6 violence at the US Capitol, the latest version of Trumpism more closely resembles fascism in its orientation and focus.

For example, Kilgore (2021) points out that pre-presidential Trumpism operated through some of the protocols associated with being a president. Although he dismissed many of the rules of governance, Trump referred to this as a "law and order" platform. However, recent events—such as the glorification of Ashli Babbitt, whom Trump called a patriot instead of someone who went to the US Capitol with the intent to do harm to congressional leaders—are characteristic of something much less focused on the rule of law.[59]

Surely mob attacks against democratic leaders fulfilling their duty, all in an attempt to overthrow the existing system, is not only shocking and alarming but also reflects a lack of respect for the rule of law and societal institutions. It's one thing to dismiss or attempt to recast the violence on January 6 as being overblown or as a peaceful protest gone wrong—which has been the way many conservatives have viewed the events. But the far right's approach to Babbitt's death, along with Trump's endorsement of rioters' behavior, that the insurrection was a good thing, is quite another, and raises many questions.[60]

Thus, while Trump undermined the democratic process and infrastructure that has existed for centuries, and while he clearly fit the mold of an aspiring dictator or authoritarian ruler, there were no Brownshirts or Blackshirts; no effort at exterminating a class of people; and his economic policies were not designed to enhance the state's control. If anything, Trump represented a greedy capitalist, determined to profit from his political and economic control of the country. But this is far different from qualifying as a fascist regime. As Polychroniou (2017) points out, to include Trump in this form of fascism is to detract from the severity of damage fascist regimes inflict on a society and its people.[61]

Rather than debating whether Trumpism is populist in origin (or even whether populism is an ideology)[62] or fascist in nature, based on what Trump and his administration have done during his presidency, there is little to no argument that it is right-wing authoritarian or even illiberal in nature. What Trump has done while president is create a space in which his legacy presents a significant shift in how democracy is understood and operates. As Aguirre (2020) points out, there are several important data points where Trump's legacy creates many concerns for the future of the United States and even for the rest of the world.[63]

For instance, Trump has demonstrated that it is possible to be elected president without the popular vote—flaws in the Electoral College, along with a subversion of democratic rule from within, serve as examples to future aspirants of the White House, as well as for leaders/rulers in other countries. What's more, once elected, the extensive claims of fraud, the creation and promotion of fake news, and the blaming of the media and anyone who disagrees with the outcome can create doubts about the legitimacy of free and fair elections.[64]

Trump has also shown that, for those who wish to succeed economically, the ruler need only circumvent or even eliminate all state regulations, particularly those that hamper efforts to portray a robust economy. Additionally, Trump and his followers have shown that with repeated and consistent proclamations, along with the regular vilification of certain groups, racism, sexism, contempt for liberal democracy, and denial of climate change and human rights, almost anything said or done can be normalized to the point where little or nothing is considered too extreme. In fact, regrettably, as some have noted, such shameless excoriation of non-White males or non-supporters is seen as a breath of fresh air in politics as well as contributing to the portrayal of Trump as a "strong" leader.[65]

Trump and Trumpism have also allowed all manner of white supremacist groups to gain some level of credibility and support, even those who advocate for the overthrow of democracy. Additionally, as was mentioned, Trump has consistently discredited science, the country's leading experts on a host of topics including public health topics and climate change, and has consistently promoted conspiracy theories and dubious "facts" that run counter to actual, available data. Perhaps no better example of Trump's anti-science stance was his handling of the COVID-19 pandemic.[66]

Another legacy data point for Trump has been his connection to the Christian Right. This has been primarily accomplished by claiming to be pro-life and by appointing conservative judges to federal courts and even the US Supreme Court. Further, Trump's apparent endorsement of religious freedom and autonomy, which is seen by critics as code for the Christian Right's agenda, have convinced Christian leaders that he wants what they want. So strong is his support among evangelical Christians on this issue that many are willing to overlook a host of ideological inconsistencies and offenses by Trump.

Finally, Trump's foreign policy is anything but a cooperative venture, and he considers the America First approach to something like international trade as a means to leveraging the relationship of the United States with other countries. This is based on the belief that the United States has been taken advantage of by other countries and, therefore, must renegotiate its position in international trade.[67]

In the end, Trumpism does not appear to have a consistent ideology nor does it have stable tenets from which to draw in assessing the behavior of its adherents. Instead, what Trump has accomplished is to create chaos, to respond inconsistently to a wide range of issues and challenges, and to constantly proclaim that he is the only person who can manage the country and its needs. The background factors that set the stage for a leader like Trump had been building among certain groups for some time, making his brand of politics ripe for support and endorsement. Unsurprisingly, Trump has been playing to the needs and emotions of his base from the beginning. This is where the problem lies: Trump, Trumpism, and even Trumpsters are not the problem, they are all symptoms of something far more dangerous and disturbing.

TRUMPSTERS: A PROFILE

In trying to make sense of who voted for Trump as well as what types of people consider themselves to be loyal followers, it would be a mistake to think of a Trump voter or supporter as the racist, xenophobic, violent, narrow-minded person who has been duped into believing the lies and inaccuracies that have become the hallmark of the Trump presidency. Certainly, there are some followers who have been misled and for whom logic and rational thinking are ineffective when describing Trump, but there are plenty of other people who voted for Trump and had different reasons for doing so.

Trump loyalists are not a fringe group of radicals who are hell-bent on destroying democracy. True, there is a subset of the population that may feel this way, but Trumpism and the antics of the former president are not a simple one-off aberration based on Trump's personality, proclivity toward sensationalism, and a constant need for attention. Trumpism has been building momentum for some time, and we should consider that there is a large segment of the American population that believes his form of leadership and government is preferable to democracy and its existing institutions.

As Fitzduff (2017) points out, it would also be a mistake to dismiss or condemn Trumpsters as ignorant, vulgar, and divisive people, who are irrational in their beliefs and are generally ill-informed on the issues.[68] Such an approach overlooks the context and meaning behind why supporting Trump makes sense to them and what it says about the direction we may be heading in this country.

In other words, Trump supporters are not a fringe group of extremists who should not be taken seriously. Instead, we need to consider the fact that 74 million people voted for Trump in 2020, and that constitutes a sizeable segment of our population. It also means that there is a large group of Americans who believe Trump and are willing to overlook extraordinarily unethical, immoral, and even illegal behavior in exchange for their issues being addressed.[69]

Consider, for example, the fact that Hillary Clinton received a bit more than 65 million (65,853,516) of the 136 million votes for president in 2016, about 48.2 percent. Trump received about 63 million (46.1 percent). Forgetting for a moment that Trump won the presidency without the majority of the popular vote—meaning, he won key states with more Electoral College delegates—63 million (62,984,825) is still a sizeable segment of the population. In that election, Trump received about 40 million votes from Republicans, about 20 million from Independents, and about three million from Democrats.[70]

In the 2020 election, Trump received even higher support from voters, where he received 74 million votes. The comments made earlier about Trump being a symptom of a larger problem is a pause point—the fact that such a large segment of voters considered him and his brand of leadership the more attractive option needs to be considered. Granted, Biden received nearly 80 million votes in 2020, and the public made an important statement about the long-term future of Trump politics, but such a large segment of supporters continues to give Trump enormous influence in the Republican Party.

So why did people vote for Trump? There are a host of reasons, as outlined in table 2.1. At one end of the spectrum are those who voted for Trump because they stood to gain financially from Trump's policies on the economy, when compared to what they thought Democrats would provide.[71] Others voted for Trump because they disliked his opponent more than they disliked him. This was particularly true in 2016 with Hillary Clinton, but even in 2020 when Biden was elected, the phrase "Let's Go Brandon!" was a pointed criticism of Biden and his presidency. Others voted for Trump because he represented their political party—and voters could feel comfortable that, at least theoretically, Trump was a Republican and stood for the main principles that the party espoused. Time has shown us that many of these voters, particularly moderate and left-leaning Republicans, are leaving the party because Trump's brand of politics is not in alignment with their views.[72]

Another reason some people likely voted for Trump was due to the entertainment value he provided. These voters liked the fact that Trump was unconventional, even a "shock" politician, where one never knew what he

Table 2.1 Reasons for Voting for Trump

Benign	Moderate	Extreme
personal gain	single-topic voter	white supremacists
disdain for opponent	Republican Party loyalist	conspiracy theorists
entertainment value	angry White workers	fascists

would say next, and there seemed to be no limits or boundaries in his comments and actions. These voters, likely drawing from Trump's celebrity status, may have viewed Trump as similar to his role on the "reality" TV show *The Apprentice*, where he challenged the status quo and routinely disparaged contestants who lost.

The same "winner take all" approach, complete with condescending comments and personal attacks, carried over into the White House. This may appear to be a fickle reason for voting for or supporting a president, but perhaps it stems from a dissatisfaction with traditional politics and a Congress that cannot seem to get any meaningful legislation passed. Trump, as a mercurial outsider who "shakes things up" and isn't afraid to be honest about what he sees, may appease voters who are cynical about our current institutions.[73]

These reasons are not likely to be seen as characteristic of a Trumpster—instead, they are more likely to be understood as reasons why some people voted for Trump: it was convenient; voting for Trump was the lesser of two evils; Trump's policies benefitted a voter segment economically; or there was an entertainment value to the outlandish way Trump talked and acted.

Others may have voted for Trump because they tend to be single-issue voters—meaning their decision to vote for him was based on where Trump stood on the topics that matter most to them. Examples could include gun control, religious freedom, or abortion. In these instances, other topics or issues matter less to a voter than their stance on their hot-button issue. It also means that single-topic voters may be more willing to overlook less than desirable behavior or positions on other matters.[74] This is an important point, and it's one we will come back to in subsequent chapters to explain what appears to be an inconsistent or misguided loyalty to Trump.

As we delve more deeply into Trump's loyal base, we will begin to see voting patterns and reasons for supporting Trump that are more disturbing and even pathological. For instance, we know that a large part of Trump's base of supporters are White, uneducated men. We also know that evangelical Christians are an important segment of Trumpsters, along with white supremacists, conspiracy theorists, fascists, and those with anti-democracy views and the belief that a dictatorship is a preferable form of government.[75]

According to most observers, including a 2021 report from the Brookings Institution, the uneducated White male has been a consistent demographic in the Trump-supporting population, representing about two-thirds of it. While Trump saw increases in support from White evangelical Christians, Republicans, rural voters, and White women, this segment of the population held steady. Part of Trump's allure for this demographic is that he appeals to their sense of fear, anger, and disillusionment about the quality of their lives.[76]

As Cherlin (2020) points out, deindustrialization, outsourcing jobs to other countries, and other factors played a significant role in the perception of working-class Whites about their current situations as well as their futures.[77] Many blue-collar workers have watched their jobs disappearing. Bradlee's (2018) book, *The Forgotten: How the People of One Pennsylvania County Elected Donald Trump and Changed America*, showed that many workers felt that they were losing jobs and their social dominance as Whites in American culture. This sense of entitlement and privilege was sometimes referred to as *cultural displacement* and reflected a belief that the government didn't care about them or their concerns.

Similarly, sociologist Arlie Hochschild's (2018) account of the working class in rural Louisiana paints a portrait of working-class Whites who feel that the American dream, based on the idea of working hard and discipline, has been taken away from them by economic and cultural factors, such as the exportation of jobs to other countries, the wage squeeze of the last few decades, and a rising economic inequality between the wealthy and poor, particularly those in the unskilled and semi-skilled manufacturing segment of the economy. In addition, an influx of immigrants and other minority groups are seen as taking opportunities from working-class Whites, all of which results in a backlash against non-Whites.

The belief in these trends has fueled the anger and resentment toward these groups, with working-class Whites feeling as though they are not getting what they think they deserve, particularly since many minorities are receiving preferential treatment at their expense. These explanations and emotions have created a climate in which many Whites feel that America has lost many of its core values: an honorable way of life defined by hard work, fair wages, and freedom to make one's own choices. What is needed is a return to a time when national pride mattered and fairness and hard work were the norm, and a desire to "make America great again."[78]

It is this dissatisfaction and perception of victimhood that led to the rise of a toxic form of politics found first in the Tea Party and later in Trumpism.[79] Add to this the stoking of fear about the presence of immigrants and other non-Whites by Trump, who confirmed and highlighted many Whites' fears about the future, and the alignment with Trump and Trumpism seems easier to understand. This is particularly true given his promises to bring back jobs to the United States and to limit immigration so that Americans would have the opportunity to get those jobs again.[80]

In short, many Whites were angry and Trump promised to fix their problems. At the same time, these supporters felt, and still feel, that the government, despite longtime politicians from both parties routinely promising to help them, failed to do so. Trump represented a change in thinking and in action, and people wanted a change. This is seen in the endorsement of Trump at the polls as well as a willingness to ignore many of his less than admirable behaviors.[81]

Of course, not everyone agrees with this account of why uneducated voters aligned themselves with Trump. As Smith and Hanley (2018) point out in their study, most Trump voters in 2016 voted for him not because they were financially stressed but because they shared his prejudices. In their analysis, while millions of voters were labeled as White working class, many of this group voted against Trump. Instead of financial reasons, however, as Smith and Hanley (2018) argue, it was more likely that they did so because the prejudices outlined by Trump, particularly those that targeted minorities and women, as well as the ones that endorsed intolerant leaders, reflected a form of authoritarianism.[82]

At the more extreme end of the spectrum are those groups that are much more vocal and angry—this includes the white supremacists, authoritarians/fascists, and conspiracy theorists, many of whom have not only bought into Trumpism completely but are even willing to engage in violence against those who disagree with them. This group of supporters also varies to some extent in terms of their zeal and enthusiasm, meaning they are not a homogeneous group either, but they tend to be closer in ideological agreement and in strategies to achieve their goals than other types of Trump supporters. It is this group that is most often portrayed as generic Trumpsters and condemned for narrow-mindedness, xenophobic, anti-democratic beliefs, and in some cases domestic terrorism. Others see this segment of Trump supporters as cult-like figures who have been duped by Trump's lies and are spurred to action by his rants, outlandish commentary, and conspiracy theories.

As it relates to white supremacists, part of the attraction to Trump is not just his language against immigrants but also his endorsement, essentially, of their actions both during his campaign and consistently during his presidency. As Haltiwanger (2020) points out, there have been numerous instances in which Trump had the opportunity to condemn the actions of white supremacists and the violence they inflict on minorities, but did not.[83]

Examples include his famous quote regarding the Charlottesville riots, where, in August 2017, Trump blamed "many sides" for the violence that occurred. The president also said there were "very fine people" on "both sides" of the protests. Similarly, during the 2020 presidential debate, when moderator Chris Wallace asked Trump: "Are you willing, tonight, to condemn white supremacists and militia groups and to say that they need to stand down?" Trump replied: "Proud Boys, stand back and stand by! But I'll tell you what, somebody's got to do something about antifa and the left."[84]

What makes this statement so extraordinary is the fact that the Proud Boys are a far-right group that has rejected the notion that it promotes white supremacy, even as its leaders regularly share white nationalist memes and have affiliations with other known extremist groups. The Southern Poverty Law Center, along with the Anti-Defamation League, considers the Proud Boys to be a hate group that espouses, among other things, white supremacist and anti-Semitic ideologies.[85]

Trump also used white supremacist language during a rally in Minnesota, where he told the crowd of virtually all White supporters that they had "good genes," a phrase that is easily linked to the views of neo-Nazis that Whites are genetically superior.[86] Thus, this segment of Trumpsters is far more likely to engage in violence, to hold racist views, and to intimidate those who disagree with Trumpism. This is also the group, along with conspiracy theorists, that is most likely to be seen by Trump critics as what it means to be a Trump supporter. Again, this represents a small but extremely vocal and active portion of the Trump base, but it does not speak for all Trumpsters or even all Trump voters.

Another segment of Trumpsters includes those who embrace conspiracy theories. It should be noted that conspiracy theories and their supporters have been around for most of American history. The difference between the conspiracy theorists of the past and the present is the speed with which information is presented and the resulting extremeness of reactions to misinformation that seem to be occurring today. The reason? Access to the internet, the rise of social media, and the weaponization of conspiracy theories encouraged by President Trump, particularly the claims about a rigged election.[87]

As Olmstead (2011) points out, the number and intensity of conspiracy theories, along with members' willingness to act on these false narratives, has increased significantly in the recent years. In January 2021, an NPR poll found that about one-third of respondents believed that voter fraud helped President Biden win the election, and about 25 percent believed that voting machines changed Trump votes to Biden ones or that cities and counties misrepresented the vote count.[88]

A similar poll conducted in 2020 found that 40 percent of Americans believed the coronavirus was made in a lab in China, despite the absence of any evidence proving this to be true. Similarly, in response to the statement (roughly paraphrased) "A group of Satan-worshipping elites who run a child sex ring are trying to control our politics and media," which is at the heart of the QAnon conspiracy theory, 17 percent said they thought the statement was true, while 37 percent said they didn't know.[89]

In sum, not only are the number of conspiracy theories increasing in size and in their reach but they are also having an effect on people's understanding of what actually occurred.[90] This impact is seen in other polls, where two-thirds of Republicans believe voter fraud got Biden elected and only about half of Republicans said they accepted the outcome of the presidential election, despite the lack of any evidence of voter fraud. Nearly 40 percent of Republicans also felt that there was a "deep state" working to undermine President Trump.[91] Clearly, the effects of conspiracy theories are being seen in how people understand and subsequently vote on issues.

Finally, there is one other group of Trumpsters worth noting. As Dean and Altemeyer (2020) point out, there is also an authoritarian influence for many, if not most, Trump supporters. They argue that there are two types of authoritarian personalities: social dominators and authoritarian followers. *Social dominators* are those people who believe in inequality between groups, believing that theirs is a group that is superior to all others. These are people who attempt to dominate everyone and gain as much power as possible.

As Dean and Altemeyer (2020) have shown, social dominators are less likely to endorse the central ideas of democracy and believe that people in subordinate positions should remain in their designated places. In this view, people born with the advantages of wealth, race, and privilege deserve to keep them. Submitting to this type of social order is said to provide safety from attacks by others—because the dominators will protect them. People with these views were attracted to Trump largely because he promised to protect White, economically vulnerable, undereducated Americans against immigrants and other non-Whites who threatened their way of life. Social dominators, as long as they remain in charge, are unconcerned about Trump's thoughts, words, or actions with regard to people who are not "real" Americans. Social dominators do not believe in right or wrong as much as they agree that lying, manipulating, and cheating gets you what you want.[92]

The second group outlined by Dean and Altemeyer (2020) is *authoritarian followers*. It is comprised of people who are submissive, fearful, and desperately want a strong leader to protect them. This belief in superiority is based on their religious training and they tend to be highly self-righteous. This group includes White evangelicals, a key component of the Trump base. While social dominators want to control other people and groups, authoritarian followers want to submit to authority and authoritarian leaders, particularly people they think should be in charge. Sometimes this group is referred to as *right-wing authoritarians* because they prefer to submit to leaders already in power. The term *right wing* is not a part of any political ideology but, rather, a set of three related attitudes:

1. Conventionalism, or the belief in old-fashioned norms and morality.
2. Authoritarian submission, meaning respectful and submissive support for existing authorities and institutions.
3. Authoritarian aggression, which involves harsh and punitive mechanisms to control people's behavior.[93]

This type of behavior is seen in Trump's supporters' willingness to accept Trump's guidance surrounding COVID-19, where many people ignored advice from medical experts and scientists about how one becomes infected and why one should wear a mask. Supporters continued to believe Trump's claims and remained supportive even when these claims were refuted with the data. It also explains why Trump followers insisted on not wearing a mask and vilifying those who did. Why? Because Trump refused to wear a mask and thought that it was an ineffective way to prevent the spread of the disease. In fact, mask wearing became an indicator to many Trump followers as a sign of disloyalty to Trump.[94]

There are also what Dean and Altemeyer (2020) refer to as *double highs*, which are people who score highly on both social dominator indicators and authoritarian follower scales. These are people who strongly believe in other people submitting to authorities, as long as those authorities include them or are affiliated with them in some way. Double highs often combine the worst elements of the two authoritarian personalities and present dangerous characteristics.[95]

One might wonder if authoritarians tend to embrace authority figures, why would they endorse a president who is known for breaking the rules and disparaging all the existing social institutions designed to maintain order in society? As Jacobs (2018) points out, there are different types of authoritarian thinking, and supporting a president like Trump is connected to the most difficult and extreme type, sometimes called *authoritarian aggressor*. These are people who take a combative approach to people they disagree with or see as a threat.[96]

The research also shows that authoritarianism involves the desire to support strong and determined authority figures, such as Trump. The things that critics of Trump find most offensive about him—his need to dominate others and conversations, his leanings toward white supremacy, his bullying language and behavior, his disparaging characterizations of those he does not like or who disagree with him—are exactly what appeals to his hardcore supporters. It also means they are likely to remain loyal in the face of virtually any scandal or inappropriate action by him.

TRUMPSTERS AS A CULT

The extreme positions taken by many Trump supporters, along with the seemingly blind faith they place in Trump, including career politicians and others who have pledged their faith in him and his tactics, where they are willing to accept virtually anything Trump says and are quick to defend his actions, is concerning.

As Bender (2021) points out, this type of fanatical loyalty is not uncommon in many areas of social life—after all, followers of the Grateful Dead rock band had some of the most loyal fans in music history. Called *Deadheads*, thousands of fans would follow the band from city to city, often leading a nomadic lifestyle to attend every concert on the Grateful Dead tour. The loyalty of fans as well as the concert experience, according to some sociologists, had a spiritual dimension, making it more than simply a rock concert.[97]

Another example of intense loyalty to a public figure could include Bruce Springsteen, a rock musician whose songs resonated with blue-collar fans about life in America.[98] Like the Deadheads, by most accounts, Springsteen fans looked upon their experiences at his concerts as more of a spiritual experience—where the music made an emotional connection not found from other musicians. Still other examples include fans of sports teams, where the intensity of the enthusiasm and loyalty to the organization, particularly when the team is losing, is a marker of a "true" fan.

Bender (2021) identifies a group that is similar to Deadheads and Springsteen fans that follow Trump. Called *Front Row Joes*, these Trump supporters, about fifteen hundred in number, actually followed Trump around the country and attended many of his rallies during the 2016 and 2020 campaigns. Given that Trump used the political rally extensively during his campaigns, averaging one in every ten days after he was sworn in as president, this is a central part of his messaging effort and a core element to his support base.

Bender (2021) points out that Front Row Joes, some of whom attended more than fifty Trump rallies, often arrived days before to be first in line for front-row seats. Front Row Joes camped out at the ticket office, often in extreme temperatures, and came from all manner of backgrounds. The excitement and adrenaline generated from attending a Trump rally, particularly from the front row, in the presence of thousands of other supporters, provided fans with a sense of purpose and that Trump was their advocate, and they could feel good about the fact that things were going to improve under his leadership. This steady diet of Trump rhetoric also reinforced the narrative of hate that characterized Trump's presidency and bred a sense of loyalty to Trump that allowed him to say and do almost anything—and his followers would remain supportive.[99]

With the exception of Front Row Joes, who are the closest in characteristics to music groupies like Deadheads or Springsteen fans, the difference between loyal music or sports fans and Trumpsters relates to the negativity the latter group demonstrates toward those who disagree with their point of view. Grateful Dead fans were not likely to engage in mean-spirited, vulgar, caustic intimidation and bullying if another fan disagreed with Grateful Dead music or anything its lead singer, Jerry Garcia, had to say. It would also be unlikely that Springsteen fans would threaten violence or someone's family because they said something disparaging about Springsteen or his music.

Even avid sports fans, perhaps the closest and most accurate comparison to Trump loyalists, some of whom are intensely loyal to their favorite teams, are not typically engaged in violence against rival fans or who question the decision-making of a coach or leader of the organization. What Trumpsters demonstrate is an entirely higher order of loyalty and blind obedience to Trump and his ideas—even when those comments are proven to be inaccurate.

Such extreme reactions have led some experts and observers to wonder if Trump supporters are acting in a way that is similar to cult followers. Is it really the case that Trump loyalists are part of a cult? Is Trump really that powerful and charismatic of a leader that he can essentially say or do anything and his supporters will continue to endorse him and ignore the consequences of his actions? These and other questions will be addressed in the next chapter.

Chapter 3

Trump, Trumpsters, and Cults

Given the extreme positions taken by former president Trump on various topics, as well as the loyalty many in his camp seem to have toward him, along with the fealty to Trump of many members of the Republican Party, it is reasonable to consider the possibility that perhaps Trump sees himself as a type of cult leader, and his supporters may resemble deviant cult members. In fact, when referring to Trump, the term *cult* has become a popular way to describe his relationship with his supporters as well as explain some of their behavior.

As discussed in the previous chapter, not all Trump voters are Trump loyalists. In addition, not all Trump supporters equally endorse Trump's behavior, language, and actions. Trump supporters come in all shapes and sizes, and not all of them embrace Trumpism completely (however it is defined), and not all of those who do embrace it are part of what researchers would consider to be a deviant cult. But what about that smaller group of extreme loyalists?

For the purposes of understanding, let's start with the idea that this is a group that reflects such a deep-seated belief in Trumpism and Trump that they might be seen as a deviant cult. To begin making some type of assessment of this trend, it is important to first discuss what constitutes a cult and what the available empirical research suggests are the characteristics that make up both cult leaders and cult followers. In the process, we may develop some understanding about whether or not all or some portion of Trumpsters are a part of a deviant cult.

OVERVIEW OF CULTS

A cult, as with many of the topics covered in this book, is complicated and challenging to define and explain. Adding to the problem is the absence of a standard or universal definition of a cult.

According to Lalich (2004), a cult can be either a clearly defined group of people or a rather loose social group tied to each other by a charismatic leader. Cults are usually linked to some type of belief system, not necessarily religious in nature, but one that calls for a high commitment from its members to some type of personal transformation. Thus, what generally defines a cult is some sort of promise of fulfillment, a methodology to achieve particular goals, and a close relationship to a charismatic leader.

Cults differ in their specific belief systems, practices, and requirements, and vary according to the level of intensity or connection to the individual member. What generally makes cults different from other types of nonconventional groups is the high level of commitment demanded of its members as well as the intensity of investment in the ideology. In other words, not all cults are the same and not all of them are necessarily bad, although some are clearly dangerous. The chances of the cult being problematic to society likely involves members who have an unhealthy and unquestioning devotion to the group and/or its leader; members who are exploited or harmed by the group leader, either physically, psychologically, or financially; and when the cult leader claims to have unique knowledge, insight, or skills that distinguish them from others.[1]

The special skill or ability of a cult leader is particularly noteworthy since it often results in controlling how cult members think, act, and feel, as well as regulating the types of relationships members form with others. The special skill also gives the leader a kind of authority that suggests their behavior or decisions should be carried out without question. The leader also attempts to isolate members from mainstream society so that they are not exposed to contrary messages or criticisms of the group or its leader.[2] Lalich (2004) refers to these features as *totalistic* and *separatist*. In these types of cults, people tend to espouse an all-encompassing belief system; have an unhealthy devotion and dependency on their leader; avoid any type of criticism of the group, its leader, or its rituals; and generally have little regard for those outside the group.[3]

Sociologists tend to see the term "cult" as an overused, pejorative term to describe any nonconventional or misunderstood group. Such a broad categorization renders the term almost useless for explaining the differences between a division of a mainstream religion, what might be referred to as a *sect*, or an entirely new religious movement that takes a radically different view of a mainstream religious ideology. These *new religious movements*, as they have come to be called, developed in the countercultural movement of the 1960s and 1970s, but because they were misunderstood by the public and religious leaders, they were simply included in the deviant label *cults*.[4]

Other features typically characteristic of cults include control, deception, and fear. Religious cults, in particular, have strong and charismatic leaders who demand almost complete submission to their wishes, ostensibly because they are chosen by God. In this way, obedience becomes significantly important for cult members.[5]

This level of control can be considerable, with some cults requiring dress codes, limits on possessions, and regulated mate selection from their members. The motivation for this control is fear of rejection, the threat of punishment by the group, or risk of disappointing God. This control extends to those members who might question the authority of the leader, where the disobedient member is seen as a rebel and not to be trusted.[6]

One way this sense of control is accomplished is through members holding each other accountable for their behavior. These are sometimes called *confession sessions*. In these events, a full disclosure of all secret sins, thoughts, temptations, and desires are expressed with members in an effort to build a bond of trust. These experiences are also a powerful tool to emotionally bond the member to the group's leader. Such sessions also serve as a mechanism of social control, where other members or the leader can use these social bonds to manipulate or blackmail someone if they decide to leave the group.[7] Still another feature of cults relates to the attempt to limit members' intellectual growth. Critical or rational thinking is often framed as prideful or sinful. In fact, a common feature of cults is a sense of anti-intellectualism and discouraging the use of science to explain phenomena. Researchers point out that cult members are often discouraged from learning philosophy, history, science, systematic theology, or any topic about which the leader lacks familiarity or agreement. Much of this anti-intellectualism comes from the fear of exposing the limitations or flaws in the leader's ideology or philosophy.[8]

The nature of secrecy is an important component in understanding cults. It is here that cult leaders and members often withhold information from the public and even members' families about the nature of the group's activities or beliefs. Such a practice helps to create a sense of isolationism among members, as it limits their exposure to people who might question the ideology or the deception presented by the cult and its leader. Such secrecy is often portrayed to members as necessary because outsiders simply can't understand the significance of the information offered by the leader, which makes members feel as though they are more insightful or special.[9]

Another key element of cults is the development of a common enemy or threat. This is designed to distract members from evaluating what the leadership of the cult is doing to members inside the organization. In fact, the organization typically portrays itself and its members as being misunderstood and unfairly persecuted.[10]

Finally, cults are often characterized by a double standard for its leaders. While control of members' behavior is a key element of cult membership, as seen in the use of various forms of shaming or discipline for even minor infractions, there is a different standard for leaders, who escape any level of accountability for their actions.[11]

Hassan (2020) argues that what really drives cult members' behavior is the leader's influence that ultimately controls all of their behavior as well as their willingness to consider any information in light of the framework presented by the group. Hassan (2020) refers to this process as the *BITE model*, which stands for behavior, information, thought, and emotion. This includes the common cult tactics of shunning and public humiliation (*behavior*) as well as creating false enemies, which generates an "us versus them" type of thinking while also instilling a fear of others.[12]

Cult activities, such as rallies, build a sense of cohesion and behavior mimicry among members and prospective recruits. They also include the discouragement of rational thinking—information that supports the cult is accepted, while information that runs contrary to the group or its identity is dismissed as "fake news" or propaganda from the "liberal media" (*information*). Hassan (2020) also points out that mind control is a fundamental part of all cults; complex ideas are reduced to buzzwords or catchphrases and alternative belief systems are framed as illegitimate. This form of mind control also forbids asking critical questions or raising concerns about the group or its leader (*thought*).

It is important to note that these phrases or simplifications are repeated over and over again—and eventually evoke a rote response that is comparable to a form of hypnosis. Finally, a common tactic used by cults is the manipulation of members' emotions, such as making them feel special ("love bombing" is a common strategy). By far the most effective emotion, however, is fear. By inspiring real or imagined threats, the leader can promise protection from danger, often claiming that they are the only ones who can do so.[13]

DIFFERENT TYPES OF CULTS

While there are a wide range of cults, with different ideologies and sizes, and while not every group or members' experience fit into each of the categories, the following offers insight into the general nature of cults as well as a glimpse into why people join them. This typology is adapted from Lalich's (2004) research on cults and cult behavior.

Eastern Religion Cults

This type of cult category is based on the general spiritual belief in enlightenment and reincarnation, or the pursuit of nirvana. Typically, the basis of the cult's ideology stems from a version of Eastern religions such as Buddhism,

Hinduism, Sufism, and so forth. Members often engage in rituals such as meditation or altered states of consciousness, the use of mantras or chanting, dietary restrictions (including fasting), and lifestyle changes such as the rejection of worldly possessions.[14]An example of this type of cult is the Hare Krishna group.

Christian-Based Cults

There are many cults that contain a foundational belief in a general Christian explanation of the world, meaning there is some version of God or a higher being as well as a vision of life after death (including cults that combine versions of Christian, Islamic, Jewish, or other traditions into a particular ideology). Typically, the leader of this type of cult claims to be a prophet or messiah, who has been chosen by God to lead the group. This gives the leader the authority to interpret scriptures and outline a lifestyle for members. A great deal of time is spent encouraging members to engage in evangelizing, making public confessions, or participating in various rituals and practices designed to prepare members for their future tasks and life after death. This includes praying, study sessions, faith healing, speaking in tongues, and other rituals.[15] For example, many of the most well-known groups, such as Jehovah's Witnesses, Branch Davidians, Peoples Temple (Jim Jones), and the Unification Church (also known as the "Moonies") have at their base a Christian ideology.

Related to various types of Christian cults are those that involve Satan worship. Sometimes called occult, satanic, or black magic cults, these are generated through the belief in supernatural powers and sometimes the worship of Satan. Among the practices and rituals performed by members of satanic cults are animal sacrifices, cutting and blood rituals, tattooing, and scarring. Evidence also exists of the physical and sexual abuse of members.[16]

New Age Cults

Another type might be broadly called New Age cults. Here the group is founded on belief in power through internal knowledge. Often the leader presents herself or himself as a mystical creature who serves as a vehicle through which members can gain greater insight into their own god-like powers. New Age groups tend to have female leaders, and members rely on artifacts such as crystals, astrology, holistic medicine, or Tarot (or other magic cards) to perform magic, channeling, chakra adjustments, faith healing, or even intergalactic experiences. Examples include groups like Heaven's Gate as well as Wicca and Witchcraft-based groups.[17]

Political Cults

Political cults are created by a perceived need to change society, including eliminating evil forces that impact a group's way of life. In some cases, members are drawn to a particular leader but they can also be attracted to an extreme ideology. Political cults can operate in secret or engage in violent activities, such as kidnapping, suicide bombings, intimidation, and other forms of violence. Sometimes groups have ritualized practices, including coded language and secret handshakes or gestures. Extreme groups often think of themselves as superior to all others and feel the need to prepare for war. This includes paramilitary and weapons training as well as engaging in accountability sessions for members who violate group rules, proof of loyalty rituals or proclamations, and a disdain for outsiders.[18]

Fundamentally, political cults are organized around a particular political dogma. As Hassan (2020) points out, Aryan Nations believes in white supremacy and has ambitions to take over the US government. The Nazi Party under Adolf Hitler is another example of a repressive regime that silenced critics and dissidents and used propaganda to keep control of the masses. Contemporary examples include Kim Jong-un in North Korea and Vladimir Putin in Russia, where both leaders control the press and prevent free thought or unbiased elections.

Like traditional cults that use deception to recruit members and mind control techniques to gain acceptance and obedience, dictators use similar techniques, particularly playing upon people's irrational fears about potential threats, with the assurance by the dictator that he will protect them. For those who are not willing to accept this type of narrative, dictators often use intimidation tactics and persecution of those who present any type of challenge or threat to the existing regime.[19]

Commercial Cults

Although a bit different from traditional cults, whose members may be seeking enlightenment, religious understanding, or self-improvement, commercial cults take advantage of people's greed—specifically their desire for wealth and power. Many consist of pyramid con games, also sometimes known as *multilevel marketing organizations*, whose members recruit others and make money not from the products or services they sell but from recruits and new members. Examples include companies like Amway and Herbalife, which offer health and beauty products with the promise of quick riches for recruits. However, the vast majority of people lose money on these schemes. While some of these organizations have been charged by federal regulators for fraudulent practices, members are often told, and believe, their failure to make money is due to a lack of effort on their part. Other dangerous examples of commercial cults include human sex trafficking rings, which recruit people who believe they will be brought closer to fulfilling their dreams of success and wealth, only to discover themselves sold for sex and labor.[20]

Personality Cults

While all cults have a charismatic leader who attracts recruits and members, personality cults are inextricably tied to a particular individual. Sometimes the person, most often a male, controls or dominates another person to such an extreme degree that they cannot think or act for themselves. While such a person could be an abusive spouse, a parent, or a therapist, on a larger scale there are leaders who have the charisma to convince a number of people of their message. For example, Korean leader Kim Jong-un is seen as a personality cult leader because he is thought by his supporters to be sent from God to rule over others. Hassan (2020) considers President Trump to be a similar figure—one who uses politics and religious right-wing ideology— anti-abortion, anti-science, anti-diversity—and white power to sell himself and the Republican Party to a loyal base of supporters, including conservative evangelical Christians.

Hassan also points out that members can use their leader to further their own agenda as well, as exemplified by right-wing advocates using Trump to sell their own political and religious ideas. The difference between this type of cult and others is that it is uniquely tied to the leader's charisma and ability to "sell" his or her ideas to followers.[21] As noted in chapter 2, there are real questions about whether Trumpism is an actual ideology or if Trump simply uses particular issues to leverage support from voters who only care about their individual issues of concern.

Groups That Are Not Cults

As we begin to analyze whether Trumpsters constitute a cult, it is reasonable to consider groups that have a loyal base of followers and *do not* meet the definition of a cult. One example of this is the US Marine Corps. With its emphasis on indoctrination, strict behavioral standards, and a loyal and intense collection of followers, many people, even those in the military, conclude that the Marine Corps constitutes a cult. However, as Singer (2003) points out, there are real differences between cohesive groups, even those that have unconventional rituals and practices, and cults.

Despite the claim made by some members of other branches of the military and even within the Marine Corps itself, there are numerous differences between a cult and the Marine Corps. For instance, from the first exposure to the organization, the Marine Corps recruit knows what the organization is and what he or she is getting into. In contrast, cult recruits often attend an activity that seems harmless and they are often asked to participate in the group without full knowledge of the organization, its goals, or their role in it. Additionally, the Marine recruit, if he or she decides to join, serves a specified period of time and separates from the group at the end. In many cult groups, membership is a lifelong commitment and choosing to leave, or even articulating the desire to leave, evokes a strong and negative reaction from the group and its leadership.[22]

While serving in the Marine Corps, members have access to medical care, public records are kept of their training and progress, and there is a designated office designed to protect Marines from exploitation (the USMC Inspector General). Nothing protects cult members from the organization or its leadership. Additionally, Marines have to follow the US Military Code of Justice, which is a military legal system that is formally recognized by society. In contrast, cults may have their own code of accountability, but they generally practice an internal system, with no appeal and no recourse to an objective entity. Being a Marine means that the recruit earns a salary, can buy property, and is free to inherit wealth from relatives. Cults, on the other hand, often require members to turn over all their possessions to the organization and its leadership.[23]

Additionally, a hallmark of being a Marine is being able to think, problem solve, and adapt to circumstances. This type of rational behavior and thinking is not a part of being a cult member—where blind obedience to the cult and its leader is paramount. The Marine recruit retains freedom of religion, politics, friends, family association, selection of spouse, and access to worldly information via television, radio, reading material, telephone, and mail; this is not so with most cults.[24]

While it is true that there is a strict code of conduct, dress code, restricted diet, regime of exercise and physical labor, and authoritarian leadership within the Marine Corps, along with peer pressure to elicit conforming behavior, what is missing in this comparison between cults and the Marine Corps is there is no deception and manipulation in the latter that is characteristic of the former. And while it is true that Marine recruits are isolated from society for a period of time during training, they are not deliberately deceived about what is expected from them or their responsibilities. In fact, it is quite the opposite—the core values of honor, courage, and commitment are an ethos that outlines the behavior of all Marines.[25]

WHY PEOPLE JOIN CULTS

Conventional wisdom tells us that only ignorant or desperate people join cults. These are people who are vulnerable to the influences of a deviant group and leader who prey upon the innocent and unknowing. Educated, rational, and logical people don't join cults, right? Actually, the evidence suggests a far different portrayal of cult members and the reasons they join these organizations. As researchers have discovered, sometimes a cult looks like a normal self-help or support group or one that appeals to people's dreams of wealth, success, and recognition.

Cults are very intentional in the types of people they seek out to recruit, and everyone is susceptible to some form of manipulation and exploitation. In fact, many cults actually look for recruits who are educated, idealistic, and optimistic about their futures. Cults seek members who are passionate about something in their lives and then cultivate that desire to draw members into the fold.

A 2017 study of former cult members found that almost two-thirds had more than a high school education. Former cult members look upon their experiences in the cult as being similar to any other group—where there was affirmation, encouragement, and like-mindedness in beliefs and activities. Cults make people feel special through what psychologists call "love bombing," or showering people with praise, encouragement, and inclusion. It is after the relationship has formed that the subtle suggestions about joining or becoming a member begin, along with activities that usually involve giving something to the organization—donations, paying for seminars or counseling sessions, buying merchandise, and so forth.[26]

Again, this can all seem rather conventional and nonthreatening—many people regularly join different types of groups for a variety of reasons. So even those who are intelligent, thoughtful, and savvy may not realize they are being indoctrinated or manipulated. In fact, many members believe the group is simply helping them to achieve their potential or dreams.[27]

Other types of people who join cults may need a sense of religious connection. Perhaps the person isn't satisfied by their church or religious ideology. As was mentioned, most new religious movements begin as an alternative (and more accurate) explanation of traditional religious doctrine. This is true of mainstream religions as well as some of the more unconventional belief systems. It is the disillusionment with the person's existing spiritual framework that provides a reason to explore cults.[28]

Related to a desire for a spiritual connection is the idea that people sometimes join cults because they are searching for the existential meaning of their lives. This is particularly true of millennials, who are generally known for wanting to live with a sense of purpose. A cult gives members that sense of meaning and direction—they aren't simply surviving their time on earth, but rather they are doing something that really matters.[29]

Still others join cults because they are searching for a sense of community or fellowship. This is a fundamental human need—humans are social creatures and we naturally seek out like-minded individuals with whom we can develop relationships. A cult provides a ready-made set of friends and colleagues who help to generate a sense of social cohesion by being associated with something much larger than what is possible as individuals.[30]

Sometimes cults become attractive to people because they are experiencing a great deal of emotional and psychological vulnerability. Perhaps they have gone through a bad relationship, experienced the loss of a loved one, are having difficulty at work, or struggle with a variety of mental health issues that result in an inability to effectively cope with life. These episodes, particularly if they are enduring, often make people vulnerable to the gentle and subtle messages of a cult.[31]

Some people are susceptible to cult influences because they lack self-confidence or need others to validate their worth. These people may have difficulty finding their own direction in life, and cults provide a space in which people can feel good about themselves. Similarly, people may join cults because they have trouble saying "no" or expressing any type of criticism toward others. These people may be coerced into joining a cult because they are conflict averse or have a fear of offending others.[32]

Sometimes people join cults because they tend to believe what they are told without any real assessment of the information. Many people need to understand the world in simple and easy to understand terms—things are black and white, right or wrong, good or bad. This lack of ability to tolerate ambiguity makes the assertions of a charismatic leader, who provides a clear message about the group, its ideology, and its members, very attractive to people who need that type of simplistic thinking in their lives.[33]

Finally, some people join cults because they are disillusioned with society in general or oppose some of the inequalities contained within it. This was a popular explanation to describe the rapid growth of new religious movements in the 1960s and 1970s and can still be used to explain the tendency of people to join cults today. The 1960s and 1970s was a time of great social unrest. Many young people became disillusioned with materialistic values and questioned the reasons the United States was engaged in controversies such as the Watergate scandal and the Vietnam War.[34]

While some rebelled through drugs or popular resistance, others turned to alternative lifestyles in the religious marketplace. This led to the development of the hippie movement of the 1960s, with an emphasis on New Age religions, experimental drug use, and free love/sex as part of the culture.

Changes in national immigration rules in the 1960s brought an influx of Asian immigrants into the United States, including teachers espousing the faiths and philosophies of the East. For some people, these were attractive alternatives to mainstream American culture.[35]

More currently, the disillusionment many people feel, as outlined in chapter 2, particularly those who have seen their jobs disappear or believe their standing in society has been disparaged as more diverse populations, become a part of the social, economic, and political landscape. This same fear about the future has been redirected toward minority groups and has allowed people to coalesce around what they believe to be appropriate in ideology or perspective.

IS TRUMP A CULT LEADER?

In Bandy X. Lee's book, *The Dangerous Case of Donald Trump* (2017), a group of highly regarded psychiatrists and mental health experts assert that there is ample evidence that Trump exhibited a pattern of behavior that made him dangerous as a president. The experts argue that Trump had narcissistic tendencies, impulsivity, delusions, paranoia, xenophobia, misogyny, an inability to admit mistakes, pathological lying, and extreme hedonism. While narcissism by itself is not a psychological disorder, there is an extreme form of it that is problematic, sometimes referred to as *malignant narcissism*, which occurs when narcissism combines with other forms of psychological disorders or pathological traits.[36]

Research on cults demonstrates that they are often led by narcissists. These are individuals who have had some sort of childhood trauma and cope with that experience by creating their own realities through the manipulation of others and the fabrication of facts, situations, and explanations for their behavior. While there are varying degrees of narcissism, and while not all narcissists become cult leaders, the following are common characteristics of extreme or abusive narcissists:

- A perception that they are always treated unfairly and embrace a victim role.
- They often interpret their opponents as evil and the narcissist's reaction or aggressive response to the offense is seen as a reasonable reaction.
- Narcissists do not believe they are ever wrong and do not apologize for their actions. Instead, they often recast the events in such a way that portrays them in a favorable light or revise the situation to be one where they gain power.

- Narcissists believe that they are beyond societal rules and should not be held accountable for their actions.
- They are very skilled at manipulating others and are often able to create a group of loyal followers who offer unconditional support.
- Narcissists are vindictive, particularly against those who disagree with them or harm them in some way. When in positions of power, narcissists will persecute their opponents with great satisfaction.
- As part of their ability to manipulate others, they convince others to commit unethical or illegal acts on their behalf.
- Narcissists are very insecure about themselves and the success of others. In fact, this high degree of jealousy convinces the narcissist that the person who is superior to them is not really successful. Instead of acknowledging the talent of those around them, narcissists must self-promote above all others.
- Narcissists are incapable of experiencing empathy or compassion for others, despite publicly proclaiming to be sensitive and caring. In reality, these traits are equated with weakness.[37]

As Hassan (2020) points out, Trump easily possesses many of these characteristics. For example, with regard to the exaggeration of talents and achievements, Trump has taken creative liberties with the extent of his expertise on a variety of topics. For instance, Trump tweeted in 2015, "There's nobody bigger or better at the military than I am." A few days later he elaborated on this point. "I know more about offense and defense than [the generals] will ever understand believe me. Believe me. Than they will ever understand. Than they will ever understand." A few other Trump examples, as noted by Hassan (2020):

- "I know our complex tax laws better than anyone who has ever run for president and am the only one who can fix them" (tweet posted on October 2, 2016).
- "Nobody has ever done so much in the first two years of a presidency as this administration. Nobody. Nobody" (political rally in Biloxi, Mississippi, November 26, 2018).[38]

Hassan (2020) also points out that narcissists often construct narratives that allow them to boast about their success and talents. This is seen in Trump's now-famous claim that his power was so great that he could "stand in the middle of Fifth Avenue and shoot somebody" and he would still win votes. His claims of sexual prowess are also noteworthy symptoms of this element of narcissism.[39]

As it relates to narcissists' belief that they are above the law and their sense of entitlement, there are numerous examples of cult leaders who display such bravado. For instance, L. Ron Hubbard believed he deserved a Nobel Prize for his Purification Residue program that purged the human body of drug and radiation residues.

In the case of Trump, as the Mueller report emerged, Trump was convinced he could pardon himself. Another example would be the question of Trump's taxes, where defying a forty-year protocol of all presidents to release their income taxes for public review, Trump refused to. Trump has also been involved in thousands of lawsuits, nearly 3,500 over the past thirty years, for nonpayment of workers at his resorts and clubs, and contractors and real estate agents.[40] Thus, there is a general sense for narcissists that the rules governing everyday behavior are beneath them and simply do not apply.

As experts note, envy and jealousy are a common feature of narcissists and it likely stems from low levels of self-esteem and a general sense of inadequacy. David Koresh, leader of the Branch Davidians, was a frustrated rock musician and was very envious of those who had made it in the music industry. Similarly, Trump projects an air of self-confidence, even arrogance, but his fascination with other world leaders such as Vladimir Putin or North Korea's Kim Jong-un, who have more control over their citizens than Trump, are taken as illustrations of his sense of insecurity.[41]

As many psychologists note, narcissists also demonstrate a lack of empathy for others. That is, they are incapable of imagining the emotions and feelings of another person in a given situation. While narcissists may be very good at reading people and often appear charming and personable, they care little about other people's pain and suffering. This is seen in many examples during the Trump administration. For instance, in 2017, after Hurricane Maria devastated the island of Puerto Rico, Trump argued with the mayor of San Juan, contending that the storm did not constitute a real catastrophe.[42]

While taking credit for the response to the storm by the Federal Emergency Management Agency (FEMA), Trump declared that the death toll had been exaggerated as another example of fake news. Trump showed a similar response at the Mexican border by separating children from their families. He also minimized the impact that a thirty-five-day government shutdown had on the nearly eight hundred thousand federal workers who were not paid during his standoff with Congress about his border wall funding.[43]

Finally, Hassan (2020) points out that malignant narcissism is the disorder that combines the pathological traits of narcissism, some of which have been outlined here, with other disorders such as antisocial behavior, paranoia, and sadism. Antisocial behavior is seen as a general disregard for societal rules, cultural norms, and morality. It is also seen in the form of pathological lying and manipulation, either for personal gain or to intimidate and make others afraid.[44]

Fact-checkers for the *Washington Post* estimate that Trump made more than thirty thousand false or misleading claims during his presidency.[45] He also used a strategy called *gaslighting*, which is the tendency to recreate words, actions, or sentiments in such a way that the person affected by them begins to question whether or not they understood what actually occurred.[46] When lies are repeated or the substance of claims is distorted, people tend to have difficulty engaging in critical thinking.

This is a classic technique used by cult leaders, who create doubt about the legitimacy of claims or the accuracy of the lies told. Such divisiveness creates a climate in which the leader is seen as misunderstood, particularly by a media that is determined to undermine him or her. All of this results in reactions by members to close ranks, to intensify the "us versus them" thinking, and to sow seeds of mistrust of the media and those who disagree with the leader.[47] According to many experts on cults, Trump also meets the criteria for cult leaders in terms of sadism, a sense of vindictiveness toward enemies, the willingness to use violence and paranoia, a desperate need for loyalty, and an obsession with real and perceived enemies.[48] As Egawa (2021) points out, the danger involved in conspiracy theories like a stolen election or the existence of a "deep state" is that they begin with an element of secrecy— stories that are not reported by the media that offer more accurate accounts of policies, trends, and behaviors. These stories are often attractive to people's existing views and perceptions of the world. Once the theory is adopted, two things occur. First, the person no longer has to evaluate the information or its source—the theory provides a ready-made "fact checking" mechanism that simplifies the issues and maps the appropriate response. Second, people who adopt or endorse a conspiracy theory no longer accept any information that is contrary to their point of view. The real danger with conspiracy theories is that, if left unchecked, the narrative expands and, coupled with a healthy dose of confirmation bias, it becomes increasingly difficult for members to reconsider any other point of view.[49]

QANON: CULT OR SOMETHING ELSE?

One final group that should be mentioned in the discussion of Trump followers and cult-like behavior, largely because it represents a rather unique blend of cultish thought with a fervent devotion to President Trump, is QAnon. This is particularly true given that conspiracy theories abound in cults. What is fascinating about QAnon is not only its makeup and configuration, complete with many of the elements of what constitutes a cult, but also the differences of opinion among experts about whether QAnon is actually a cult. There is little doubt, however, about its influence, particularly as it relates to members' willingness to engage in violence, as evidenced by the participation of QAnon members in the January 6 assault on the US Capitol in 2021.

QAnon began in 2017 after a post on the website 4chan, an internet forum known for questionable activity and various conspiracy theories. Later this site became *8chan*, with the same level of dubious distinction and questionable credibility of its content and users. The person who made the post called themselves Q Clearance Patriot, a reference to a security clearance provided by the government. In the message, the poster claimed to be part of a small military intelligence team, with the goal of disseminating information about a secret war taking place. This war, essentially a larger battle between good and evil, was about to end, with the outcome resulting in the end of evil, the shutdown of child trafficking organizations, the elimination of what was called the "deep state," and the beginning of real and meaningful freedom.[50]

The deep state is comprised of Democrats, Hollywood elite, business leaders, wealthy liberal celebrities, the medical establishment, and the mass media, who are controlled by Barack Obama and Hillary Clinton. These people influence movies, music, and television with Satanic symbols designed to weaken our resolve and ability to think for ourselves. This is accomplished by forcing vaccines and distributing unhealthy fast food and antibiotics to keep us as physical and mental slaves to their wishes. Deep state operatives were said to have tried to assassinate Donald Trump many times and to have done everything they could to interfere with his effectiveness as a president and protector. The most important dimension of the deep state is that most people have no idea it exists nor do people seem to care to learn more about it.[51]

These posts, or "drops," are available to the public, and readers are encouraged to research the information and draw their own conclusions. Unlike other conspiracy theories or cult messages, QAnon wants dialogue among its readership. The content of the information is cryptic pieces of intelligence that often appear to be indecipherable collections of symbols, codes, or memes. Essentially, drops focus on the inevitable outcome of accountability of those who have committed offenses against the country, with imminent arrests and indictments of leaders such as Hillary Clinton, Barack Obama, and others, who will be found guilty of treason and/or sex trafficking.[52]

However, the messages are vague, unintelligible, and, most importantly, unverifiable. These drops often ask rhetorical questions, offer riddles, or provide affirmations of what readers may have heard in other news forums. Drops can be texts, links, tweets, photos, songs, or posts with amalgamations of information using military jargon (Rothschild 2021). However, only a select few people, called Anons, are able to understand what the coded texts actually mean.[53]

QAnon technically remains anonymous because on the message boards users do not register accounts using email addresses. Instead, they are identified by what are called "tripcodes," which are scrambled versions of the password used to log in. Users, then, only have a username and password, and the latter is visible in public posts in its "hashed" or scrambled form. This means that those who post have a consistent tripcode that identifies them. However, these codes are easy to hack, and a review of the process shows that many times users have had to change this information or even move to a different message board because, they claim, enemies have compromised their accounts.[54]

Drops are repeated again and again by fans and many have become catch-phrases, such as "Where we go one, we go all." In addition to the content of the information presented, the frequency of the drops is also inconsistent, with some days containing multiple posts and then no posts for weeks at a time.[55] What is important is that Q followers use these drops as central to the movement and the Anons have become media sensations on YouTube, Twitter, and blogs, where they interpret messages and their meaning and tie them to the ultimate message of QAnon. This is important since many of these decoders develop large numbers of followers on social media, which can translate into huge profits.[56]

What makes QAnon so confusing is that it consists of an amalgamation of myth, conspiracy theories, assumptions, jargon, symbols, and descriptions that are difficult to define conclusively. QAnon can be understood as a conspiracy theory, but it contains elements of cult movements, new religious movements, political doctrine, and even some con artistry.[57]

For Q followers, those who wish to fight in Q's war, all a person has to do is read the drops and participate in the discussions. This makes QAnon different from other conspiracy theories, which require the reader to be passive. However, as a *digital soldier* (another catchphrase of the group), all one needs to do is respond to posts, make YouTube videos, or decode posts on Twitter and share them with others. The attraction, according to some experts, is that QAnon lets people feel like they are a part of something bigger than themselves.[58]

In other words, participating in QAnon gives people a sense of noble purpose—after all, they are contributing to the battle between good and evil. It is also easier for members to believe the rhetoric of QAnon since it is not difficult to believe that leaders of this country are greedy, incompetent, or apathetic to the struggles and issues of the general public. QAnon also gives members a target to hate—there is an easy scapegoat for those people who feel as though they have been deprived of the life they imagined.[59]

An added benefit is that QAnon also contains a mechanism where people can feel they are doing something about the problem. This is attractive to people who question authority, distrust the media, and want to do their own research. In the end, QAnon tells a story, one that some people want to believe and that appeals to many people who feel rejected by society. And that story began with the prediction that Hillary Clinton was going to be arrested for treasonous acts, and once convicted, the entire cabal would be revealed. This is the storm that is referenced by QAnon.[60]

ARE TRUMPSTERS CULT FOLLOWERS?

As was mentioned, cult members typically have a level of blind obedience and loyalty to their leader and to the organization, often with such a high degree of commitment that they will condemn anyone who disagrees with them, including their closest friends and family. Members will also often lose sight of any ethical, moral, or legal compass if it runs counter to what the leader commands them to do.

Hassan (2020) points out that many extreme Trump followers have been convinced by Trump that there is an assortment of threats against him (and them). He has also convinced his supporters that villains exist (including the mainstream media) who threaten the American way of life. This is seen in the media's continued efforts to slander and attack Trump as well as the stealing of an election that he won in a landslide. It also includes a distorted version of events that occurred at the US Capitol, which is said to be a protest by patriots who were trying to secure what had been taken from them.

To a group of people who are already known for their divisive and radical view of the world, seemingly separated from reality (there is, after all, a deep state that is actively trying to destroy the country and the leader who is trying to uphold all that has made America great), such a position is consistent with how cult members react to threats to their leader or their group. As the research on cult leaders shows, cultists always blame others for bad things that happen to them, they construct nonexistent enemies and threats that are ripe with conspiracy theory logic, and employ an approach that allows for the suspension of rational thinking, prudent decision-making, and respect for the core elements of a civilized society.[61]

As it relates to the January 6 attack on the US Capitol, while there remains some debate about whether Trump called on his followers to storm the Capitol, he did predict what would happen on that day. In cult parlance, he "prophesied" a day of reckoning. The riot and the behavior of its participants, by their own accounts, were carried out because their leader told them to do so. Most experts note that such actions and perceptions of events have all the characteristics of typical cult behavior.[62]

As it relates to the election fraud, people who are caught up in cult thinking aren't interested in logical or objective truth, regardless of who presents it or how much evidence exists to support it. Instead, they rely on their leader's claims, particularly if that leader asserts that the facts are "fake news," "alternative facts," or are part of a larger "witch hunt" or conspiracy to mislead them. In the minds of many Trumpsters, their own truths and their own facts and sources of information supersede anything anyone else can offer.[63]

Comparisons to Other Countries

It might be tempting to conclude that Trump and Trumpsters constitute a cult—as a leader, Trump displays many of the characteristics and tactics noted in the literature on cults. Similarly, some of his followers appear to have been duped into believing virtually anything he says or does, even to the point of dismissing hard evidence that contradicts many of his statements.

This is also consistent with cult followers, who see the world in simple terms and believe their leader makes the country a better place or makes them better people. It also serves to isolate Trumpsters from others since there is no middle ground, there is no disagreeing with them, and they are fiercely loyal to Trump. Yet, while Trump may be a narcissist or even a malignant narcissist and he may suffer from any number of psychopathologies that may make him unfit to serve as the president of the United States, it doesn't necessarily mean he is a cult leader.

What Trump seems to promote is a brand of populism that borders on dictatorship and anti-democratic rule. Perhaps most telling, Trump's approach to governing the country is more similar to what has happened in Hungary under Prime Minister Viktor Orbán and his Fidesz Party.[64] Orbán has built his empire on the idea that democracy has failed and globalization has negatively impacted many nations across Europe. The impact of these trends has led citizens to a general mistrust of existing institutions and political elites who have lost touch with the needs of the people. What is needed, Orbán argues, is a political party and leadership that centers its efforts on "making Hungary great again." This sense of nationalism is seen in Hungary's opposition to immigration, where Hungary built a border wall designed to limit immigration into that country.[65]

Under Orbán's leadership, voting districts were redrawn to favor the Fidesz Party, along with the revamping of the court system by the appointment of dozens of right-wing judges. The media was also redesigned so that the flow of accurate information from independent sources was limited, along with the creation of a massive propaganda machine to promote a singular and pro-Orbán narrative. Included in this narrative was a revision of Hungary's history and educational curricula, particularly its involvement in the Holocaust of World War II, all designed to provide a different narrative that minimized Hungary's culpability for past misdeeds and a sanitized version of its present and future. Bribery, corruption, intimidation, and persecution were all part of the new regime, including a particular effort to seek out and persecute enemies of the new regime. Orbán's version of populism, at its core, uses hatred and misinformation to mislead the public into believing that a dictatorship is the solution to its problems.[66]

The familiarity of these strategies is the result of Trump's great admiration for Orbán's version of governance. In fact, Steve Bannon, former advisor to Trump, observed that Orbán's strategies were "Trump before Trump"— meaning, Orbán's strategies were the foundation of Trump's vision for the United States.[67] Trump even invited Orbán to visit the White House and expressed great admiration for the Hungarian leader when he said Orbán had done a "tremendous job" leading his country and that he was respected "all over Europe."[68]

Orbán and Trump are not the only authoritarian nationalists—there appears to be a strong inclination for this in countries such as Brazil, Russia, Turkey, India, China, the Philippines, and other countries. While it might be tempting to limit comparisons of Trump to Orbán, or to consider Trumpsters as a unique segment of the population found only in the United States, such a perspective would be misguided.

In fact, there is growing and significant evidence that far-right views are becoming much more popular and part of mainstream politics in other countries across Europe. For example, a recent survey found that people in Europe are witnessing a rise in far-right violence and terrorism as part of an overall appetite for populist rhetoric and the election of far-right leaders. According to a survey of more than eleven thousand people in eight European countries, there is a growing threat of far-right political views and belief in conspiracy theories similar to what has been seen in the United States. In the *State of Hate* report, which is a collaboration between three European advocacy groups, there is growing concern about the dangers of the election of far-right leaders such as Andrzej Duda in Poland and Giorgia Meloni in Italy, along with the escalation of far-right violence and terrorism across Europe.[69]

The popularity of far-right leaders is consistent with the acceptance of much of the rhetoric offered by extremist groups. The false claim that Hollywood, government, media, and other officials are involved in child smuggling and exploitation, reminiscent of one of QAnon's key accusations in the United States, has garnered strong support in some European countries. For example, according to the survey, about a third of the respondents in Poland and 21 percent in Germany believe the QAnon narrative as true. The survey also reports that 39 percent of people in Italy and 45 percent in

Hungary adhere to the idea that elites are orchestrating immigration with a goal to weaken Europe and European identity.[70]

These beliefs often translate into a general mistrust of government and the questioning of democracy's viability. In France, for example, about two-thirds of the people surveyed think their political system is broken. Even countries like Great Britain show some shaky confidence in democratic rule, where only 6 percent think their system of government works well. However, not all countries in Europe agree with a lack of trust in democracy. Some countries remain strong in their belief in democratic rule, such as Germany, where 60 percent of Germans think their democracy is working well.[71]

As in the United States, anti-immigration policies, the pandemic, secularization, the loss of jobs, escalating costs of living, and other issues in countries across Europe have resulted in people's heightened fears about the future and the role of government. These problems have been decades in the making, and the latest concerns about inflation and the war between Russia and Ukraine have only elevated those concerns.

Adding to this has been the rebranding by some far-right extremist groups to soften their messaging to appeal to the masses by focusing on the preservation and restoration of their country's culture; messages that promote nationalism and target the challenges brought on by immigration and globalization, making what is occurring in Europe not that different from the brand of populism that has gained popularity in the United States.[72]

Similar to the Trump message in the United States, the narrative in Europe attempts to capitalize on people's dissatisfaction with their lives and their loss of cultural identity, while leaders promise positive changes if they are elected—and it is working. For example, in Italy, Giorgia Meloni has become the country's first female prime minister after her party, the Brothers of Italy, a far-right group with neofascist roots, claimed the greatest percentage of votes in that country's election in 2022. Similarly in Sweden, a far-right group called the Sweden Democrats received the second-highest number of votes in the 2022 election after the left-leaning Social Democrats.[73]

These European leaders, for whom Trump has openly expressed admiration, are not seen as cult leaders in their countries. Rather, they are seen as they are: dictators who have dismantled any effort to limit their control and power. The difference between the brand of populism offered by leaders such as Orbán and Vladimir Putin in Russia is that these leaders and their countries generally dislike a capitalist economy. In the United States, however, Trump appears to have struck a balance between those who endorse capitalist rule and those who eschew the oversight that democracy imposes on their pursuit of profit.[74]

Similarly, Trumpsters, many of whom have authoritarian tendencies, are misguided in their thinking and beliefs about Trump and may have been deceived into a strange sense of misdirected loyalty toward him. As some followers engage in a form of cognitive dissonance, such a tendency does not, by itself, constitute a cult following.

CONCLUSION

As was mentioned in chapter 2, there are multiple dimensions related to being a Trump follower. For some, perhaps all the criteria discussed in this chapter apply to them—and perhaps, at an extreme, a few do resemble and act like cult members. But let's also remember that there are those who have not been deceived and know exactly what Trump is doing and don't care as long as they are getting what they want from him—his offensive behavior may simply be seen as a cost of doing business with someone who can get the results they desire. It also explains how and why so many current members of the Republican Party seem willing to hold their nose as they swallow Trump's narratives because it ensures a healthy political future for them.

There is also a group who actually agree with Trump and think he's fine—everyone else has it wrong; they believe critics are foolish in their inability to see that Trump is exactly what the country needs—democracy doesn't work and it is better to put someone in charge who can get things restored to their proper order and form. If Trump "breaks some eggs" in effecting change, so be it. While it is understandable that we fear what we don't understand and there is much about Trumpism and Trumpsters that confuses people, labeling them a deviant cult serves little purpose. That they hold very different views from other groups should be a reason to invite more dialogue, not to separate themselves from the larger collective.

Finally, as it relates to QAnon, given its diverse structure and configuration, experts disagree on whether it actually constitutes a cult. For example, most experts contend that distinguishing a cult from a social movement requires that there is a charismatic leader who becomes an object of worship. This leader is typically totalitarian and demands total control over believers. Second, there is an intentional effort to use thought and mind control over its members. Third, the group is destructive—meaning, members are willing to engage in violence to further its goals.[75]

Ross (2014) argues that QAnon meets some of these criteria but not all of them. QAnon has a leader, Q, and, indirectly, Trump, but as he points out, Q is not always visible and in control of the organization. In this way, QAnon is more of a movement than a cult. Second, there is no direct mind or thought control involved. QAnon has created an online world where people can attack unbelievers or collaborate with like-minded followers, but it lacks the direct mind control element that is seen in cults. However, as Ross (2014) points out, there is little question about the group's willingness to engage in violence.[76] In the end, QAnon has some of the features of a cult, but not to the degree one would use to define them as one.[77]

Similarly, Juergensmeyer (2000) argues that QAnon is more of a worldview than an actual cult. He argues that QAnon's loyalty toward President Trump has less to do with behavior or thought control than it does with the rejection of traditional political norms or authority. That is, QAnon members intensely believe in the idea that there are enemies everywhere and endorse the nationalistic rhetoric offered by Trump. But it was not QAnon that created the rhetoric in the first place; Trump was offering it with his America First approach that vilified immigrants and the media as enemies of the people.[78]

Other scholars, such as Stein (2016), are similarly uncertain about the configuration of QAnon as a cult. Similarly to other scholars, he argues that in terms of ideology and belief, QAnon seems to have cult-like features: an "us versus them" worldview, along with members' total devotion to the cause, including the exclusion of family and friends if they disagree. Additionally, some of the violent commentary, threats, and actions—the impending storm, the predicted arrests and public executions, designed to make the world a better place, are critical to understanding how difficult it is for members to leave QAnon. As Stein (2016) notes, the driving force behind any cult is fear and secrecy, and QAnon has an ample supply of both in its ideology and actions.[79]

As Rothschild (2021) points out, in addition to the elements of fear, secrecy, and the influence of a charismatic leader, there can be little doubt that the violence used by QAnon members is significant and serious. One need only look at the events of January 6 at the US Capitol to realize that it is far from a harmless group of conspiracy theorists who offer counter explanations for events. As Trump has promoted and endorsed conspiracy theories as part of his platform, the result has been the belief by groups like QAnon that their ideology, behavior, and willingness to engage in violence is appropriate, supported, and accepted.[80]

Chapter 4

Trump, Trumpsters, and White Supremacists

In chapter 3, we explored the idea of whether or not Trumpsters were part of a cult. This common assertion is based on the idea that many Trumpsters were and are unwilling to recognize the challenges presented by President Trump's behavior, comments, and beliefs. It is also based on disturbing reports that have emerged regarding the role of Trump supporters in the violence during the January 6 attack on the US Capitol.

As was mentioned in chapter 3, there is a great deal to unpack in such a discussion, starting with the idea that not all Trump voters are Trumpsters; not all Trumpsters embrace the rhetoric and narrative offered by the former president; and not all of them embrace Trump's inappropriate comments, behaviors, policies, and decisions. And while there are reasons to be concerned about the thoughts and actions of some extreme Trumpsters, particularly their willingness to engage in intimidation and violence, the available scholarly research on deviant cults suggests that while many Trump supporters have displayed thoughts, beliefs, and cult-like behavior, identifying Trumpsters as a cult is not a simple nor clear-cut process. This is true even of those who are ardent followers of QAnon, a group known to be strong supporters of former president Trump.

In this chapter, we explore another dimension of Trumpsters: those who embrace an ideology of white supremacy. Embedded in this discussion will be a description of white nationalism, as this is an integral part of the debate and controversy on Trump's stand on race-related issues.

THE RISE OF WHITE SUPREMACY GROUPS

White supremacy is not a new concept in the United States. It can be argued that the growth of the country geographically, militarily, and even economically can be traced back to the violence used against Native Americans. This form of white superiority was also seen in the enslavement of Blacks, which even had legal and religious justifications tied to it. In fact, some experts argue that the most obvious and disappointing period in American history relates to the violence that occurred during and after Reconstruction, where many Whites were convinced that Black Americans were disrupting their way of life and granting them equal rights would undermine democracy.[1]

The violence was not limited to members of hate groups but also included laws that were enacted to restrict Blacks' freedoms, coupled with rhetoric from politicians on the evils of Black equality. The impact of these actions is still felt today as the mechanisms, such as the criminal justice system, have continued to perpetuate the disenfranchisement of Blacks and other minorities under the banner of law and order. According to Mulligan et al. (2021), through the early part of the twentieth century, many Americans, including political leaders, embraced the idea of a racially pure White America. While the extent of violence against Blacks decreased after the civil rights movement and the formal end of Jim Crow laws, there continued to be an influence from white supremacist groups, who were responsible for violence against and hatred of minorities in many communities around the country.[2]

In more recent times, there was an increase in white nationalist group activities after President Barack Obama was elected. It has been long understood in the literature that membership in hate groups tends to rise during difficult economic times. Minorities and immigrants are often blamed for the problems many Whites experience, either because they are perceived to be taking jobs away from Whites, or policies and practices used to provide minorities with preferential treatment result in a disadvantage for Whites. With the election of President Obama, the first Black president of the United States, coupled with the 2008 economic recession, a pivotal moment was created that spurred the rise and popularity of white supremacist groups. Additionally, the impact of globalization, outsourcing of jobs by corporations, and the shortages of labor in some industries contributes to a narrative for white supremacists that the economic and political problems many working-class and poor Whites have encountered are a result of decisions and policies that favor others over White people.[3]

As illustrated by Mulligan et al. (2021), today's white supremacist movement finds its basis in these ideas but also a more magnified "white genocide" conspiracy theory, which argues that the White race is threatened by the increase in diversity, interracial marriage, and demographic changes to the country brought about, in part, by immigration. This theory contends that the preservation of white culture and the economic, social, and political power of White men is critically important to the future of the country. This platform is the basis for many white nationalist/white supremacist groups such as neo-Nazis, Christian Identity adherents, the alt-right, and those who espouse anti-immigrant, anti-Muslim, and anti-Semitic beliefs.

Additionally, white supremacist ideologies and misogyny are seen as another iteration of the threat non-Whites present to White men. While not all misogynists are racists, nor are all racists misogynists, attempts at any form of equality, whether they are based on race or gender, are seen as similar types of threats that should be addressed.[4]

Another threat to White men relates to Jews, where many white supremacist groups argue that the "Zionist Occupation Government" focuses on Jewish control of the government in the United States. There is also overlap with the QAnon conspiracy, which is built on long-standing anti-Semitic beliefs, and self-organized militias, some of which hold anti-immigrant and anti-Muslim views. While many scoff at the ideologies of white supremacist groups, there is evidence of increased support for such views, as seen in 2020, when two members of Congress who support QAnon and often use white supremacist language were elected. Such developments suggest that some of these ideas have reached mainstream status.[5]

Perhaps nowhere has the white supremacy rhetoric reached a more dangerous level of credibility than with the election of President Trump. During his campaign, as well as his time in office, Trump disparaged immigrants, women, Blacks, and other minorities in a variety of ways, including his famous Muslim ban, the appointment of a noted white supremacist as a senior policy advisor, and a general unwillingness to condemn white supremacist violence. Additionally, as white supremacist attacks grew in number and intensity, Trump advocated against allocating more resources toward addressing the threats that white supremacy groups posed.[6]

This latter reaction has carried significance, particularly when, in October 2020, the Department of Homeland Security identified domestic violent extremism as a significant threat, noting that white supremacist extremists have become "exceptionally lethal" in their attacks. Other groups, such as the Anti-Defamation League (ADL) have reported a rise in violence by white supremacist organizations against Blacks, Hispanics, Jewish, Muslim, and Sikh communities, and there appears to be an increase in members as well as informal supporters of white supremacist ideology.

Part of the explanation for the increase in recruitment and support relates to the ways in which white supremacist groups distribute information, attempt to attract members, and secure funding. A large part of this effort has been to transform the narrative from the hatred of others (which remains a feature of some groups) to a more nuanced and morally digestible message of celebrating white culture.[7]

The logic behind this approach is that the promotion of white culture and coded language relating to white superiority is much more likely to garner mainstream credibility. In addition, many white supremacist organizations make extensive use of online outreach to prospective members and have targeted military and veterans communities as well as appealed to law enforcement and first responders. As we will see, the Oath Keepers as an organization serves as an illustration of how white superiority can be parlayed into a patriotic message of defending the US Constitution or protecting the freedoms of the common man.[8]

WHITE NATIONALISM VERSUS
WHITE SUPREMACY: DEFINED

President Trump's critics are quick to point out that his comments spur the actions of groups in this country that spawn hatred and violence against others, particularly minorities. While President Trump cannot be held responsible for the actions of others or how his comments are interpreted, such commentary raises a variety of questions about the extent to which some groups feel threatened by the demographic changes occurring in the United States. It also raises many questions about Trump's words and deeds that seem to lend support to white supremacists.

Some observers might argue, for example, that the challenges related to immigration in this country are symptomatic of a much larger set of problems that relate to political, social, and economic hegemony; white privilege; the inevitable consequences of capitalism; and the growing inequalities around the world. Changes to the demographic profile of the United States, in part due to immigration, have caused some people to conclude that diversity, a hallmark of a democratic society, is unpatriotic.

The fear generated from the "threat" of diversity is part of the reason for the popularity of the slogan "Make America Great Again." It is also one of the reasons for the rise in popularity of white nationalism. While nationalism is not a new concept, President Trump's apparent support for it has emboldened some groups to encourage the use of violence against other groups, and it has resulted in the promotion of an extreme form of cultural, political, and economic isolationism in the United States.

White Nationalism

What exactly is white nationalism? President Trump claims that he rejects racist ideology and is "the least racist person there is,"[9] and he has chosen to use the term *nationalism* to describe an emphasis on promoting American culture. Nationalism is also seen in Trump's efforts to place the United States at the forefront of his domestic and foreign policy decisions. For Trump and his supporters, "making America great again" involves having a particular cultural identity rather than a culture based on ideals and values that transcend any particular dominant group.

According to most experts, white nationalism, like white supremacy, places the interests of White people over those of other racial groups. White supremacists and white nationalists both believe that racial discrimination should be incorporated into law and policy because White people are innately superior to people of other races and should maintain political and economic dominance.[10]

The problem with white nationalism, however, is not that it is overtly racist, although some would undoubtedly argue that it is synonymous with white supremacy. As some experts have noted, the real problem is that whiteness has been the default category in terms of political, economic, and cultural power, and the preservation of whiteness inevitably contains elements of racism and discrimination. For many Americans, the culture and nation as a whole are simply extensions of what they have always known—whites are in power, and they determine the course of the country. However, when threats to what people have come to know and understand about what it means to live in the United States emerge, the reaction is generally elevated levels of fear and anxiety about the future.[11]

Such fears are heightened by demographic shifts, such as decreasing birth rates for Whites and the increase in minority representation, particularly in positions of power. Such shifts are perceived as reducing the size and scope of White influence. This is why supporters of white nationalism argue that the United States should protect its White majority by limiting immigration as well as prohibiting other strategies that enhance multiculturalism.[12]

As is often the case when fear drives decision-making, there is a tendency to romanticize the past as a happier time, such as portraying the country as more unified and stable. As it relates to immigration, Trump's narrative and policies are described as an effort to return to a time when there was greater unity in this country—meaning less diversity. Trump's comments about what immigration has "done" to Europe reflects such a position.[13]

What makes this fear so dangerous is that, as the messaging and rhetoric surrounding the threat grows, so does the level of fear about the problem. This can result in the public becoming susceptible to manipulation of the facts and ignoring effective and reasonable solutions to the problem. That is, the gloom and doom rhetoric, coupled with outlandish claims including factually incorrect information, promoted again and again, can easily lead to justifying all manner of decisions that would otherwise be seen as unacceptable and counter to what has "made America great" in the past. In such a scenario, what would normally be seen and understood as racist or discriminatory becomes blurred, and the decisions begin to sound reasonable to the public.[14]

THE ALT-RIGHT MOVEMENT AND WHITE
SUPREMACY/NATIONALISM

According to the Southern Poverty Law Center, the alt-right movement was created in 2008 to describe a set of far-right ideals centered on white identity and the preservation of traditional Western civilization, which has at its core white supremacy and superiority. The alt-right is an ideology that celebrates what might be called *contemporary conservatism*, with an emphasis on liberty, freedom, free markets, and capitalism.[15]

The Anti-Defamation League contends that many alt-right adherents, including those in the United States, claim to be *Identitarians*, who promote racism and intolerance under the guise of preserving the ethnic and cultural origins of their respective countries. Others in the alt-right are referred to as *radical traditionalists*, comprised of members who claim to be supportive of traditional Christian values but do so from a white supremacist perspective. Still others in the alt-right identify as *white nationalists* who want to preserve the White majority in the United States, claiming that Whites losing their majority status is equivalent to white genocide.[16]

Another segment of the alt-right refers to themselves as *neo-reactionaries*, who reject liberal democracy and ideas associated with the Enlightenment. Some neo-reactionaries refer to themselves as *race realists*, or as human biodiversity advocates or *HBDs*, based on a belief that a person's race governs their behavior and intelligence—with Whites being superior to non-Whites. However they define themselves, alt-righters reject egalitarianism, democracy, universalism, and multiculturalism. Many alt-righters also blame Jews for allegedly promoting anti-White policies such as immigration and diversity.[17]

Alt-Right Rhetoric

As was mentioned, the alt-right movement consists of many dimensions, but in the end what they have in common is a connection to some form of white supremacy. As part of the narrative, alt-right members use various terms that mitigate the inflammatory nature of the white supremacist doctrine. For example, instead of inflammatory comments about race, some alt-right members use the term "culture" or argue they are promoting "Western Civilization" instead of white identity or white culture.[18]

The alt-right also tends to attract young, White men. Many of these young men are active on various message boards, many of which have been disbanded, such as 4chan, 8chan, and Reddit, mentioned in the QAnon section of chapter 3. It is on these anonymous boards that the racist and supremacist narratives are most easily seen, where women, minorities, and Jews are common targets for ridicule and vilification.[19]

Another aspect of the alt-right is its connection to the world of misogyny, broadly known as the "manosphere." In this narrative, there is a belief that men are increasingly being stripped of power by feminists and their supporters. Others view women not as equals or those who can make meaningful contributions to society but simply as a means to sexual gratification.[20]

As Hemmer (2016) points out in her book *Messengers of the Right*, alt-right members espouse racist ideology and anti-Semitic activities not based on a platform of hate but as a form of free speech. They also reject the mainstream conservative political view and are distrustful of free market systems since they believe that profit can easily circumvent the need to protect Whites' interests. Alt-right members often see themselves as "true" conservatives since many mainstream conservatives have become race traitors, or what are sometimes derisively called *cuckold conservatives*.[21] Hemmer (2016) also points out that some alt-right members, sometimes referred to as *alt-lite*, try to distance themselves from their white supremacist colleagues and claim instead that they simply hold views that are against immigration, globalism, feminism, and liberal views, which are seen as actively attempting to eliminate American culture.[22]

WHITE SUPREMACY AND THE TRUMP ADMINISTRATION

President Trump's political platform capitalized on the fears and anxieties about demographic changes, and efforts to promote minorities, such as affirmative action, were identified as a threat to the American way of life. His slogan, "Make America Great Again," suggested that America was no longer great. One of the reasons for this, he argued, was based on the country's inability to put "our" needs before others. As a symbolic and literal display of this form of isolationism, Trump remained committed to building a massive wall along the Mexican border and to make it more difficult for people, particularly from non-European countries, to immigrate to the United States and become citizens.[23]

Another example of Trump's acceptance of white supremacy was his appointment of Steve Bannon, a self-proclaimed white nationalist and leader of the alt-right movement, as his senior counselor and chief strategist. This decision brought the topic of white supremacy/nationalism into the mainstream discussion about American culture, politics, and economic decisions. While Bannon eventually left the White House, the fact that he was given such an important position was an alarming and disturbing development in the Trump administration.[24]

The intersection between white nationalism, race, and the Trump administration was seen in several policy decisions and commentary. While President Trump claimed he was not a racist and his proclamations of nationalism focused on the protection of the United States, critics point to a number of examples where his rhetoric and policies raised serious questions about whether there were racist undertones to his agenda.

For instance, Srikantiah and Sinnar (2019) contend that President Trump's position on immigration was really designed to preserve the country's predominantly white identity. They argue that evidence of this was seen in Trump's opposition to the removal of Confederate monuments, which he described as a threat to "our culture." His comments following the death of a protestor in Charlottesville, Virginia, which was the largest gathering of white supremacists in years, when he stated there were some "very fine people on both sides of the debate," raised many questions about his feelings regarding race. In fact, Trump began his presidential campaign by denouncing Mexican immigrants as "rapists" and has described undocumented immigrants as "animals."[25]

Additionally, some experts point out that Trump described the need to prevent immigrants from "shithole countries," a reference to Haiti, El Salvador, Honduras, Guatemala, and some African nations, from coming to the United States. He also suggested that immigration is generally a cultural threat to the United States, not simply one related to economic or national security. As an illustration, in describing the immigration issues in Europe, Trump stated that it changed the fabric of Europe and that Europeans were "losing their culture." Trump further stated, "We don't want what is happening with immigration in Europe to happen with us!"[26]

While some might claim that these comments may indicate a lack of sensitivity or perhaps a fundamental lack of understanding of the complexity of the issues, questions remain about whether Trump's claims and policies were actually race-neutral (Srikantiah and Sinnar 2019). For instance, in 2017, Trump ultimately succeeded in passing a Muslim travel ban, which prevented certain people from Muslim countries from entering the United States. Additionally, the Trump administration ended the temporary protected status for noncitizens from El Salvador, Haiti, Nicaragua, and Sudan that protected people who were unable to return home because of the civil unrest in those countries.[27]

Trump also attempted to end the Deferred Action for Childhood Arrivals (DACA) program, which allows children who entered the country without documentation to obtain work permits. This had racial undertones, since the vast majority of DACA recipients are Latinx and people of color. The administration had also targeted Mexican and Central American asylum seekers fleeing their countries due to violence by reducing the overall number of accepted asylum applications and making it more difficult to meet the criteria needed for admission.

The Trump administration also initially implemented policies that separated children from their families. The backlash from this latter decision ultimately led Trump to reverse this policy, but only because of the overwhelmingly negative response by the American public. Finally, the Trump administration escalated immigration enforcement and detention and took steps to process deportation cases quickly, without adequate due process or giving noncitizens a chance to prepare an adequate defense.[28]

As Srikantiah and Sinnar (2019) point out, while these changes were not specific to particular immigrants, the effects of these decisions fell heavily on noncitizens of color. When they are considered along with his public statements about certain groups, there remains important concerns about whether these policies were part of a comprehensive immigration policy or whether the underlying justification for them involved elements of white nationalism.

In sum, white nationalism and what has been more broadly referred to as the alt-right movement suggest that any attempt to dilute the American culture from its natural selection based on racial purity is a threat to national security.[29]

Trump's Stance on White Supremacy Groups

There have been a number of questions regarding Trump's position on white supremacy groups. On one hand, it is clear that his brand of populism as well as many of his public statements have been taken by many white supremacist groups as an endorsement of both ideology and violence against minority groups. Added to this is the fact that during the 2016 and 2020 campaigns, Trump was reluctant to condemn these groups, likely out of fear of alienating a portion of his base of support. In fact, in those instances when Trump actually denounced white supremacist groups in any way, it was often the result of a backlash of negative publicity for his comments that appeared to endorse them.

The controversy about Trump's stance on white supremacy became heated during the 2020 presidential debate when moderator Chris Wallace of Fox News pointedly asked Trump, "Are you willing, tonight, to condemn white supremacists and militia groups and to say that they need to stand down?" Trump's response was to ask for a name of a white supremacist group—to which, in response, President Biden mentioned the Proud Boys, a far-right neo-Nazi group that had been blamed for violence at protest rallies in recent weeks. However, instead of following the request by Wallace, Trump said,

"Proud Boys, stand back and stand by! But I'll tell you what, somebody's got to do something about antifa and the left."[30]

Not only did the Proud Boys quickly take to social media to proclaim that the president was supportive of their efforts, Democrats and even some Republicans reacted strongly to the lack of condemnation by Trump. Observers pointed out that the unwillingness to denounce the group was actually a form of endorsement that likely increased the Proud Boys' recruiting efforts. According to some experts, particularly those who track far-right groups, the conclusion from the debate was that Trump legitimized the Proud Boys in an extraordinary and unique way, particularly by a sitting US president.[31]

Days later, Trump attempted to repair the damage, but by then, coupled with several other previous statements that appeared to endorse white supremacist groups, Trump's response seemed contrived and less emphatic. Still, as Neuman (2020) points out, Trump told Fox News reporters that he condemns right-wing hate groups such as the KKK and the Proud Boys.

Later, in speaking to the press, Trump said: "Let me be clear again: I condemn the KKK. I condemn all white supremacists. I condemn the Proud Boys. I don't know much about the Proud Boys, almost nothing, but I condemn that." Trump also wanted President Biden to make a similar condemnation of Antifa, an anti-fascist group that Trump and his followers have blamed for many acts of violence across the country.[32]

The lukewarm statement during the presidential debate was not the first instance in which Trump failed to denounce or reject white supremacy groups. In August 2017, for example, after a white supremacist rally in Charlottesville, Virginia, resulted in the death of a protestor, Trump initially refused to condemn the organizers of the rally or the violence that ensued. Trump originally blamed left-wing counter-protestors and argued that there was "blame on both sides of the event." In his now famous quote, Trump said there were some "very fine people on both sides." Two days after that statement, facing widespread criticism from both Democrats and Republicans, Trump walked back his comment saying he denounced "the KKK, neo-Nazis, white supremacists, and other hate groups."[33]

Another example of Trump's racist, xenophobic rhetoric was seen in Minnesota at a rally where Trump told a crowd of nearly all White supporters that they had "good genes," echoing the views of neo-Nazis that White people are genetically superior.[34] These moments are part of a long list of disparaging comments about minorities, particularly immigrants from Central America, along with criticisms of protestors as part of the Black Lives Matter movement.

PROUD BOYS, BOOGALOO BOIS, AND OTHER
WHITE SUPREMACIST TRUMP SUPPORTERS

Proud Boys

As one of the staunchest supporters of President Trump, which was high-lighted in the 2020 presidential election debate, the Proud Boys are perhaps the most visible, violent, and active white supremacist group of Trumpsters. According to many organizations that track white supremacist groups, such as the Southern Poverty Law Center (SPLC), the Anti-Defamation League, the Armed Conflict Location and Event Data Project (ACLED), and other researchers such as Kriner and Lewis (2021), and despite the fact that the United States has not yet identified the Proud Boys as a terrorist organiza-tion, the Canadian government did so in 2021.[35] As we will see, there can be little doubt about what the Proud Boys represent or their allegiance to President Trump.

The Proud Boys may be best conceptualized as a quasi-street gang that has taken on paramilitary characteristics, with a political agenda. Often seen in their "colors"—black-and-yellow Fred Perry shirts—and often shouting *uhuru* (a Swahili word for "freedom"), the group attends events, demon-strations, and rallies that either promote an alt-right agenda or attempt to disrupt left-leaning gatherings and demonstrations. They also have a sig-nificant online presence, where their racist, white supremacist, xenophobic, anti-feminist, and anti-immigration stances are presented.[36]

As it is with most groups with an agenda, the purpose in participating in these events is to garner media attention for their cause, recruit poten-tial members, and spread disinformation about political groups and events that have taken place. Most recently, the Proud Boys embraced President Trump's "Stop the Steal" campaign, which alleged voter fraud in the elec-tion of President Biden. The group is far from an intellectual collection of like-minded members—instead, their actions have been described as akin to the kind of street-level violence and intimidation seen in Europe and other countries. Within the MAGA movement, the revival of the "Stop the Steal" narrative quickly became a focused rallying cry for Proud Boys activities and rhetoric. On December 12, 2020, hundreds of Proud Boys par-ticipated in a demonstration against the 2020 presidential election results in Washington, DC.[37]

The Proud Boys do not describe themselves as a militia. Instead, members refer to the Proud Boys as a "men's drinking club," or a fraternal organiza-tion. The organization emerged in 2016 as part of the alt-right movement and "men's rights" narrative. Of particular noteworthiness is the Proud Boys' stance as hyper-masculine, xenophobic, and willing to employ violence to achieve political and social goals.[38]

Its current national leader, Enrique Tarrio, serves as the national chairman for the Proud Boys, but allegations of Tarrio's role as a confidential informant, particularly after the January 6 violence at the US Capitol,[39] has created questions about the direction of the national organization in the future. Like many extremist groups, at the local level, the Proud Boys are made up of chapters that work autonomously.[40] Where these chapters of Proud Boys align is in their opposition to far-left movements—Proud Boys have regularly stood in opposition to immigration, feminism, social justice movements such as Black Lives Matter, LGBTQIA movements, and most notoriously anti-fascist (often referred to as antifa) mobilization.[41]

Proud Boys have also identified Democrats and liberals as evil and corrupt, and often refer to them as cultural Marxists or communists. In fact, the Proud Boys has remained consistent in its conservative rhetoric, including a willingness, until the January 6 violence, to be supportive of law enforcement. The Proud Boys endorsed the "Blue Lives Matter" movement, even framing their efforts as colleagues and "brothers in arms" with the law enforcement community. That changed just before the January 6 violence, when the organization stated that "the police are starting to become a problem," even though "we've had their back for years."[42]

After the murder of Heather Heyer at the Unite the Right rally in Charlottesville, Virginia, the Proud Boys leadership attempted to publicly distance the group from the alt-right movement and made concerted efforts to diminish the public's perception that they are a racist organization. However, members frequently display racist and fascist iconography on apparel ("Right-Wing Death Squad" images, "6 million was not enough," swastikas, etc.), and several members and chapters have openly shown affinity for overtly fascist organizations.[43]

In the end, most experts agree that the Proud Boys are a right-wing extremist organization; with some agencies, such as the SPLC and the Anti-Defamation League, categorizing the Proud Boys as a hate group. At the very least, by any reasonable assessment, the Proud Boys are a far-right group that promotes white supremacy, maintains affiliations with known extremists, and promotes misogynistic, Islamophobic, transphobic, anti-Semitic, and anti-immigration rhetoric.[44]

It is not clear how many men are members of the Proud Boys—some researchers have estimated between three thousand and eight thousand members in the United States, while the Proud Boys leadership has previously suggested upwards of twenty-two thousand globally.[45] Despite the variance in membership estimations, what is missing from the discussion is how many individuals sympathize with the Proud Boys but do not hold formal membership in the organization. As with other extremist movements, this is important since a focus on formal membership overlooks the ability of the group to incite violence by others who are in alignment with the group but do not self-identify as formal members of the organization.[46]

Like any criminal gang, the initiation ritual for prospective members is designed to demonstrate a recruit's commitment to the organization and to adopt an identity that is consistent with the organization's goals. This is no less true with the Proud Boys. Their initiation ritual illustrates how violence is a fundamental feature of the organization and the initiation protocols serve to reinforce the acceptability of violence to further its political causes. The initiation process involves four steps, beginning with the individual proclaiming himself to be a Proud Boy. The second step is a form of physical initiation similar to a "jumping in" process found in gangs, where members collectively assault the recruit.

In this particular ritual, the Proud Boy recruit is beaten until he can name five breakfast cereal brands. A third step in becoming a full member of the Proud Boys involves the recruit getting a tattoo of the Proud Boys logo. Finally, full membership is achieved once the recruit, having completed the first three steps, demonstrates his commitment to the organization by engaging in some form of violence to enhance the Proud Boys' agenda, known as "serving the cause."[47]

In addition to attending demonstrations for far-right extremist causes, along with efforts to interfere and intimidate protestors and demonstrators who disagree with their alt-right tendencies, the Proud Boys have a significant online presence that uses disparaging jokes, memes, and online baiting (or inserting anti-feminist or anti-immigration comments on others' posts) designed to escalate debates as well as serve as a recruiting tool.[48]

Boogaloo Bois

The "boogaloo" movement—named for a 1980s break-dancing movie and characterized by members who carry weapons and wear Hawaiian shirts, is a loosely organized group with many splinter sects associated with it, from its original neo-Nazi and white supremacist roots to newer versions that are sometimes described as more libertarian. At its base, the overall goal of the boogaloo movement is the overthrow of the government, including starting a second civil war to achieve that goal.[49]

According to the SPLC, the movement began in early 2010 and was characterized by racial violence. According to the National Institute for Research and Education on Human Rights, the neo-Nazi version of Boogaloo Bois believes that the destruction of the government begins by starting a race war. By allowing other groups to kill each other, with Whites ultimately prevailing, the United States will be rid of all its current problems related to race, social class, and sexual orientation.[50]

The libertarian version of Boogaloo Bois, some of whom are Black and Hispanic, reject the white supremacist label and instead believe in defending the rights of individuals against the government. Many members wear Hawaiian shirts and body armor, and carry weapons. These members are generally anti-police, since law enforcement represents the oppressive government, and Boogaloo Bois have been known to attack police officers.[51] The "boogaloo" name is a code word for the second civil war and came from the 1984 movie *Breakin' 2: Electric Boogaloo*. The plot of the movie is about break-dancing teens who try to save their community center from greedy corporate developers and corrupt politicians.[52]

The Hawaiian shirts come from the popular term on boogaloo websites and message boards: "Big Luau," a Hawaiian ritual involving a tradition of roasting pigs that translates into a reference to killing police officers. The Big Luau is also code for the event that will result in the destruction of government and birth of a new society.[53]

Like many white supremacist organizations, Boogaloo Bois makes extensive use of social media such as Facebook, Reddit, and YouTube. One estimate shows that there are about 125 Facebook groups related to the boogaloo movement, with tens of thousands of members. While Facebook has attempted to limit these groups, in part by banning the use of the term "boogaloo" and related words, the group continues to garner followers through other propaganda campaigns.[54]

Since the pandemic lockdown, experts have noted that many members of the Boogaloo Bois have escalated the use of violence, with a number of celebrated cases involving members killing police officers or planning violent attacks during demonstrations related to the George Floyd death or Black Lives Matter movement.[55]

Oath Keepers

According to McQueen (2021), the Oath Keepers is an anti-government, right-wing political organization committed to supporting and defending their interpretation of the US Constitution. The group was created on the belief that the federal government is part of a conspiracy designed to keep citizens from expressing their rights and freedoms. The name "Oath Keepers" comes from the oath that military personnel and law enforcement take when they join those organizations and keep regardless of who is in charge of a particular entity or agency.[56] This is significant because the oath transcends any particular leader—if the behavior or actions of the leader violate the US Constitution, Oath Keepers are required to refuse to follow the leader's wishes.

The Oath Keepers began as a political blog in 2009 by Army veteran Stuart Rhodes, who graduated from Yale Law School and became a trial lawyer before being disbarred in 2015. As an organization, the Oath Keepers evolved from these discussions and has, at its core, an ideology that centers around a duty based on the formal promises made upon entering a profession of public service. That ideology focuses almost exclusively on protecting citizens' natural and constitutional rights. This is accomplished by minimizing or even dismissing orders of their appointed leaders if he or she is perceived as running counter to the US Constitution. In addition, Oath Keepers pledge to obey commands as long as they do not violate ten specific organizational rules.

While in theory such an ideological position sounds noble and reasonable—after all, it is based on the ideas founded in the military and law enforcement—by some accounts, such as Jackson (2020) in *Oath Keepers: Patriotism and the Edge of Violence in a Right-Wing Antigovernment Group*, there are themes of nativism, Islamophobia, a dislike of leftist groups, and elements of white supremacy found in various chapters of the organization. This is true despite the fact that the Oath Keepers claim to reject white supremacy and are not a militia group.[57]

The Oath Keepers is structured as a nonprofit organization and is led by a board of directors. Stewart Rhodes serves as the organization's president alongside other leaders, characteristic of the typical roles found in a nonprofit organization (e.g., treasurer, secretary, and executive director). At the local chapter level, the Oath Keepers organize around state and county militias.[58]

Before their participation in the January 6 US Capitol assault, the Oath Keepers were involved in several confrontations with local and federal authorities, as well as with far-left political protesters and rioters. These confrontations have all been nonviolent, but the Oath Keepers' heavily armed presence at emotionally charged events remains a significant concern due to the potential for violence. They typically arrive on the scene well armed, wearing body armor and other military-like clothing and equipment.[59]

The Oath Keepers' members leverage their law enforcement and military experience and they are very capable and willing to engage with lethal force, but it is also clear they understand that any deadly action must be justifiable as a proportionate act of self-defense. Most research on this group estimates it to contain about five thousand members, making it one of the largest groups in the militia movement, Although the Oath Keepers' organizational structure is fluid, and its size is not fully known, as seen in the action of some of its members on January 6, they pose a significant threat should they decide to employ the strategies and tactics for which they were trained.[60]

The Oath Keepers also have an ideological connection to colonial America and British tyranny, which generates a sense of perceived righteousness and purpose that has some public appeal and helps to recruit new members. In addition, the organization's notable variety of operations—defending ranches, guarding city businesses, and even conducting humanitarian relief—gives it wider appeal to the general public.

After all, the Oath Keepers portray themselves as defensive in nature, they claim that they are protective of the common man, and have the competency of military and law enforcement training to employ sufficient restraint as the situation warrants. All of these are part of the narrative presented to the public and promote the idea that the group is simply present at events to protect those who need it. However, at an extreme, the group has a pattern of vigilantism and believes that they have the authority to determine when a right is being violated and whether a forceful response is warranted. It is this latter concern, as well as an ideological foundation strongly influenced by conspiracy theory, that has led many experts to conclude that it is simply another form of extremist group. In the end, perhaps more so than any other far-right group, the Oath Keepers have a legitimacy and appeal that other militia or extremist groups cannot match.[61]

In 2021, a group called Distributed Denial of Secrets hacked into the server of the Oath Keepers and distributed the names of members and those who had paid membership dues. More sensitive information, including the group's purported membership rolls, have been made available to media organizations and researchers. Some accounts of what had been discovered show that Oath Keepers members include police officers, former military personnel, sheriffs, teachers, and other government employees. While the Anti-Defamation League had estimated the size of the Oath Keepers to be in the hundreds, this information, along with hundreds of email correspondences between members, shows that number to be grossly underestimated. According to one account, membership in the Oath Keepers was approximately thirty-eight thousand.[62]

Countering White Supremacists: Antifa

In response to white supremacists, authoritarians, and fascists, some groups have organized in opposition to the violence. Labeled *anti-fascist*, these organizations have existed for decades. For instance, anti-fascist groups fought against dictators Mussolini and Hitler during World War II.[63]

More recently, anti-fascist groups have emerged to counter neo-Nazi groups and to address the racism and discrimination that continues to plague the United States. Known as *Antifa*, or anti-fascist, these groups are defined by their ideological stance in opposition to white supremacist groups and their platform of hate. Antifa groups are characterized by a left-leaning political view, a tendency to be against capitalism (largely because it tends to promote inequalities), and an eschewal of racism, sexism, and homophobia.[64]

The movement does not have a unified structure, national leadership, or identifying feature; instead, it is comprised of a number of local organizations focused on preventing neo-Nazis and white supremacists from gaining political or social acceptance by the public more so than promoting a particular agenda. Bray (2017) argues that one main strategy used by Antifa groups is confronting white supremacists at rallies and demonstrations as well as offering protection to counter-protestors at these events. Another common strategy used by Antifa groups is uncovering personal information about white supremacists and publicly identifying members. Called *doxing*, this tactic is designed to discourage people from joining hate organizations since it can have social and economic implications.[65]

Antifa became the focus of considerable national attention after the killing of George Floyd and the protests related to his death. President Trump, Attorney General Bill Barr, and other officials have blamed Antifa for the violence at these demonstrations, including the rioting and looting that occurred. In fact, Trump promised that Antifa would be identified as a terrorist organization because they were responsible for the vandalism and violence by radical left-wing groups. Trump also blamed Antifa for the violence that occurred at the Charlottesville, Virginia, rally—this is what led to his comment that "many sides," meaning in addition to the neo-Nazis and white supremacists, were to blame for the violence.[66] The violence that typically emerges from the meeting of Antifa groups and white supremacists reveals their tendency and willingness to participate in violence to further their cause. Such actions lead to questions about whether Antifa is substantially different from the white supremacists they purport to counter.[67]

WHITE SUPREMACY GROUPS AND THE
VIOLENCE AT THE US CAPITOL

As the evidence surrounding the events of the January 6 violence at the US Capitol continues to mount, what has become obvious is that many of the participants were active members of a white supremacist group, sympathizers of those organizations, or part of a wide collection of people who would not normally be seen as radical extremists but were willing attack congressional leaders for simply trying to perform their prescribed duties.[68]

It is indeed disturbing to learn that some members of the Oath Keepers were actively involved in the January 6 violence at the US Capitol, with several members identified as former and current military and law enforcement personnel whose sworn duty is to uphold their oath of office. Similarly, members of the Proud Boys have been charged in connection with the violence that occurred on January 6, along with other individuals who had some affiliation with the group.

Perhaps most disturbing, however, were those people who, on the surface, appeared to be normal, law-abiding citizens who had careers, homes, families, and every reason to avoid the events that took place. These were businesspersons, attorneys, physicians, and others who saw themselves as patriots attempting to remedy a great injustice, despite the fact that the only evidence of that injustice was Donald Trump's proclamation that it was occurring.[69] Moreover, it was not a spontaneous reaction by a mob caught up in a frenzy of emotion, acting in a way that was counter to their normal behavior. There is significant evidence that the events at the US Capitol were planned well in advance and there remain serious questions about whether President Trump knew or had indirect involvement in the planned attack.[70]

These developments go beyond a small number of overzealous supporters of Trump following his directions, as many who participated in the violence are now claiming. Instead, the alarming direction of white supremacy appears to have gone beyond the fringes of smaller groups like the Proud Boys, Boogaloo Bois, Oath Keepers, neo-Nazis, and the like and has permeated into mainstream discourse about the direction of the country for many other Americans.

MAKING SENSE OF WHITE SUPREMACISTS AND TRUMP SUPPORTERS

As Byman (2021) points out, the events at the US Capitol indicate a willingness between white supremacists and anti-government extremists, along with conspiracy theorists and misguided Trump supporters, to collaborate on a coordinated use of violence against innocent victims. As the white supremacist movement has morphed beyond the traditional Ku Klux Klansman or the neo-Nazi skinhead, and has developed subtler messages of hate and leveraged the use of social media to spread its ideology to mainstream America, it has highlighted the fear that many Whites have harbored about the future of white hegemony.

The white supremacist movement has also spread to other countries and has capitalized on what is known as the *Great Replacement Theory*. This idea contends that many countries in Europe and the United States have been and continue to be diluted by non-Whites such as Blacks, Hispanics, Arabs, and other immigrants. The fear is that these other groups will replace Whites and eventually cause the White race to become extinct.[71]

The "great replacement" idea has been promoted by the white supremacist movement, since it supports the idea of a "white genocide." The theory has also become a rallying cry for many white supremacists in what is known as the "fourteen words": "We must secure the existence of our people and a future for white children."[72] In a telling moment during the 2017 rally in Charlottesville, Virginia, white supremacists were heard chanting the phrases "Jews will not replace us" and "You will not replace us," as they marched: clear references to the theory.[73]

This theory and the white supremacy movement in general depends on the distribution of propaganda via social media in various forms, making it an ideal recruitment tool for both members and supporters of the ideology. The latter are an understudied area of white superiority/supremacy, since there is a tendency to focus on active and current membership in various white supremacist organizations. What is also sometimes overlooked are the lone-wolf actors who are not necessarily members but engage in deadly attacks in the name of either white supremacy, in general, or on behalf of a particular group.[74]

Moving forward, changes made by the Biden administration regarding things like immigration as well as vaccination mandates and other restrictive policy changes may only spur white supremacists and anti-government groups to escalate their agendas and activities. This is particularly true as Trump has continued to proclaim election fraud and has the support of many Republicans in Congress, who believed that unless their party was successful, the election must have been tainted.

This comes on the heels of a recent poll that shows nearly a third of Republicans believe that violence may be the only way to rescue the country from the problems it currently faces. This poll also points out that nearly 68 percent of Republicans believe the presidential election was stolen from Donald Trump, compared to 26 percent of Independents and 6 percent of Democrats.[75] That figure rises to 82 percent among Republicans who trust and watch Fox News.

The latter is important, as evidence has revealed that hosts of Fox News were aware of the level of danger occurring at the US Capitol (as seen by their texts to White House officials urging President Trump to stop the assault) despite on-air claims that the events of January 6 were nonviolent in nature. As experts have noted, the Republican Party has clearly been radicalized. The implication of this, of course, is that by raising questions about free and fair elections, extremist views have been given greater legitimacy and fuel the conspiracy theory machine that seems to have impacted and continues to be impacting many citizens.[76]

The justification for such thinking is achieved by calling attention to the similarities between the current government and what took place prior to the American Revolution. Such effort, of course, is an attempt to exploit feelings of patriotism, to cast a wide recruitment net for prospective members, as well as reinforce claims that only Trump can save society. While these are not necessarily new messages by any means, current events, including efforts by some groups to alter voting laws and vaccination mandates, and the inability of Congress to pass meaningful legislation to help Americans in need, all point toward an opportunity to intensify the messages and their value.[77]

In the larger context of our discussions about Trump and Trumpsters, we need to consider the fact that the traction given to white supremacist groups is not confined only to fringe organizations that have long been a part of the American experiment. Rather, as a result of deft packaging and subtle marketing and distribution through social media, hate groups have been able to make significant inroads into mainstream politics.

As Klein (2020) points out in his book *Why We're Polarized*, this is problematic for a number of reasons, not the least of which is that our political beliefs have become a main identity marker, making any discussion of white superiority and racism in the political realm a reality for most people. In other words, it is one thing to argue that white supremacist groups are troubling but remain on the edges of society; but it is quite another when we consider the fact that we have allowed those narratives and rhetoric to gain a foothold in our thinking about our place in the world. The implications are disturbing.[78]

Of course, this is exacerbated by a president whose platform has dehumanized some groups while celebrating the privilege of others. Still, in the end, we are responsible for much of what has happened in this country regarding the rise in popularity of hatred and beliefs in white superiority. As much as we would like to point a finger at a culprit or set of conspiratorial actors, most notably Trump and the co-opted and radicalized Republican Party, ultimately, we are the ones who have allowed these ideas to seep into our thinking and influence our behavior.

Perhaps most telling, while the intensity and extremism seen in the events surrounding the Trump administration may be more alarming than in the past, this is not the first time that people in the United States have had misguided notions and actions about other groups. One need only look at events in American history as reminders of our potential to ignore the evidence and allow fear to justify the mistreatment of others.

Chapter 5

The Christian Right as Trumpsters

As we have seen in previous chapters, some Trump followers have extreme views on politics, in general, as well as perceptions of President Trump and his policies, in particular. In chapter 4, we explored how some Trumpsters embrace the idea of white supremacy, including the use of violence as a means to achieving white superiority or preserving of White domination in America.

There is also considerable support for Trump by evangelical Christians. Many Christians even think he has been sent by God to restore the country. While it is easy to dismiss some followers that demonstrate extreme positions such as neo-Nazis, members of hate groups, or even those who espouse outlandish conspiracy theories, some experts point out that the Christian Right might be initially seen as a more mainline group with a reasonable perspective. However, as we will see, some members of this group also espouse extremist views as they attempt to implement a narrow and intolerant ideology.

This chapter offers a description of the Christian Right, as well as an explanation of how and why Trump has been able to convince so many members of this group to support him. This is true despite the fact that much of Trump's behavior and beliefs run counter to a Christian ideological and behavioral framework. In an attempt to reconcile these inconsistencies, part of the explanation for Christian support of Trump relates to the tendency of voters to focus on single issues, such as abortion, rather than a more holistic view of Trumpism and Trump's behavior.

In fact, in the case of the Christian Right, there are actually multiple issues at play in addition to abortion, some of which overlap with white supremacist ideology. Like their white supremacist counterparts, who have learned the value of nuancing the message of the ideology they embrace, similar strategies are used by the Christian Right in their support for Trump. Examples include topics broadly framing the issue as one of "religious freedom" or "parent's rights." These are often seen by critics as code for the Christian

Right's attempt to assert its narrow ideology over other competing religious and secular frameworks.

As Graham (2020) points out, there is division among American Christians about Trump. On one side are those who insist that the president is a Christian hero who is standing up for religious rights. On the other side are critics who contend that White evangelical Christians have justified supporting Trump not because of an ideological stance on any topic, but because they are like any other interest group who want their agenda furthered. Graham (2020) points out that many members of the evangelical Christian community see themselves as a marginalized group, and by supporting Trump, they can secure the protection they need and have policies relating to abortion, same-sex marriage, and traditional views of the family passed that reflect their beliefs.[1]

Gerson (2018) notes that while questions remain about whether Trump is an actual believer, despite surrounding himself with cabinet members who are, there is little doubt that he has seen his role as a protector of the evangelical Christian community. As a result, many Christians view Trump as a divinely inspired savior who will further the Christian Right's agenda.[2]

THE CHRISTIAN RIGHT DEFINED

What exactly do we mean when we talk about the Christian Right? While it may seem a simple matter to define the Christian Right (CR) as ostensibly all Christians who espouse conservative views, as with the discussion of cults and white supremacists, this is not a homogeneous group, despite the fact that they may have similar religious beliefs. As Wacker (n.d.) points out, public opinion polls at the end of the 1980s found that the CR was made up largely of evangelical Protestants, but not all members of the CR were shown to be evangelical Protestants and many evangelical Protestants did not agree with the CR. Generally speaking, the CR drew support from politically conservative Catholics, Jews, Mormons, and even some people who espoused nonreligious beliefs.[3]

For many groups, such as the Amish or other deeply conservative denominations, the political dimension of the CR had little value: they felt that participation in politics was not part of their ideological mission. Other Christian groups showed more liberal theological beliefs than the CR and were not interested in helping candidates win elections. Instead, they wanted to help people in need and focus on setting a Christian example for others. As Wacker (n.d.) notes, one way to understand the CR and its relationship to evangelical Christians is seen in figure 5.1. Wacker points out that the CR emerged as a

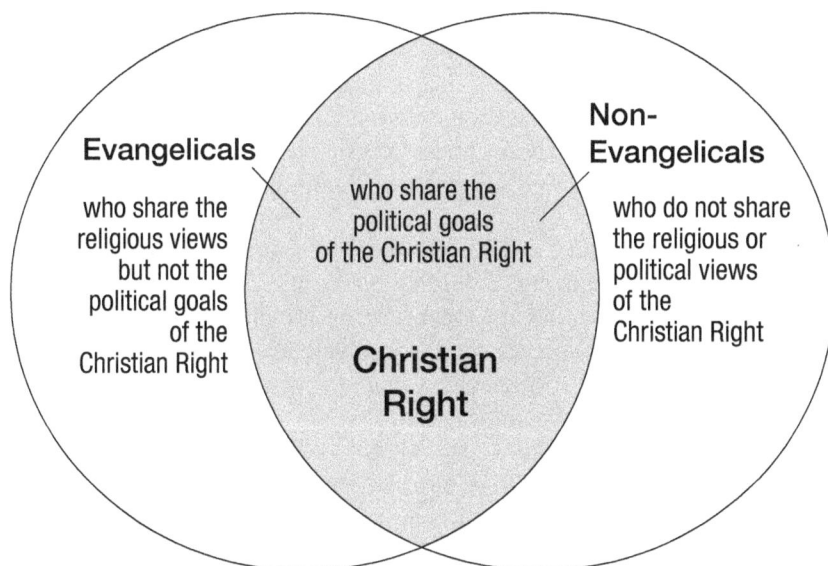

Figure 5.1. The Diversity of the Christian Right

Source: Wacker, Grant. (n.d.). "The Christian Right." National Humanities Center. Available at: http://nationalhumanitiescenter.org/tserve/twenty/tkeyinfo/chr_rght.htm.

response by some Christians who became politically active in part because they felt it was the only viable way to further their ideological message.[4]

A BRIEF HISTORY OF THE CHRISTIAN RIGHT

While one can argue that the CR's views come from the development of things like teaching evolutionism in public schools or the rise of communism after World War II, the more significant developments came as a result of events that occurred in the 1960s in the United States. This includes the civil rights movement, the hippie movement, anti–Vietnam War demonstrations, the women's movement, new ideas about sexuality, and the development of new religious movements. After the Supreme Court banned prayer and Bible readings in public schools, many traditional Christians felt the only way to prevent further dismantling of the Christian ideology was to participate in the political process.[5]

In general, when examining the history and development of the CR, we see a clear pattern of dissatisfaction with the direction of the country by many members of the Christian community as well as the perception that religious freedom and traditional morality was under attack. In order to restore the social order to its proper place, many Christians felt that a more pronounced and even extreme response was needed. The CR stressed traditional family values, free market economics, and a hard-line foreign policy approach, as well as a negative response to secular culture in America. In the development of its current form, we see the rise and fall of groups such as the Moral Majority, the Christian Coalition, and others that have attempted to influence social policy decisions as well as provide economic support to candidates that align with those views.[6]

While the history of the CR is based on a Christian fundamentalist approach, today's version sees a loose confederation of groups such as the Southern Baptist Convention, the Presbyterian Church of America, Catholics, Mormons, Jews, and other cultural conservatives who band together to protest abortion rights, pornography, same-sex marriage, and other current social issues. While the theological split that occurred among conservative Protestants in the early part of the twentieth century was the beginning of the CR, the decades between the 1920s and the 1980s were critical in terms of the consolidation of groups around issues in law, politics, and special interests.[7]

Foundations of the Christian Right

An essential part of the theological divisions between Protestant groups was seen in the reaction to the famous Scopes trial of the 1920s. In that case, some Protestants favored more modern interpretations of Christian teachings to reflect the scientific theories proposed by Darwin's evolutionary theory. This group also endorsed the idea of challenging traditional views of the origins of biblical scripture. In contrast, a second group of "fundamentalists" disputed such claims and retained the core views of the inerrancy of scripture, the divinity of Christ, and the reality of scriptural miracles.[8]

Against the backdrop of the Scopes trial, which involved teaching evolutionary theory in public schools, was the conflict over alcohol (seen in the Eighteenth Amendment to the US Constitution, also known as Prohibition) as well as the changing role of women in society. Fundamentalists, in an attempt to maintain control over churches and the narrative, took an isolationist approach by creating independent colleges such as Bob Jones College in 1927, which later became Bob Jones University.[9]

Over time, many conservative Protestants wrestled with the isolationist approach and the belief that fundamentalists needed to become more socially and politically active. During the Great Depression, some fundamentalist groups took issue with Roosevelt's New Deal policies, as it signaled the centralization of the power of the federal government, seen by some as a trend similar to the biblical prophecy that powerful regimes were destined to fall.[10]

By the 1950s, many fundamentalists came to view communism as a threat, particularly the example of the Soviet Union, that foreshadowed what could happen unless Protestant groups became more politically active. In fact, some fundamentalists, most notably Billy Graham, took issue with the passive isolationist approach and interpreted political and social activism as a form of evangelism. This early version of political involvement was accelerated during the 1960s as a new generation of neo-evangelicals began focusing on some of the more pressing social issues of the era.[11]

This aggressive form of political activism was highlighted by fundamentalists' relationship with the Republican Party. By the late 1960s and early 1970s, the infamous Southern Strategy served to identify the more pressing anxieties of Whites and White conservatives about the changing nature of race relations and the family structure in America. It was also during this time that concerns about secularization and the ambivalence of traditional values and culture led to the rise of a "law and order" campaign by Richard Nixon. This "get tough" approach to crime resonated with fundamentalist Christians, as it was seen as a counter to the radical trends of the previous decade.

In fact, similar to President Trump's impeachment trials, the Watergate scandal and Nixon's resignation was a watershed event in galvanizing fundamentalists and evangelical conservatives into an organized and cohesive political force that remained loyal to the president. This was not done because of any concerns about his culpability but, rather, because Nixon, like Trump, represented a response and reaction to the previous decade's dissatisfaction with the direction of the country.[12]

The Moral Majority and the Christian Coalition

An important step in the development of political activism by the CR was the creation of the Moral Majority by Southern Baptist minister Jerry Falwell. The decision to create the organization was based on the large following that Falwell had created as well as his strong views on the threats posed to the evangelical community, specifically communism and the moral decline of America. Falwell created Lynchburg Baptist College in 1971, which ultimately became Liberty University. By 1980, the Moral Majority boasted more than 2 million members and became a centerpiece of Falwell's influence.[13]

Many religious conservatives also felt the government was limiting their religious freedom. The highlighted case was when, in 1976, the Internal Revenue Service revoked Bob Jones University's tax-exempt status because of its racially discriminatory practices in the admissions process. The IRS used the *Green v. Connally* (1971) ruling that justified the revocation of the tax-exempt status of any organization that engaged in racial discrimination.[14] At that time, Bob Jones University had a policy that prohibited the admission of Black students. However, in response to the backlash of opposition, along with the IRS threats, the university eventually relented and admitted married

Black students and then, ultimately, unmarried Blacks. However, university officials prohibited interracial dating.

At the same time, there were a series of controversial US Supreme Court decisions in the 1960s that regulated the operation of public schools, specifically prayer and Bible readings on campus. The *Green* case, coupled with three landmark rulings that affected the role of religion in public schools, *Engel v. Vitale* (1962), *Murray v. Curlett* (1963), and *Abington School District v. Schempp* (1963), led many religious conservatives to view these decisions as part of a secular attack on religion and religious freedom.[15]

Falwell's Moral Majority also took issue with the US Supreme Court decision in 1973 on abortion. While one can debate the merits of the case and abortion as a singular cause of the development of the Christian Right, one has to consider the context in which that ruling occurred. In fact, some experts argue that this case, more than any other, galvanized the collaboration of many like-minded groups into the CR in the late 1970s. The ruling brought Protestants and Catholics, along with other non-Protestants, into dialogue and became a rallying point for the claim that religious freedom was under attack.

This was particularly true given the Scopes trial and other rulings that demonstrated to Christians the secular viewpoint was dominating society, and unless religious groups responded collectively, the trend was likely the end of religious freedom in general. Advocating nonviolent techniques once championed by civil rights activists in the South, many Christian leaders promoted the idea that all Christians had a moral and theological obligation to resist unjust laws and to use nonviolent means of protest to defend and protect the sanctity of the American family. Falwell adopted this approach, sometimes referred to as *cobelligerency*, as a central concept for his Moral Majority.[16]

By the end of the 1980s, abortion remained legal, women were involved in the workforce as never before, and prayer in public schools remained illegal, and the value of the Moral Majority was seen in setting the stage for the rise of the CR movement as a political force, which has remained solid since the late 1970s.[17] That is, much of the success of the CR came on the heels of the decline of the Moral Majority and the contributions of the Christian Coalition, which is credited to Pat Robertson, a Southern Baptist minister who was the host of the widely popular *700 Club* and who founded the Christian Broadcasting Network and the Family Channel cable network.

After a failed presidential campaign, Robertson used his millions of followers to create the Christian Coalition, with the goal of supporting Republican candidates, offering voters direction on issues, educating local activists and building local political machines, and ultimately serving as an intermediary between Christians and Republican candidates. The Christian Coalition is often seen as the second generation of the CR. The IRS, citing the overt political activity of the Christian Coalition, eventually denied its application for

501(c)(3) tax-exempt status in the late 1990s. Today the organization persists as an advocacy group but at a much lower level of activity.[18]

THE CONTEMPORARY CHRISTIAN RIGHT

One could argue that the Moral Majority and the Christian Coalition were short-term efforts to identify single-issue topics with voters and getting conservative Christians connected to the Republican Party in general. While these two organizations promoted a narrow agenda, as they waned in popularity and effectiveness, other groups followed with a set of long-term goals, including efforts to shape societal morality and mainline efforts to spread the message. Examples include James Dobson's Focus on the Family and the Heritage Foundation, which were designed to build more lasting and durable relationships between religious leaders and policymakers.

In other words, instead of attempting to elect particular candidates, as was the case with the Moral Majority and the Christian Coalition, these organizations attempt to influence policy decisions regardless of which candidate occupies the White House or which party holds the majority in Congress. By focusing on larger social issues that are confronting American democracy, these organizations attempt to shape the country's sense of morality and further their agenda by leveraging relationships between religious leaders and high-profile politicians.[19]

Political candidates understand the significant influence members of the CR represent and evidence of this was seen in the support of Donald Trump in 2016, which garnered the endorsement of leaders such as Pat Robertson, James Dobson, and many others in the CR movement. The linkages between Christian conservatism and the Republican Party are critical to the success of both groups, so much so that religious leaders are often willing to overlook ideological challenges, such as the questions about Trump's actual religious beliefs and his immoral past and present behavior, in exchange for policy considerations on the appointment of conservative judges, abortion, the role of Israel, religious freedom, as well as what is taught in public schools.[20]

Ideological Stance

Religious leaders such as Jerry Falwell, Pat Robertson, and Phyllis Schlafly linked their beliefs to a romantic view of American life in the past. The CR has been extraordinarily successful in getting the message out, particularly its ability to capitalize on the public's fear of the future. Essentially, there are four basic ideas that surround the CR perspective. These are: the assumption that moral absolutes exist, including the creation of sexual identities and gender roles; the preferability of capitalism to other economic models such as communism; the importance of hard work and self-sufficiency; and the sanctity of unborn life. The source of these moral absolutes is found in the Bible, and questioning or modifying these absolutes threatens the very existence of society. These four principles are the basis of the CR stance on a variety of issues such as reproductive rights, the role of women in society, transgender issues, welfare, and other contemporary topics.[21]

The Christian Right's Need for Strong Leaders

Another interesting dimension of the CR is its heavy reliance on traditional views about men and women, with the former being considered the dominant voice within families, in economic decisions, and in politics. As Du Mez (2020) points out, there is a long history of fascination with strong (White), masculine leaders within the church as well as an attraction to leaders who display a type of image that personifies strength and aggression.[22]

The basis for this need for a strong rescuer is, of course, the deep-seated fear by many in the CR that they are under attack. Feminism is a threat to traditional views of women and of the family structure. According to scriptural interpretation, the traditional American family was a patriarchy, with the male being the physical, social, and spiritual leader of the family. Communism, homosexuality, and civil rights are all serious threats to family values in general and Christianity in particular.[23]

Many Christian leaders, for example, have long had a penchant for strong and militant leaders; after all, scripture is replete with examples of heroic and masculine figures. Within the CR, people like Franklin Graham, Pat Boone, James Dobson, Pat Robertson, and other contemporary leaders continue to identify with and endorse what Du Mez (2020) refers to as "John Wayne types" of political leaders, despite a host of inconsistencies in the personalities, morals, ethics, and behaviors of those leaders who promise their protection. It is for this reason, Du Mez (2020) points out, that evangelical Christians of all types were willing to overlook Trump's less than Christian behavior and commentary. And given Trump's comfort level with thinking of himself as a decisive and strong leader, the repeated xenophobic, racist, and disparaging comments about anyone other than White Christians are often ignored by CR leaders while they continue to embrace Trump's obviously non-Christian messaging. Du Mez (2020) offers the observation that this reaction is not unique to Trump, given the history of the CR movement.[24]

CHRISTIAN RIGHT TOPICS OF IMPORTANCE

Stacking the Courts With Conservative Judges

In aligning with the CR's agenda, the appointment of Trump's three Supreme Court nominees led to a 6–3 conservative majority. Some among the Christian Right believed that their appointment would make eventual reversal of *Roe v. Wade* more likely.[25] Overall, the appointment of these Christian conservatives to the Supreme Court is expected to advance the religious freedom agenda of the CR and parry the secular movement that threatens the Christian way of life. Trump clearly catered to this audience in his comments about the prevailing threat of a growing totalitarian influence on the left that sought to restrict religious expression. Promising to protect Christians' ability to pray without fear of attack from secularists, Trump argued to uphold "religious liberty for all."[26]

Trump nominated 274 conservative federal judges, with a total of 245 appointed.[27] What is missing from this discussion, however, is the CR's claim of the need to protect religious expression and liberty of *all* religious groups to worship, pray, and engage in religious activities. Instead, a thread that runs through the CR narrative is that religious liberty or freedom really means those freedoms are reserved for conservative Christians to pray, worship, and engage in religious activities. Part of the ideological differences with the fundamentalist approach is a narrow view of what constitutes "appropriate" interpretations of scripture and of the values outlined in the Christian doctrine (e.g., anti-homosexuality; anti-same-sex marriage; promotion of traditional family values; Christian prayers in public schools).

What was also missing from the discussion of Trump's efforts to stack the Supreme Court was the willingness to manipulate the process of confirmation based on political affiliation. During President Obama's administration, who nominated Merrick Garland after Justice Antonin Scalia had passed away, Senate Majority Leader Mitch McConnell famously stated that the confirmation of Merrick Garland was inappropriate during an election year, arguing that the next president should decide if that nomination was acceptable.[28] Yet, when the same set of circumstances presented themselves during the 2020 election, after the death of Justice Ruth Bader Ginsburg, McConnell and the Senate did the exact opposite, confirming Amy Coney Barrett in less than thirty days.[29]

Few on the CR had any objections to the "gaming" of the system or the process, largely because the outcome was in favor of their agenda, a clear contradiction of protocol and any degree of fairness. In fact, in a 2021 article, McConnell promised to block any Supreme Court nominees by President Biden if Republicans controlled the House and the Senate in 2024.[30]

Fortunately, this promise was not acted upon, as Biden nominated and the Senate confirmed Ketanji Brown Jackson to the Supreme Court in 2022.[31]

Religious Freedom

As was mentioned, many conservative Christians believe that their freedoms are being threatened by secularists and other groups who do not share their beliefs. This infringement was seen in a 2015 lawsuit in Colorado, where a Christian baker refused to bake a customized cake for a same-sex couple because of his religious beliefs.[32] Other examples of infringement on religious freedoms include the elimination of prayer in public schools or even the ability to worship during the COVID pandemic.[33]

In the larger sense, religious freedom is a bit of a paradox for many Christians and Christian religious groups. As Little (n.d.) points out, Christians have always struggled to reconcile individual religious freedom and religious uniformity. On the one hand, Christians generally believe that they are separate and different from others based on political, ethnic, or national lineage and instead are bound together by God and His rules. And because they make this decision to follow God's word freely and individually, they should be granted the ability to do so regardless of political affiliation or other forms of social control.[34]

At the same time, Christians believe that salvation and the common good can only be achieved through religious conformity and that may require an imposition of a single religious view rather than a plurality of beliefs. In November 2021, Michael Flynn, former national security advisor to President Trump, called for a single religion in a speech to a conservative Christian audience on the ReAwaken America tour. Flynn stated, "If we are going to have one nation under God, which we must, we have to have one religion. One nation under God and one religion under God, right? All of us, working together."[35]

Such a view was widely condemned by many Democrats, former colleagues, and others. However, it was a telling commentary about how some conservative Christians view the idea of religious freedom. What we do not know from these accounts is how the audience of the speech reacted to Flynn's statements. While Flynn is clearly advocating a version of the CR that is on the extreme end of the religious freedom debate, his comments raise a larger question that many Christians have grappled with: Christians are required to submit to worldly governments and leaders but how does this reconcile with obedience to God when the two forms of obedience conflict? How is the authority of worldly leaders to be employed in the service of God?[36]

There are, obviously, many different and conflicting answers to these basic questions and the rise of the CR calls attention to a narrow interpretation of scriptures and even a willingness to overlook some incongruities—is religious freedom only meant for some groups and not others? Should Christians overlook behavior and actions of leaders that run counter to scripture if they offer favor to them in ways other leaders have not? Can Christians really overlook what the Bible says about helping others if those others do not agree with Christian ideology?

For the CR, it appears that the answers to some of these deep and complicated questions suggest that their role as victims warrants special consideration when it comes to some forms of freedom of expression. One such example involves the CR's reaction to limits on social interaction and worship during a worldwide pandemic.

Religious Freedom and the COVID Pandemic

Despite Trump's dismissal of the seriousness of the pandemic, as the realities of COVID-19 became self-evident, including the lack of competence and leadership in addressing the problem, Trump pushed the responsibility for action to individual states. Some states shut down religious services completely; others allowed them to function as normal. Many members of the CR argued that such strategies, which were not unique to churches and religious groups (restaurants, schools, and businesses shut down as well), was another attack on religious freedom.

Many in the CR did not accept the medical reasons behind closing churches or limiting worship services and instead subscribed to conspiracy theories that secular groups were attempting to limit and ultimately eliminate the right of religious groups to gather and worship. In fact, some Christians even believed that COVID-19 was a "phantom plague" that was created and circulated by the government as a way to limit all manner of freedoms.[37]

As Stewart (2020) points out, within the CR is a group known as Christian nationalists. Christian nationalism is a powerful ideological component of the CR that first came to prominence during the Reagan presidency. Christian nationalists seek to acquire power so as to impose their religious vision on all of American society, and Trump was a means to trying to achieve this goal. Christian nationalists claim to be the public voice of theologically conservative Christian Americans. In fact, many have noted that some Christian nationalists are also white supremacists.[38]

According to Perry et al. (2020), Christian nationalists are more likely to believe in conspiracy theories, to distrust the media, and to distrust scientists. As it relates specifically to the pandemic and religious worship, Perry et al. (2020) argues that American Christian nationalists were likely to scorn social distancing recommendations and claim that coronavirus-related lockdown orders threatened both the economy and people's liberty.[39]

According to many experts, the issue of forced mask wearing and vaccination, which started as a public health issue, was transformed into one about religious and political freedom. As Kenneth Resnicow, professor of public health at the University of Michigan, argues, historically, mandatory vaccinations have long been accepted as standard practice for children who wish to attend public schools, while other vaccination mandates have been seen as an acceptable responsibility of all citizens for the common good. Examples such as polio, measles, and other vaccinations are routinely required as government mandates, yet during the COVID-19 pandemic, the topic became weaponized and transformed into one related to autonomy and fear.[40] For many members of the CR, public health demands have been transformed into matters of religious autonomy, with the CR using it as another illustration of an attack on their beliefs.

Abortion

Perhaps more than any other social issue, abortion is a centerpiece of the CR framework. Until 2022, when the *Roe* decision was overturned by the US Supreme Court, the *Roe v. Wade* case had been the law of the land since 1973. Even prior to overturning the *Roe* decision, states were beginning to pass laws banning all types of abortions. For example, in 2021, Texas passed a new abortion law, known as Senate Bill 8, that prohibits most abortions after about six weeks and makes no exceptions for pregnancies resulting from incest or rape.[41]

The law has been in place since September 2021 and allows ordinary citizens to sue those who violate the law, with awards of up to $10,000 per illegal abortion. Patients cannot be sued, but doctors, staff, and anyone who assists the patient in any way can become a defendant in the lawsuit. As a result of this new law, the number of abortions performed in Texas decreased by nearly half in the weeks after the law went into effect.[42]

In a 2021 ruling, the US Supreme Court allowed abortion providers in Texas to challenge a state law that bans most abortions after six weeks, allowing them to sue at least some state officials in federal court despite the procedural hurdles imposed by the law's unusual structure. But the Supreme Court refused to block the law in the meantime, saying that lower courts should consider the matter.[43]

This decision came on the heels of another ruling by the US Supreme Court, in which a case challenged Mississippi's abortion law that bans most abortions after fifteen weeks. While *Roe* prohibited states from banning abortion before fetal viability, which has been identified at about twenty-three to twenty-four weeks into a pregnancy (the point at which fetuses can sustain life outside the womb), the court's conservative majority seemed prepared to uphold the Mississippi law, and several justices indicated that they would vote to overrule *Roe* outright, a decision that ultimately occurred in 2022.[44]

The Mississippi law differed from Texas's law, sometimes referred to as the *Texas Heartbeat Act*, in that it eliminates the viability standard in the *Roe* case by barring abortions once fetal cardiac activity can be detected, which typically occurs at around six weeks of pregnancy. Such a timeline occurs often before the mother even knows she is pregnant.[45] The issue of abortion is far from resolved, and while the *Roe* standard is no longer applicable, President Biden has promised to sign any legislation by members of Congress that makes abortion legal in the near future.[46]

Parental Control of Public Schools

As was mentioned, part of the reason for the political activism of the CR stems from US Supreme Court decisions regarding prayer in public schools as well as the teaching of evolutionism as part of the curriculum. A 2021 gubernatorial election in Virginia highlighted another topic that has become a focus of the CR: the teaching of critical race theory and parental control over schools.[47]

While the debate over the teaching of critical race theory (CRT) has remained a focus of the Republican Party, with many candidates and elected officials, including President Trump, arguing against its use in schools, much of what is presented about the theory is inaccurately portrayed, and, perhaps more importantly, its connection to the CR forces a manufactured choice between believing biblical scripture or accepting the theory as a worldview. Politicians are quick to capitalize on this debate, when, in fact, the controversy focuses more on accepting the notion of white privilege than adopting a Christian worldview.[48]

Thus, like many issues discussed in this book, the issues are rather complex and yet many of the nuances stemming from their discussion get ignored, manipulated, or distorted into sound bites that require the public to choose one side or the other. In the process, we have allowed ourselves to be forced into a decision to pick a side without fully understanding or appreciating the actual issue at hand. CRT, particularly for the CR, is perhaps the best example.[49]

While a full discussion of CRT is beyond the scope of this book, it is important to understand how and in what ways Christians and other conservatives have understood the theory and its implications. CRT is an academic concept that has circulated for decades. At its core, the racism and discrimination that exists in the US, particularly against Black Americans, is not the result of individuals who discriminate on the basis of race, but is instead a structural product that is an integral part of the existing US legal system as well as many social policies—some of which were actually created to address the problems of racial discrimination.[50]

The basic tenets of CRT emerged out of a framework for legal analysis in the late 1970s and early 1980s created by legal scholars Derrick Bell, Kimberlé Crenshaw, and Richard Delgado, among others, and focused on how the legal system has systematically discriminated against Blacks and Latinxs. Individual explanations of racism and discrimination cannot account for the widespread use of laws and policies, some of which are championed as "color blind" in their scope.

An example of such discrimination was the redlining policies of the 1960s and 1970s related to housing for Blacks in certain neighborhoods, which resulted in fewer families of color being eligible for mortgages. Today those same patterns are seen in policies that limit the construction of affordable housing in White neighborhoods. It is critically important to note that CRT is normally reserved for graduate students and is typically seen as an academic explanation for the persistent discrimination that exists in US society, not something offered to elementary, middle, or high school students.[51]

The problem is that the academic and accurate understanding of CRT differs from its presentation in the popular media and how it is portrayed by politicians and policymakers, particularly conservative Republicans. Thus, there is a good deal of confusion over what CRT means, as well as its relationship to other terms, like "anti-racism" and "social justice." This misunderstanding lumps all manner of diversity programs into a category labeled as CRT, regardless of whether any information about the theory is included in those training seminars.

For example, as Sawchuck (2021) points out, the Heritage Foundation, a noted conservative organization, attributed a host of social issues to CRT including the 2020 Black Lives Matter protests, LGBTQIA clubs in schools, diversity training in federal agencies and organizations, California's recent ethnic studies model curriculum, and the free-speech debate on college campuses.[52]

In reality, CRT asserts that racism is part of everyday life, largely because of the way race and racism has influenced the operation of society for so long. The implication, of course, is that anyone, even those who do not intend to be racist or even those who believe they are treating others equally, may be inadvertently fueling racism and discriminatory practices. Other critics contend that CRT discriminates against Whites in order to achieve equality. This is readily evident by those who advocate for policies that explicitly take race into account. However, CRT puts an emphasis on outcomes, not on individuals' beliefs, and it calls on these outcomes to be examined and rectified. Of course, there are many disagreements about the extent to which race should play a role in policy decisions, but ignoring its presence is not the solution either.[53]

Scholars who study CRT in education look at how policies and practices in K–12 education contribute to persistent racial inequalities in education, and advocate for ways to change them. This includes topics such as the racial segregation that continues to exist in many schools across the country; how some schools, particularly those with large Black and Latinx student populations, are underfunded compared to White schools; and that the disproportionality of academic failure among minority students along with the lack of admission, persistence, and graduation among Black and Latinx students is seen at all levels of education.[54]

CRT is also not a synonym for culturally relevant teaching, which emerged in the 1990s. This teaching approach seeks to affirm students' ethnic and racial backgrounds and is intellectually rigorous. But it is related in that one of its aims is to help students identify and critique the causes of social inequality in their own lives. Many educators support, to one degree or another, culturally relevant teaching and other strategies to make schools feel safe and supportive for Black students and other underserved populations. But they don't necessarily identify these activities as CRT-related.[55]

Many of the popular depictions of CRT suggest that schools are teaching that Whites are inherently privileged and that Blacks and people of color are oppressed and victimized. Additionally, popular notions of CRT suggest that the only way to achieve racial injustice involves discriminating against Whites in part because the US was founded upon racism and racist ideas. In short, the rejection of CRT is based on misguided notions of what the theory actually is and the extent to which it is actually being taught in public schools.[56]

Despite this confusion about both the substance and extent of CRT in schools, many states are passing laws banning it in public schools. The problem extends beyond CRT, however. Putting aside for the moment that many policymakers cannot articulate an accurate description of CRT or the extent to which it is being taught in public schools, many of the bills introduced to prohibit it have been so vaguely written and raise so many questions that teachers and administrators are confused about what they can actually address in the classroom.[57]

The rationale behind the laws and of teaching CRT in general is that the subject is harmful to or manipulative of students and what they learn in the classroom. Such a position is not new in education. Whether it was the threat of socialism or Marxism in the early twentieth century; the suggestion by the John Birch Society to ban books that encouraged students to consider the economic inequality that existed in the 1950s; disagreements about multiculturalism or teaching students about American history, including what actually occurred during the enslavement of African Americans; or the exclusion and violence toward Native Americans, the idea of limiting student exposure to ideas and banning books in schools to prevent students from being poisoned with alternative explanations of events is not an innovative approach to education. The most recent example that has exacerbated the debate about the importance of CRT is found in the 1619 Project by *The New York Times*, which attempts to accurately document the history and impact of slavery for Blacks, along with their contributions to reforming and reshaping democracy.[58]

Critics argue that the anti-CRT rhetoric, including strategies such as book banning, are consistent with the CR worldview that suggests either a separatist approach, which is illustrated in the popularity of homeschooling around the country (where many of the curricula have a strong religious influence) or the restriction of topics that threaten the existing narrative presented by the CR that focuses on the control and obedience of children.[59]

Political Voice for Christian Organizations

One of the things that the CR has endeavored to achieve is having a significant voice in the political process. However, a federal law places limits on how much nonprofit organizations who wish to be exempt from paying taxes can contribute to political campaigns. Known as the "Johnson Amendment," the law came from President Lyndon B. Johnson, who, when he was the Senate minority leader, introduced an amendment to section 501(c)(3) of the federal tax code dealing with tax-exempt charitable organizations. The goal was to restrict the involvement in partisan politics of organizations that wanted to be exempt from paying taxes. The rule states:

> Under the Internal Revenue Code, all section 501(c)(3) organizations are absolutely prohibited from directly or indirectly participating in, or intervening in, any political campaign on behalf of (or in opposition to) any candidate for elective public office. Contributions to political campaign funds or public statements of position (verbal or written) made on behalf of the organization in favor of or in opposition to any candidate for public office clearly violate the prohibition against political campaign activity. Violating this prohibition may result in denial or revocation of tax-exempt status and the imposition of certain excise taxes.[60]

Many on the religious right see this as a roadblock to free speech. In 2017, as president, Trump said, "I've gotten rid of the Johnson Amendment . . . I signed an executive order so that now . . . ministers and preachers and rabbis and whoever it may be, they can speak. You know, you couldn't speak politically before, now you can."[61]

The concern, of course, is that if religious organizations were allowed to make political contributions, they could become little more than lobby groups. While Trump signed the executive order, such a move did not eliminate the amendment. Only Congress can change a law. What most experts note is that Trump instructed the IRS to be lenient in enforcing the law, which was rarely done in the past. Additionally, most pastors have been vocal in their political views anyway so Trump's order accomplished little, other than as a symbolic act to show support for the CR.[62]

Immigration

Consistent with the efforts to have a single framework of understanding, coupled with an unwillingness to embrace diversity and pluralism, immigration is squarely in the crosshairs of CR advocates. Trump's efforts to limit immigration during his administration, similar to conservative presidents before him, such as Nixon, Reagan, and Bush, are in alignment with CR ideology. This is true despite many members of the Christian community, sometimes referred to as the Christian Left (see below), who argue that there are several passages in the Bible that call believers to welcome strangers, to help those in need, and to embrace Christ's message about those without a home.[63]

Voter Suppression

As the results of the 2020 election became a reality for conservatives and Christians, many continued to buy into the lie presented by Trump that the election was stolen from him. This is true despite any evidence of widespread voter fraud or misrepresentation. It is also true that many Christians continue to believe that the resulting efforts by many Republicans at the state level to change the voting laws, which primarily make it more difficult for the poor and people of color, most of whom historically vote Democratic, to cast their ballots, is actually an attempt to preserve election integrity.

One has to wonder why so much energy and effort is being spent dedicated to a problem that has not proven to be an issue other than the fact that Republicans and Trump claim it is so. It is also curious that the same people who want to pass laws to preserve the integrity of the electoral process use the fact of their party's loss as evidence that fraud exists. The flawed conclusion, of course, is that as long as the preferred candidate wins, the integrity of the election is secured. What is unclear is how the outcome in one's favor demonstrates a fair and impartial election occurred.[64]

In Texas, a new law, the Election Integrity Protection Act of 2021, severely restricts voting access in Texas, with the biggest impact on voters of color. Critics argue that this is the most obvious attempt to suppress votes since the Jim Crow era. A January 2021 survey by the American Enterprise Institute found that evangelical conservatives were far more inclined than other Republicans to believe Trump's lies about widespread election fraud, as well as conspiracy theories about QAnon, Antifa, and the "deep state." Belief in Trump's "big lie" is now being seen in the mobilization of Christian support for a wave of voter suppression efforts.[65]

The justification for these efforts is not necessarily that Christians have lost confidence in the election system, although that is undoubtedly what Trump is attempting to promote. If the concern was that efforts needed to be undertaken to ensure the election process is fair, one would think there would be greater support for federal legislation on how elections are managed and supervised. Critics argue that what is happening instead is that laws are being passed to limit voters who would likely vote for someone other than Trump, thereby giving Christians the assurance that he and other Republicans would be more likely to win in the future.[66]

According to the Public Religion Research Institute (2020), White evangelical Protestants now make up 14 percent of Americans, down from 23 percent in 2006, which is the largest decrease in affiliation for any group.[67] Even though White evangelicals made up 34 percent of Trump's voters, giving him 84 percent of their votes, it did not win him reelection. In fact, so dependent has Trump become on this group that had he not gotten such strong support, estimates show that President Biden would have won by an even greater margin.[68]

At the same time, Trump and the Republican Party do not seem sufficiently interested in cultivating other minority groups who will make up a larger portion of the voter population. While there may be some incremental changes, such as what we saw with the Latinx population who voted for Trump in 2020, Republicans, Christians, and Trump seem to be banking on stoking fears among White voters as well as limiting the ability of non-Whites to participate in the democratic process. One might wonder about the inconsistency of such a practice, particularly among Christians. After all, fairness and kindness should be the hallmarks of the Christian model and fair play is antithetical to things like voter suppression. However, as some experts have noted, one must also consider that, for many Evangelical Christians, fairness in democracy may not be the goal.[69]

The loss of Republican Senate seats in Georgia resulted in a number of new laws passed that restricted voters' ability to get to the ballot box. Examples included eliminating drop-box sites, imposing more restrictive rules for absentee ballots, and prohibiting judges from extending voting hours at precincts experiencing long waits, all under the guise of stopping fraud. There was also a racial undertone to this legislation, where one provision, which received a strong and negative backlash from the public, included eliminating Sunday voting, which has long been a strategy by Black churches to encourage members to vote. Given that most people of color tend to vote for the Democratic candidate, one can easily see the rationale behind this and other provisions in the legislation. Also of note is the law that criminalizes providing water or food to voters standing in line and empowers state officials to replace local election officials with appointees from their own party.[70]

Congress has the power to protect American voters from these kinds of restrictions. The Freedom to Vote Act would create nationwide automatic voter registration, restore voting rights of the formerly incarcerated, and expand voting by mail and early voting, while shoring up the security of election infrastructure. This bill, which remains stalled in the Senate, is a comprehensive package of voting, redistricting, and campaign finance reforms. It includes national standards for voting that would ensure access to the ballot across state lines. The John Lewis Voting Rights Advancement Act, which passed in the House, complements the Freedom to Vote Act. It prevents changes to voting rules that discriminate on the basis of race or membership in language minority groups from being implemented, and it restores voters' ability to challenge discriminatory laws.[71]

The delays in passing this legislation, along with the number of new laws passed by Republican-controlled legislatures in many states, including the ability of states to insert party loyalists into the state election oversight process, suggest that there are questions about whether ensuring a fair election or ensuring people's right to vote are actually the goals. However, by any account, most experts argue that this process, particularly voter access, is critical to a functioning democracy. As we have seen in other countries, sham elections and the illusion of an operating democracy is no democracy at all, particularly if there is no meaningful level of accountability of leaders who attempt to manipulate elections to act in their own self-interest rather than what its citizens want or what is best for the country.

THE CHRISTIAN LEFT

Not all Christians accept the CR's portrayal of a Christian worldview. In fact, there is another version, sometimes referred to as the Christian Left, that takes a different approach to the politics of the CR. A discussion of the Christian Left suggests a contextual reading of the Bible and its teachings. This perspective, popularized in the 1960s and continuing today, focuses on new ways of understanding Christ's life and work. It also promotes a more active participation in the work surrounding social justice. Black theology, for example, argues that the legacy of slavery provides Black Americans a unique insight into the story of Christ and His suffering. Similarly, queer theologians offer context of understanding of marginalized groups and the mistreatment of those who are seen as different by others.[72]

This liberal approach to Christianity in general, with its focus on social justice, has resulted in greater understanding, awareness, and activism on a variety of issues such as immigration, racial equity, climate change, women's reproductive rights, and access to housing and health care as fundamental rights. While not a homogeneous group, the Christian Left has not gotten the same level of notoriety or political support as the CR, in part because of its lack of intentionality to develop a political and media platform. The diversity of beliefs surrounding the Christian Left also means that there is far less agreement on the boundaries or parameters of the movement than is seen with the CR.[73]

According to some reports, most progressive Christians identify as Democrats, but about one-third report being Republican or centrist in their views. Interestingly, many liberal Christian churches struggle with meaningful LGBTQIA issues, where some churches welcome members of the LGBTQIA community, but do not perform same-sex weddings or ordain LGBTQIA members into the ministry. Despite these shortcomings, the Christian Left's focus on civic engagement, community organizing, and social justice requires empathy for the challenges faced by traditionally marginalized groups, along with the need for intentional and meaningful interaction with people who are different from them.[74]

THE CHRISTIAN RIGHT AS TRUMPSTERS

How does the history of the CR movement along with its current structure help in understanding Trump followers? As was mentioned, the CR has taken rather extreme positions on a number of controversial and complex issues. As a starting point, most Christians who support Trump believe he has been divinely chosen by God to be their protector. They also overlook many of Trump's transgressions by claiming that God often selects flawed people to become leaders, such as King David in the Bible. While many CR supporters acknowledge Trump's failures as a Christian, as an ethical or moral leader, or even accept him as someone who is narcissistic and a pathological liar, they do believe he has a God-centered agenda. This was reflected in the selection of his cabinet, which contained a host of devout Christians, including Vice President Mike Pence, Attorney General William Barr, Secretary of

State Mike Pompeo, Secretary of Education Betsy DeVos, and Secretary of Housing and Urban Development Ben Carson.[75]

Other Christians claim they support Trump because he has delivered on his promises to the things that matter to them. Specifically, he has fulfilled his promise to nominate many conservative federal judges, including three appointees to the US Supreme Court with the goal of overturning the *Roe v. Wade* decision on abortion, something that was ultimately achieved in 2022. Christians also point to Trump's promise to protect religious freedoms of Christians from those who want to prohibit forms of religious activities, worship, and prayer in public schools.

Both Trump and his Christian supporters have wrapped their agendas into a mainstream and acceptable package—victimhood. For the CR and Christian Trump supporters, the public message is the promotion of religious freedom, which is being denied through attacks by the secular left wing, even though the CR agenda does not include the freedom for everyone to practice whatever they believe. Instead, religious freedom consists of a controlled and narrow view of Christianity that requires loyalty, obedience, and a strict form of submission to religious leaders. For Trump, the public message was to protect society and "Make America Great Again," a task that only he could accomplish. Such noble intentions were hampered by attacks from the left and Trump's consistent claims of victimhood were seen in the various "hoaxes," "witch hunts," and "fake news" designed to keep him from improving life in America.

Trump's critics point out that this was delusional—in reality, what we saw was a pattern of behavior that ignored the rule of law and democratic principles, and justified questionable actions that bordered on criminal behavior, none of which would have been tolerated if they had been committed by a member of a rival political party. Critics also point out that many members of the CR are not very different from other extremists outlined in this book, such as white supremacists or cult members. While they may adopt a Christian framework, which should generally suggest a moral and ethical way of life, a more humanistic approach to helping the less fortunate, the CR tends to reflect many of the same characteristics that most interest groups adopt. In other words, the CR has an agenda and they are not above playing fast and loose with the rules of society in furthering their cause. Similar to other groups, the CR also tends to embrace a persona that they are somehow being mistreated, oppressed, and exploited, or are missing out on the things to which they are entitled.

For the CR, what likely drove and continues to drive much of the loyalty to Trump is not Trump himself but, rather, fear—that they will be marginalized and their agenda overlooked; that their beliefs will not be part of public policy, particularly as it relates to abortion, religious freedom, and parental control. This fear also pushes supporters to engage in cognitive dissonance when it comes to Trump's actions—this is what drives supporters to the conclusion that Trump is a divinely inspired leader or has similarities to flawed biblical leaders. Yet because he is seen as supportive of the CR agenda, and because he portrays himself as a strong and forceful leader, much of what Trump represents can be overlooked, minimized, or ignored. This occurs despite the fact that many CR members are highly educated and otherwise thoughtful Christians, who follow a noble and moral framework as a way of life. Yet, when it comes to Trump, they act, think, and speak in ways that are remarkably similar to their extremist counterparts.

In the next chapter, we explore perhaps the most alarming criticism of Trump: where observers have noted the similarities between Trump and the rise of Adolf Hitler and Nazism in Germany during World War II. Such comparisons are extraordinary and disturbing at many levels and warrant some type of commentary and examination.

Chapter 6

Trumpsters as Nazis

In the preceding chapters, we examined Trumpism as well as whether Trumpsters are a cult, are white supremacists, and why members of the Christian Right endorse Trump. In this chapter, we begin to frame the reasons why people support Trump, which is due in part to people's need to align themselves in groups. An added feature of this tendency toward others is that there is an embedded sense of cultural elitism, which makes people feel better about themselves and the groups to which they belong. At an extreme, however, group identification and loyalty result in the narrowing of perspective, the inability to respect different points of view, and the mistreatment of others. Such intensity also likely results in conflict and tension between groups and a limiting of contact and interaction.

As it relates to Trumpsters, this tendency is highlighted in the controversial discussion of whether Trump and Trumpsters are similar to members of the Nazi Party under Adolf Hitler in Germany in the 1930s. This discussion was quite popular during Trump's presidency, and as such, it is worthy of some type of analysis and commentary.

HOW TRIBES FORM: TRUST AND LOYALTY IN RELATIONSHIPS

We begin this discussion with an overview of *ethnocentrism*, a concept that is pivotal to understanding what happens in groups as well as how loyalty and trust develop within them. It is within this larger discussion that we can glean a better understanding of comparisons of Trump and Trumpsters to the extremism seen in the rise of Nazism in Germany prior to and during World War II. As we will see, given people's inclinations toward elitism and exclusivity, the type of extremism seen either in Germany in the 1930s or in Trump supporters today is not surprising.

Why Groups?

To begin, the notion of grouping is understood by many experts in the social sciences as a necessary element of survival. That is, we are wired to be a part of a group and our physical abilities essentially require it. Generally speaking, we are weaker than other species, humans have a long period of physical and emotional development compared to other animals, and our ability to survive independently as lone individuals significantly limits our survivability. In other words, we need groups to survive and our ability to identify, accommodate, and cooperate with others, as in groups, is critically important. We need connection to others beyond physical survival, and these connections are at the heart of how relationships are formed. This is significant because being a part of a group creates and sustains what many psychologists define as our *social identity*, or who we think we are as individuals.

At its core, sociology contends that much of how we act, who we perceive ourselves to be, and how we see and understand the world is based on the groups to which we belong. While there is an individual component to a person's social identity, sociologists argue this is less significant and that a person's identity is heavily tied to an affiliation with a group. This puts great emphasis on the group to deliver an individual's value; in other words, the success or failure of that group triggers a positive or negative response at the individual level. Identification with a group can be so strong that it can easily result in misguided loyalties (doing, saying, and feeling things that would not be the case under other circumstances as an individual) as well as often changing one's worldview to better align with the group's perspective.

A critical part of group belonging are the boundaries that distinguish members from nonmembers. Sociologist William Graham Sumner coined the terms *ingroup* and *outgroup* to describe people's feelings toward members of their own and other groups. Being a part of an ingroup generates feelings of belongingness and a sense of identity and exclusivity. In contrast, outgroups serve as sources of competitiveness or even hostility and disdain, even if there is no inherent conflict between groups. In other words, at the collective level, this ingroup/outgroup distinction brings group members closer together in solidarity and, at some level, all outgroups are seen as potential threats or possible enemies. Ingroup members typically view themselves positively (and often as superior) and they also tend to view members of outgroups negatively.[1]

One consequence of our strong need to belong and our social identification with groups is *ethnocentrism*. The term "ethnocentrism" was coined in 1906 by William Graham Sumner in his book *Folkways: A Study of the Sociological Importance of Usages, Manners, Customs, Mores and Morals*.[2] Ethnocentrism is the tendency to judge other groups by the standards of one's own, thinking the latter is superior. That is, ethnocentrism is a form of cultural arrogance or elitism, that can easily lead to prejudice, discrimination, racism, and a host of negative behaviors toward others. This tendency can be overt, such as a self-proclamation of superiority over all others, or it can be at an unconscious level, where a person or group simply treats others as less significant or entitled to access to economic, social, and political resources. In either case, ethnocentrism offers a rather narrow view of the world. There are two key points relating to ethnocentrism. First, all human societies tend to divide the world into "us" and "them" groups; and second, people tend to trust and remain loyal to fellow ingroup members.[3]

At times, ethnocentrism is confused with things like patriotism or feeling a strong sense of loyalty and affiliation to a group. While being proud of an affiliation or attraction to a given group can be healthy, ethnocentrism is an extreme and learned behavior that demonstrates a level of insecurity and can easily lead to oppression, racism, discrimination, dishonesty, war, and all manner of negative behaviors. It can also result in the justification of almost any action, since the air of superiority that comes from ethnocentrism often results in people and groups feeling that they are above societal rules/laws that govern society.[4]

Is it reasonable to think that all groups believe they are superior to others? This is a difficult question to answer, but it seems fair to state that some cultures and groups are more progressive and diverse than others. This suggests that some individuals may feel a sense of loyalty and pride towards their group, but such bonding does not manifest itself in the mistreatment of others. People also tend to fear things that are different or difficult to understand and, in extreme cases, will go to considerable lengths to avoid or negate that fear. As was mentioned, while groups were historically used as a form of protection from the natural elements and predators, there is also a natural tendency for people to want to join groups whose members see and understand the world the same way.

It is with all this in mind that we turn our attention to the factors that led to the rise of Nazism and Adolf Hitler's prominence in 1930s Germany. This sets the stage for understanding how many observers note that President Trump and his followers are dangerously close in word and deed to this historically maligned group.

WORLD WAR I: MILITARISM, ALLIANCES, IMPERIALISM, AND NATIONALISM

The issues and problems associated with Nazism in Germany during World War II were really a product of what transpired before, during, and after World

War I. In fact, one could argue that the circumstances in Europe prior to the start of World War I are directly related to the concepts of ethnocentrism and ingroup/outgroup dynamics mentioned earlier. In order to really understand what happened in Germany during World War II, it is important to offer a somewhat brief explanation of what occurred prior to that infamous period.[5]

Prior to World War I, many countries in Europe benefitted from an improved economy, a stable social and political landscape in their respective countries, leading to a type of prosperity and entitlement that is reflective of an ethnocentric bias. As these countries began to enjoy success, the people inevitably began to see their way of life as the most successful, the most efficient, and the most appropriate for all other countries to emulate. The problem, of course, was that people in these different countries all felt that way, leading to a rise in nationalism. It also led to a substantial level of concern about rival countries and the possibilities of war.[6]

Many experts on World War I actually attribute the problems to four main factors—the rise of militarism, alliances, imperialism, and nationalism, sometimes referred to as M.A.I.N. These combined factors created and perpetuated tensions between nations that only required a catalyst to trigger a violent reaction.[7]

That event, by most accounts, was the assassination of Austro-Hungarian Archduke Franz Ferdinand in June 1914. As one country blamed another for the events, existing treaties and agreements required various countries to show their allegiance to each other, all of which escalated many long-standing conflicts and gave Germany an opportunity to demonstrate its superiority.[8]

Nationalism

In general, nationalism is the idea that people identify with one another in a given country based on attitudes, values, beliefs, and cultural traditions. Nationalism becomes more common in those places where groups come together based on a common purpose and, in some cases, to declare unity against a common threat. In Europe in the nineteenth century, this need for an identity anchor among people resulted in certain nations viewing other countries with great suspicion—many countries did not trust one another and saw each other as potential rivals. Nationalism also explains the high degree of tension and unrest within many countries in Europe prior to World War I. Historians point out that virtually every European nation experienced a growth in nationalism in the years prior to World War I, and this fear and mistrust led to a buildup of each country's military capabilities. In other words, an increase in nationalism is often accompanied by an increase in militarism.[9]

Militarism

This idea can be defined as the growth or expansion of the ability of a country to engage in war. As was mentioned, militarism is often seen as a consequence of nationalism, as each country feels the need to protect themselves from other countries, particularly those that may feel entitled to encroach on or even take over another nation. Militarism is problematic because not only does it present a costly strategy to a given country, the inevitable arms races that occurred in Europe prior to 1914 made it far easier for nations to engage in military conflict as a demonstration of their superiority.[10]

Imperialism

Imperialism generally refers to a country's oversight and authority over another. This political, economic, and/or cultural dominance usually occurs as a result of an invasion or exerting its political or economic control of the other country. As it relates to World War I, imperialism can best be seen when European countries attempted to capture and control portions of Africa in the decades prior to World War I. Often referred to by historians as the "Scramble for Africa," European nations fought against each other for African territory and control over different regions on the continent.[11]

While Germany wanted to exert a greater level of imperialism and expand its presence in Africa, it lacked the colonies there as well as in Asia compared to other European countries, such as Great Britain and France. In fact, these two countries had dominated the colonization of other countries, something Germany resented. For example, in 1914, Great Britain had a total of fifty-six colonies around the world, France had twenty-nine, and Germany had just ten. Ultimately, this tension and mistrust between Germany and other countries set the stage for war in 1914.[12]

Alliances

Another important factor in understanding the onset of World War I was the alliances and treaties between countries in an effort to protect themselves from invasion. In Europe prior to World War I, there were essentially two main agreements: the Triple Alliance and the Triple Entente. The former was an agreement between Germany, Austria-Hungary, and Italy, which held that each member nation would come to the military aid and defense of the other member nations in the event that they were attacked.[13]

The Triple Alliance eventually led to a competing agreement, called the Triple Entente between Britain, France, and Russia. The Triple Entente was not a true military alliance like the Triple Alliance. Interestingly, the main terms of the Triple Entente agreement were kept secret, which prevented members from understanding how to respond to Germany as it escalated the war in Europe. Following the assassination of Austrian Archduke Franz Ferdinand, tensions among these nations were heightened as a result of this confusion.[14]

The member nations of the Triple Entente maintained their loyalty with one another, and when war broke out in 1914, the three nations entered World War I as the Allied Powers. The Allied Powers of World War I faced off against the Central Powers, which included Germany, Austria-Hungary, Bulgaria, and the Ottoman Empire. Italy, which had previously been a member of the Triple Alliance, actually flipped sides and instead joined the Allied Powers.[15]

The Events of World War I

Ethnocentrism was on full display during Germany's involvement in World War I. As Germany felt they were the superior race and took steps to expand their control of Europe and beyond, with a supreme confidence in their military capabilities, they actually thought their efforts would result in a quick and decisive victory in Europe. This was true despite the fact that Germany was actually fighting a war on two separate fronts: the Eastern front, which engaged Russia, and the Western front, where Germany and its allies engaged in a long and intense struggle with its enemies. A quick victory did not occur, and a long and brutal war ensued with an estimated nearly 9 million military personnel killed and more than 37 million wounded during the conflict.[16]

The US involvement in World War I did not occur until several instances of German submarines sinking passenger and commercial ships. It was after the sinking of the *Lusitania* cruise ship, which carried civilian passengers, that the United States aligned with other Allied countries to defeat Germany.[17] Germany and its allies ultimately surrendered on November 11, 1918.[18] In the end, in addition to the millions of deaths and injuries, there was an extraordinary amount of physical devastation in various countries in Europe, in part due to the brutal manner in which Germany waged war. By most historical accounts, the cumulative effect of Germany's efforts left most of Europe and the world badly damaged.[19]

The Aftermath of World War I: Setting the Stage for Hitler

With Germany's defeat in World War I, other European nations made demands on the country, including reparations for the costs of war. Germany also had to surrender much of its autonomy and identity, particularly after US President Woodrow Wilson wrote the Treaty of Versailles, a document that was an attempt to secure peace but also to hold Germany accountable for the war.[20]

In fact, the Treaty of Versailles outlined a series of requirements that Germany had to follow, including the loss of territories, which proved to have a devastating impact on the German economy. Additionally, Germany lost its colonies in Africa and was required to pay hundreds of millions of dollars to compensate other countries for the costs of the war.[21]

Finally, the treaty prohibited Germany from having a navy or air force, and allowed them only a small army of one hundred thousand soldiers. Perhaps more importantly, the treaty imposed a democratic form of government on the German people, something they were not familiar with. In essence, World War I was a humiliating defeat for Germany, particularly since it saw itself as superior to all others in the world. As such, the Treaty of Versailles was not well received by German leaders, who saw it as a bitter insult to the country and its people.[22]

Some observers at the time noted that while the Treaty of Versailles was a forced peace treaty, which made Germany accept responsibility for its actions, others saw it as vindictive and the source for retaliation in the future. In 1918, the newly created democratic government, called the *Weimar Republic*, was imposed on Germany. According to most historians, two very different moods characterized Weimar politics and society. On the one hand, some observers asserted there was a sense of excitement and creativity in German society. For instance, in the early 1920s, as a democracy, Germany had a new constitution that established separate branches of government, and many groups were eligible to nominate candidates for leadership roles through elections, which was unprecedented in Germany. Women, who constituted about a third of the German workforce after World War I, also took on new roles in Weimar society. Women were eligible to vote, hold political office, and had a voice in the development of social policy. Socially, German citizens enjoyed greater freedom of expression in art, music, and dance, and the overall development of the Weimar culture flourished. In this way, significant social changes were occurring in Germany and its people generally felt a renewed sense of optimism about social life and their future.[23]

At the same time, however, not all Germans were comfortable with the new form of government or the many changes taking place. In fact, historians note that many Germans felt anxious and fearful. The dramatic changes in their way of life, particularly the relaxation of political and social restrictions, a common feature of German rule for decades, was not only uncomfortable for many people but also, for some, worth rebelling against.[24]

Many also feared the changes to the economy throughout Europe, which appeared to them to be a form of communism, would spread to Germany. This fear was heightened by the hyperinflation that occurred in Germany after its surrender, which devalued the German currency. The economic problems in Germany were magnified by the Great Depression in the 1930s, which, as a worldwide economic crisis, significantly impacted the already-struggling German economy.[25]

In fact, as some historians note, this fear translated into violent clashes among differing groups throughout the Weimar government, ultimately leaving the public fearful of the effect these tensions would have on Germany in the future. Of particular concern was the development of and enthusiasm for far-right groups, including the growing influence of anti-democratic, anti-Marxist, and anti-Semitic groups. The latter, which was part of a larger anti-Semitic movement, actually blamed Jews for the German defeat in World War I. This makes sense, given the ethnocentric bias felt by many German people, who naturally thought they were superior to all other groups, but particularly Jews. Of particular note was the rise of the Nazi Party, with its extreme views on white superiority, the hatred of Jews, and its demand for a return to its previous non-democratic form of government.[26]

As was mentioned, Germany was forced to bear an enormous economic burden to make reparations for the costs of the war. When Germany could not meet its obligations for these payments, France and Belgium took control of Germany's Ruhr region, an important industrial area, which infuriated the German people, who already felt they were being slighted by the parameters of the Treaty of Versailles. This led workers all across Germany to strike, which resulted in the closing of many German industries. The predictable consequence of such actions was further increases in unemployment, already problematic due to the struggling economy, which presented additional challenges for the Weimar government. The severity of the crisis, exacerbated by the Great Depression, provided the impetus for the rise of the Nazi Party and its leader, Adolf Hitler.[27]

THE RISE OF NAZISM AND HITLER IN GERMANY

The story of the rise of the Nazi Party and its leader, Adolf Hitler, is a fascinating example of how easily the public can be manipulated, particularly in those instances where social, political, and economic life are wracked by fear and a sense of victimhood. While the reconstruction of Germany serves as an important backdrop to Hitler's rise to power, of greater importance was Hitler's message of superiority. That is, despite the fact that there were many gaps in Hitler's rhetoric, including a lack of substance to his solutions to the problems plaguing Germany (which largely consisted of disparaging commentary about Jews, communists, and others who did not believe in the natural superiority of the German people), Hitler capitalized on a set of circumstances and convinced the public that he alone could fix the problems in Germany.

In 1919, a German locksmith named Anton Drexler, along with two other friends, Gottfried Feder and Dietrich Eckart, formed the German Workers' Party (GWP), which was later renamed the National Socialist German Workers' Party (NSDAP), more commonly known as the Nazi Party. Drexler opposed the surrender of Germany in World War I, as well as the terms of the Treaty of Versailles. He believed that Germans were part of the Aryan master race and thought that capitalism was dominated by Jews who profited from World War I at Germany's expense.[28]

Additionally, Drexler believed that the violence and instability occurring in Germany was largely the result of the Weimar government being out of touch with what the German people needed and wanted from their leaders. As a result, he formed a far-right political party that emphasized nationalism combined with a form of economic socialism that would challenge the spread of communism in Germany.[29]

Ironically, the German army worried that the GWP was a left-wing revolutionary group and sent one of its education officers, Adolf Hitler, an Austrian-born corporal, who saw combat in World War I, to spy on the organization. Hitler found that the GWP's ideas were similar to his own views, particularly its focus on nationalism and anti-Semitic rhetoric, and became a member of the group in 1920. As a charismatic leader with a gift for public speaking, Hitler quickly became the party's leader, replacing Drexler, and saw the party as a revolutionary organization whose aim was the overthrow of the Weimar Republic. Hitler believed the Weimar government was controlled by the socialists, Jews, and the government officials who had betrayed the German soldiers in 1918 by signing the peace treaty.[30]

Hitler had always been hostile to socialist ideas, especially those that involved racial or sexual equality. However, socialism was a popular political philosophy in Germany after World War I. This was reflected in the growth of the German Social Democrat Party (SDP), the largest political party in Germany. Hitler redefined socialism by placing the word "National" before it, renaming the group the National Socialist German Worker's Party. Members of the party referred to themselves as Nationalsozialisten (National Socialists), but rarely called themselves Nazis. The reason for this was that the popular use of the word "Nazi" was seen as a derogatory phrase for a backward peasant, an awkward and clumsy person.[31]

The Nazi Party ideology is centered on the belief in the superiority of the so-called Aryan race (or "German blood"). For the Nazis, German blood determined whether one was considered a citizen. Those without German blood were not citizens and therefore should be deprived of the rights and benefits of citizenship. For instance, in an effort to appeal to the working class and socialists, the Nazi program included several measures that would redistribute income and profit-sharing in large industries, nationalize trusts, and increase old-age pensions and free education to German citizens.[32]

Additionally, equal rights were to only be given to German citizens. Jews and other "aliens" who were German citizens would lose their rights of citizenship, and the country would not permit the immigration of non-Germans. That year, the party announced that only persons of "pure Aryan descent" could become party members. If the person had a spouse, the spouse also had to be a racially pure Aryan. Party members could not be related either directly or indirectly to a "non-Aryan." Even before it had become legally forbidden by the Nuremberg Laws in 1935, the Nazis banned sexual relations and marriages between party members and Jews.[33]

The precarious status of Germany, including the political and social unrest, coupled with economic challenges caused by hyperinflation, served as an important opportunity for Hitler and the party to take control. The party grew quickly, largely due to Hitler's appeal to a loyal base of unemployed young men, small business owners, former soldiers who fought in World War I, and others who were members of rival parties to the Weimar government. As the country's economic problems intensified, and the limits of the Weimar government to remedy these challenges became apparent, more people showed their support for Hitler and his party.[34]

With a growing base of support, in the early 1920s, Hitler attempted a coup to overthrow the government in the state of Bavaria on November 23, 1923. Known as *the Beer Hall Putsch*, the attempt failed, and Hitler and several colleagues were arrested and tried for treason. Rather than being seen as a criminal, the public had a high regard for Hitler—where he was seen as the people's hero. While Hitler was ultimately convicted, instead of being deported (he and his colleagues on trial were not German citizens), a judge sympathetic to the Nazi cause gave Hitler and his codefendants the minimum sentence of five years in prison. Hitler only served nine months of his term before the remainder of his term was suspended and he was released.[35]

It was during these months in prison that Hitler wrote *Mein Kampf* (My Struggle). According to many historians, the book is a mixture of autobiography, political ideas, and an explanation of propaganda techniques. A substantial theme of *Mein Kampf* was Hitler's belief in Aryan superiority, which was being threatened by the Jewish race. Jews, he argued, were lazy and had not made any meaningful contributions to the world. However, Hitler contended, Jews controlled the largest political party in Germany, the German Social Democrat Party, along with many leading businesses and newspapers that spread a distorted message to German citizens.[36] A conspiracy theorist, Hitler also believed that the Jews were collaborating with communists to take over the world. He pointed to the example of such a partnership in Russia, which now threatened all of Europe.[37]

As Hitler was released from prison, he discovered Germany had changed. In 1924, the German economy had begun to improve. By 1928, the country had recovered from the war and business was booming. As a result, fewer Germans seemed interested in the hatred that Hitler and his Nazi Party promoted. However, the stock market crash and Great Depression that began in 1929 presented Hitler with his greatest opportunity to seize control of Germany and to create a narrative appealing to the German people.[38]

On one hand, the circumstances of the Depression prompted many members of the Communist Party in Germany to contend that the government should take over all German land and industry from capitalists, who were only interested in profits for themselves. Communists promised to distribute German wealth according to the common good. In contrast, the Nazis blamed the Jews, communists, liberals, and pacifists for the German economic crisis in the first place and promised to restore Germany's pride in their nation as well as end the Depression, campaigning with slogans such as "Work, Freedom, and Bread!"[39]

Many German citizens saw what the Nazi rhetoric presented as an attractive alternative to democracy and communism. Among them were wealthy industrialists who were alarmed by the growth of the Communist Party and did not want to be forced to give up what they owned. While Hitler wanted to "Make Germany Great Again," what he offered as a solution depended very much on the audience. In rural areas, he promised tax cuts for farmers and government action to protect food prices. In working-class areas, he spoke of the redistribution of wealth and attacked the high profits of capitalists, particularly those made by the large chain stores.[40]

When he spoke to industrialists, however, Hitler focused his comments on plans to destroy communism, to reduce the power of the trade union movement (a communist idea), and to enhance profits through embracing capitalism. Regardless of these solutions proposed to various audiences, Hitler's main idea was to blame Germany's problems on the Treaty of Versailles and the reparations it enforced. Instead of concrete solutions, Hitler centered his messages on the hatred of Jews, the persecution and victimization of Germans by other countries, and the belief that Germans were the superior race.[41]

This narrative worked, and Hitler and the Nazi Party grew in size and popularity. In 1932, Hitler became a German citizen so that he could run for president in that year's spring election. Hitler finished second, but the popularity of the Nazi message was seen in an increased number of elected officials in the legislature. Hitler had also amassed a large quasi-army of stormtroopers, who outnumbered the German army by a 4 to 1 margin (recall that the Treaty of Versailles only allowed a German army of one hundred thousand troops).

This group routinely engaged in street-level violence against those who did not support Hitler and the Nazi Party, particularly the communists. German officials began to fear that Hitler would take over power by staging a coup.[42]

As the communists began gaining some support among the voters, Hitler escalated the urgency of his rhetoric to proclaim communists were taking over the country and the only way to preserve the German way of life was to support him and the Nazi Party. The Nazi Party's stormtroopers also escalated the level of violence, particularly against the communists. Both of these tactics left the German middle class and wealthy industrialists worried about a communist takeover. This was particularly true as the Great Depression began to impact German society.[43]

A group of prominent industrialists, who feared a revolution was about to occur, sent a petition to the German president, Paul von Hindenburg, asking for Hitler to become chancellor. Hindenburg reluctantly agreed to their request and at the age of forty-three, Hitler became the new chancellor of Germany on January 30, 1933. It is worth noting that Hitler was neither elected as chancellor nor necessarily even endorsed by the German president for that position. Instead, he was named to that position as a way to capitalize on Hitler's popularity (as the Weimar government was declining in popularity) while allowing time for a solution to emerge for the economy and the country.[44]

Historians note that Hindenburg and his allies believed they could contain Hitler's radical ideas, coupled with the belief that Hitler would eventually see the value in a more moderate approach to the problems facing the German people. In fact, President Hindenburg did not believe that Hitler would be successful in his efforts and concluded that when Hitler ultimately failed, they could step in and take credit for rescuing the country. What they did not anticipate was the manner in which Hitler and the Nazis transformed German democratic rule into a dictatorship and changed the country's future forever.[45]

For instance, Hitler assumed total control of the government and the Nazi Party, taking the title of *Führer*. Building upon his popularity with the people and his promise to "make Germany great again," Hitler wasted no time in implementing his plans to take over Europe and elevate the German people to their superior status by abolishing labor unions and other political parties and imprisoning his political opponents. In 1933, Hitler withdrew Germany from the League of Nations and began to rebuild the German armed forces beyond what was permitted by the Treaty of Versailles. Ultimately, Hitler took over neighboring territories, which culminated in the invasion of Poland and the start of World War II on September 1, 1939.[46]

By the time the conflict ended, there were an estimated 15 million military deaths and more than 25 million injured in World War II. As with all numbers relating to wartime deaths and injuries, this number is an approximation and does not include the estimated 45 million civilian deaths that occurred during the war.[47]

Adding to the carnage was Germany's attempt to engage in genocide, where more than 6 million Jews were murdered in concentration camps—Germany's answer to the "Jewish problem." In fact, one could easily argue that the Holocaust was the defining feature of Germany's attempt to take over Europe and impose its form of racial superiority on the world. The images of the brutality committed by Germany and its military, coupled with the support of the Nazi Party–political machine, remain vivid reminders of the impact of ethnocentrism and its effect on society.[48]

THE DEBATE ABOUT TRUMP, HITLER, AND THE NAZI PARTY

From the outset of his candidacy, many of Trump's critics have offered comparisons between his actions as a candidate and as president, as well as the behavior of many of his followers, to the events that led up to both world wars; with some observers identifying many similarities between Trump and Hitler. While some of these debates intensified during Trump's presidency, experts have noted that the debate died down a bit near the end of Trump's time in the White House, largely due to the congressional midterm elections that saw Democrats maintain their majority rule in the House of Representatives and a slim majority in the Senate.

However, the events following Biden's election as president in 2020, along with the violence that occurred in January at the US Capitol, re-energized the discussion, particularly in 2022, as the evidence from the congressional committee on the January 6 violence continues to mount that Trump may have attempted to interfere with the 2020 election and perhaps committed criminal acts in his efforts to overturn the results.

More importantly, the response by so many Republicans, who continue to claim that the election was "stolen" from Trump, along with public opinion polls that show a large portion of the general public continues to accept the narrative that Trump actually won the election, raises many questions about the common threads between the German people's allegiance to Hitler prior to World War II and the unfailing support many Americans show toward Trump.

It is worth noting, then, that this debate about comparing Trump and Trumpsters to Hitler and Nazis in Germany continues to spark controversy. As Rosenfeld (2019) notes, there are many levels to this debate and scholars and experts sharply disagree on the extent to which such a comparison of Trump to one of the most ruthless and notorious figures of the twentieth century has any relevance or credibility.[49]

Rosenfeld (2019) contends there are essentially two periods in the comparisons of Trump to Hitler. The first phase began when Trump announced his candidacy for president in 2015 and ended with his election in 2016, while the second essentially focused on the period from his election through 2018. Some of these comparisons were made as a criticism of Trump while others were more thoughtful commentaries regarding how leaders in general and Republicans in particular were able to square their support for Trump with the ideology of the Republican Party and conservatism. In the end, critics take what Rosenfeld (2019) calls an alarmist view while the latter assessment offers a more nuanced approach to the comparisons, instead arguing that Trump's behavior reflects a great deal of similarity to other historical figures.[50]

Alarmist Views of Trump and Hitler

Within the alarmist view, there are four related arguments: The first points out that Trump was literally like Hitler as a leader, while the second view essentially argues that Trump as president differed from Hitler, but his actions paralleled the German leader. A third and related view argues that while the two men may be different leaders, with some debate about whether or not Trump acted as Hitler did, the real danger lies in the fact that, if unchecked, Trump could have (and still might), indeed, become a version of Hitler. Finally, the fourth view contends that while Trump, as president, was not like Hitler nor was he a Nazi, he was and is, in fact, a fascist. Alternatively, some contend that while Trump isn't a conventional fascist, perhaps he is an American version of it. Finally, still another variation on this theme contends that Trump is arguably a fascist, but the real threat comes from many of his supporters who embrace fascist ideas.

Rosenfeld (2019) observes that the most vocal critics of Trump compare him directly to Hitler. The basis for this position, which began in 2015 and continues to the present, is derived from Trump's comments about banning Muslims from traveling to the United States and the disparaging way he referred to immigrants from Central America (similar to the way Hitler talked about Jews), as well as eerie similarities between Trump's slogan "Make America Great Again" and Hitler's "Make Germany Great Again" sentiment. As Trump made proclamations and policy decisions, politicians inside the United States as well as foreign leaders and other critics made numerous comparisons between Trump's decisions and Hitler's in a previous era. Moreover, these comparisons were not discouraged by Trump, who allegedly kept a book of Hitler's speeches by his bedside. Trump has routinely admired dictators, such as Hitler, Vladimir Putin of Russia, and Viktor Mihály Orbán of Hungary, so it is not surprising that many of the ideas and decisions made by such leaders would be incorporated into Trump's decision-making.[51]

A variation on the Trump-as-Hitler model suggests that while Trump, as president, was not an exact copy of Hitler, there is substantial evidence that his behavior was similar to the German leader's. This perspective notes both men's narcissistic personality traits, shared tendency toward the role of bully, and casual relationship with the truth—often spreading lies about opponents and themselves as part of a propaganda machine that manipulates people and the press to convey an image as a form of self-promotion. Other similarities include Trump's approach to immigrants, particularly those from Central America and Muslim countries, as analogous to Hitler's persecution of Jews during the 1930s. In fact, one historian notes that Trump's decision to stop issuing passports to certain Hispanic/Latinx Americans is similar to Hitler's Nuremberg Laws. Additionally, Trump's family separation policies at the US-Mexico border, in 2018 and beyond, had a similar flavor to Hitler's efforts to remove Jews from Germany. Thus, there were and are many instances of parallel decision-making as well as perceptions of problems and solutions that make comparisons of Trump to Hitler compelling.[52]

In fact, in his 2021 book, *Betrayal: The Final Act of the Trump Show*, former White House chief of staff John Kelly alleges that Trump said, "Well, Hitler did a lot of good things," a quote Trump has denied.[53] Similarly, Michael Bender, in his 2021 book, *Frankly, We Did Win This Election: The Inside Story of How Trump Lost*, quotes Trump as saying, in reference to protestors, "That's how you're supposed to handle these people, crack their skulls!"[54]

A third alarmist view notes that many of Trump's actions and perceptions of problems make it very possible that, if left unchecked and not held sufficiently accountable, he could easily transform himself into a Hitler-like leader. In his book, *Hitler: Ascent, 1889–1939*, Volker Ullrich points out that Hitler was prone to shameless self-promotion, an overwhelming sense of self-importance (considering himself to be a genius), and possessed an intense level of ethnocentrism, coupled with an adept propaganda machine that exploited people's willingness to accept fraud, deceit, and lies as part of his platform. Ullrich points out that Hitler's rise to power could have been prevented had the public at large not accepted his outlandish claims, told over and over again, and his policies, which were dismissed as part of his celebrity. In his book, Ullrich makes a parallel comparison to Trump, although not by specifically naming him.[55]

Other critics have warned of the consequences of allowing a leader like Trump to act unchecked, with the likelihood of Trump, believing in his own infallibility, representing a significant danger to the Republican Party and the country as a whole. Such a "one party" state, complete with Trump's own version of loyalists who support gun rights and Second Amendment freedoms, could easily replicate what Hitler created with his stormtroopers. Other critics note that Trump's election could be seen as a parallel to Germany's Reichstag Fire, implying that, in a national emergency or crisis, Trump would likely act as Hitler did in the 1930s.[56]

The suggestion and the warning, of course, was that Trump, as Hitler did, would incrementally take over the United States. Similar to Hitler's transformation of Germany, the process occurred gradually, with the support of the people who did not realize the monster they were creating. In a similar vein, the same thing could have occurred, and could still occur, in the United States under Donald Trump. This perspective is articulated by Cornel West, who, after observing many of Trump's actions and comments, asserted that Trump, as president, was becoming the American version of Hitler.[57]

Another version of the alarmist view offers the idea that Trump may not be Hitler, may not even have acted like Hitler, but instead framed his actions, narratives, ideology, and policies as president along the lines of fascism. This point was discussed in greater length in chapter 2, where insight into the definition of fascism and its variations are applied to Trump's presidency. The applicability of fascism with Trump's presidency was underscored by Timothy Snyder's book *On Tyranny*, which warns of the consequences for the United States with a leader like Trump in office. More specifically, Trump's efforts to dismantle many of the existing institutions that are pivotal to the operation of a democracy, coupled with the disinformation, lies, and false claims, essentially were the makings of fascism in America.[58]

Snyder's comments have been echoed by Jason Stanley's book *How Fascism Works*, as well as by comments made by former secretary of state Madeleine Albright, who wrote *Fascism: A Warning*—both have pointed out that Trump, as president, qualified as a fascist.[59] What is remarkable about those who contend Trump was and is a fascist is that they typically argue that a US version of a fascist would be quite different from traditional characterizations such as Mussolini or Hitler. In fact, most of these predictions argue that a modern-day fascist leader in the United States would appear under the guise of a change agent, as someone who would avoid the traditional trappings of fascist rule and instead employ a carefully crafted manipulation of the public, similar to an infomercial huckster, celebrity, or television personality. The modern-day fascist in the United States would be portrayed as a populist who capitalizes on the public's need for a savior, a defender, a protector, and someone who is clearly not a professional politician.

Finally, and perhaps most relevant for this discussion, is the perspective that Trump wasn't (and isn't) a fascist, or even like Hitler, but his supporters hold many fascist ideas and rhetoric. As many commentators have noted, from the beginning of his presidential bid, Trump was endorsed by many extremist right-wing groups and he did little to dissuade them from support-ing him. After his election, Trump doubled down on this base of support, as described in chapter 5 on white supremacists, appointing white supremacist Steve Bannon to a White House position.

Further, evidence of Trump's position on white supremacy is seen in his comments supporting white supremacists after the Charlottesville rally in 2017, along with numerous comments in the media of Trump's "dog whistles" of support for white supremacists. What is important to consider here is that a number of scholars point out that Trump's base was comparable to that of classic fascist parties. In fact, in 2016, German Studies historian James Skidmore noted that Trump's supporters actually resembled Hitler's: "both were angry and frustrated people who felt threatened by a world that is changing in ways they don't understand."[60]

Other scholars offer comparisons between the present United States and the Weimar Republic of the 1930s. As it unfolded in Germany in the 1930s when Hitler was appointed chancellor, German officials thought they could contain and control him and ultimately use his efforts against him. As some scholars have argued, a similar line of thinking may have occurred in the Republican Party in dealing with Trump. Both groups were tragically mis-taken. Perhaps most significant is the parallel between the current Republican Party's attempts to dismantle democracy and the Prussian efforts to over-throw the Weimar Republic. As was mentioned in chapter 2, while there are undoubtedly ideological proponents in the Republican Party who see the value in deconstructing democracy in the United States, there are likely far more opportunists within the party whose naked ambition for power leads them to support Trump and his ideas only for political gain. In all of this, however, is the support from a large segment of the public who have endorsed these ideas, continue to believe the false narratives and the rhetoric, and who believe Trump, or someone like him, is the solution to the country's problems.

Realist Views of Trump and Hitler

A second group of observers disagree with the alarmist views about Trump being like or similar to a latter-day Hitler. These *realists* argue that Trump, as president, was not even a fascist because he did not meet the criteria normally used to identify fascism. Moreover, realists contend that the United States is not similar to the Weimar Republic, largely because it is and has remained far more stable and therefore less vulnerable to a fascist takeover. Perhaps most telling, realists argue that comparisons to Hitler are pejorative and detract from the significance of what occurred in Nazi Germany, particularly the Holocaust.

Realists contend that comparing Trump to Hitler fails because he was, as president, not a fascist. That is, Trumpism lacked a clear ideology; it lacked a base of support that endorses fascism; Trump endorsed democracy while fascism calls attention to its limitations, as Hitler did with the Weimar government. Additionally, Trump did not possess an aggressive foreign policy; while Hitler was obsessed with taking over Europe, Trump's policies were more in alignment with an America First approach to foreign relations. Where Trump exhibited fascist behavior was in his nationalist orientation, his tendency to vilify and scapegoat certain groups, particularly immigrants, his penchant for endorsing conspiracy theories and other lies and mistruths, his admiration for and emulation of dictators and demagogical demeanor, and his strong support of and contribution to the propaganda machine that continued to mislead the public and misinform the citizenry about events and trends.[61]

As was mentioned in chapter 2, one of the features (and criticisms) of Trumpism is its lack of clearly defined ideology. Other than demonizing other groups and the efforts to endorse authoritarianism, Trump lacked the vision and skill to dismantle democratic institutions and take over as a dictator. Similarly, Trump did not, in principle, oppose democracy. Unlike other fascist leaders, such as Mussolini or Hitler, who almost immediately began to seize control of societal institutions, Trump had no rational or violent plan to overthrow democracy. Instead, he embraced a portion of the established system and simply ignored some of the boundaries of checks and balances. While he may have tried to run the country like one of his businesses, with an autocratic rule and a careless disregard for federal laws, and while he may have had disdain for the Constitution since it limited his ability to operate in his usual fashion, realists argue that Trump never tried to overtly overthrow the government—at least prior to the events of January 6. In other words, while Hitler always opposed democracy, Trump tried to get reelected by voters instead of simply trying to take control.[62]

Realists also point out that Trump did not support organized violence in the same way that Hitler used a private paramilitary force like his stormtroopers. Historians note that Hitler routinely used arrest, torture, and imprisonment on opponents. Realists also point out that Trump did not have an aggressive foreign policy. In fact, one could argue that his America First slogan was more akin to an isolationist approach because he attempted to remove the United States from its global military role. Perhaps this was due to the fact that Trump never served in the military, but there were clear distinctions in his use of the military to solve political or economic problems that are in contrast to fascist regimes of the past.

Finally, realists point out that Trump is unlike fascists in that he did not support or endorse typical fascist economic policies. Instead, Trump embraced a free market system and tried to eliminate social programs such as Medicare,

Social Security, and welfare. Thus, in many ways, realists argue, Trump does not meet the benchmarks of fascist rule nor does the United States resemble the Weimar Republic in its configuration or vulnerabilities. An added point is that fascism is a more left-leaning ideology, making it difficult to assert that Trump aligned himself with this type of governing, particularly given the United States had a long tradition of a functioning democracy, whereas the Weimar government had been in existence for a much shorter period.[63]

Assessing the Trump as Hitler Debate

Considering both the alarmist and realist views on the comparison of Trump to Hitler, what are we to make of this debate? Was Trump a modern-day Hitler, determined to rule as a dictator and desiring the extermination of an entire group of people, as Hitler did with the Jews? As president, was Trump like Hitler in that he had endorsed white supremacy and stoked the violent extremists to do the dirty work of eliminating minorities? Did Trump have, at his disposal, a group of violent fanatics, like Hitler's stormtroopers, who took exception to anyone who disagreed with Trump's ideas and policies? Are Trumpsters simply a modern-day version of this group, with some being less prone to violence but nonetheless inflexible in their thinking and intolerant of anyone who disagrees with Trumpism?

Is it reasonable to consider the idea that Trump admired and even modeled many of his strategies based on Hitler's, particularly his propaganda machine that fed the public a steady stream of lies and half-truths, and created a narrative of fear, hatred, loathing, and white superiority? Is it reasonable to assume that Trump, if given the chance, would have dispensed with many of the checks and balances that prevented him from running the country as he would one of his companies? In other words, would Trump have dispensed with democracy and the US Constitution if it interfered with his interests and goals?

Is it reasonable to consider that Trump, a masterful manipulator, was more interested in self-aggrandizement at the expense of others and in the accumulation of power than in actually trying to "make America great again"? Is it reasonable to consider that the United States is at a stage where it resembles the social and political upheaval that characterized Germany during the Weimar Republic, making it susceptible to the influences of a maniacal leader who promises to restore the United States to a previous era of comfort and security for its people? Of course, this perspective is not necessarily accurate or even adhered to by a large segment of the population.

Finally, is it reasonable to consider that the shocking manner in which Trump led the country, coupled with the questionable judgements, actions, and policies as president that raised questions about his competency, has inevitably led to comparisons to other ruthless and incompetent leaders of the past, such as Hitler? On balance, it seems understandable that these conclusions and references to Hitler and Nazi Germany could be interpreted as predictive—the United States had not had a president like Trump before and it is fair that some of his actions would be framed in light of his similarities to a leader like Hitler.

While much of this debate by scholars focuses on whether or not Trump met the criteria or benchmarks of definition (Trump is or isn't a fascist based on how one defines the term; Trump is or isn't an aspirational Hitler because he created and expanded an enormously successful propaganda machine that consistently fed the public misinformation and outright lies about various topics and his role in them), there are parallels between Hitler's actions and Trump's that warrant examination and concern.

To ignore the similarities or the possible consequences of various actions would be misguided. What is important to remember is that while there are similarities between the two leaders, Hitler was not the only leader who employed these types of strategies or held the perspectives and beliefs that we see in Trump. For instance, Trump's stance on immigration was nearly identical to that of President Ronald Reagan's while he was in office, and Trump's law and order campaign was a veritable carbon copy of President Richard Nixon's.

Most importantly, and somewhat missing from the larger discussion, however, is the fact that in the case of Trump and Hitler, government officials, along with a large portion of the general public, endorsed, praised, and supported much of what both leaders attempted to accomplish. This is at the heart of the story; that people, in Trump's case, the 74 million people who voted for him, generally think what he tried to do was not only acceptable, but believed, then and now, the narrative and the rhetoric. This has created a serious and significant challenge in polarizing the country, politically, socially, and even economically. How and why did we end up here? This will be the subject of the next chapter.

Chapter 7

How Trumpism and Trumpsters Have Changed Social Life in America

A recurring theme of this book has been that Trump is not the source of the many problems facing the United States. For all his inappropriate and offensive behavior—his tendencies toward white supremacy, his disparaging comments and mistreatment of other groups, his willingness to engage in shameless self-promotion and outright lies, his policies promoting a form of national and international selfishness, his dictatorial manner in dispensing with the rule of law and democratic principles when it suits him—Trump isn't the problem. In fact, other politicians who model Trump's approach and who present their own threats to democracy and the future of this country aren't the problem either.

It isn't even the case that Trumpsters, whether they are white supremacists, cult followers, misguided evangelical Christians, or a Republican Party that has fractured into something that contradicts itself on many issues, are the problem. As we continue to explore the idea of Trump and Trumpsters, with an eye toward understanding who they are, what they are about, and why there are so many of them, we begin to see important glimpses of ourselves as a society. Trump and Trumpsters are not an accident or aberration, as was mentioned in chapter 1; the Trump phenomenon can be seen as part of a social movement that has been growing for some time and has accelerated the reshaping of social life in the United States in ways we had not expected.

Trump adeptly capitalized on much of what already existed—and his talent for maximizing the narrative and expertly manipulating the public into believing his tales only exacerbated what many people already felt. There are reasons for these feelings, of course, and we will offer insight into their sources, but we should not make the mistake of thinking that the elimination of Trump from the political landscape would remove the tensions existing between various groups. Following the Trump era, there will be others who have learned from his mistakes and who will present similar but more sophisticated narratives; ones that potentially have even greater appeal but are equally dangerous.

While many of the problems facing this country are complex and require careful thought and consideration, we are unlikely to get any closer to solving them if we remain so adamantly opposed to each other and unwilling to consider others' perspectives. The problem is that we are spending enormous amounts of time, energy, and money finding ways to oppose each other rather than finding reasonable compromises or solutions. In other words, *we* are the problem, and as long as we continue to dedicate ourselves to deepening divisions rather than forging solutions, the problem will persist.

The real question, then, is why have we become so separated and polarized from one another? To do this, we need to revisit our understanding of concepts like ethnocentrism and the ingroup and outgroup dynamic, since they are important factors in grasping how we became so divided in the first place. When we witness the extremism, anger, and intolerance of Trump and Trumpsters, what we are really seeing is fear. It makes sense, then, to unpack the source of that fear, since it influences how we relate to one another.

This is particularly true in those instances where politicians and other leaders convince people that those fears are justified. The outcome is predictable, particularly since many of us engage in a type of lazy thinking about the world and have an unrealistic and distorted sense of entitlement about our place in it.

SORTING, SEPARATISM, AND SOCIAL LIFE

As was mentioned in chapter 6, much of what we see in Trump loyalists are influences generated by strong inclinations toward ethnocentrism and ingroup/outgroup behavior. Humans naturally come together in groups because we need social interaction and social relationships. The influence of these groups, including those we dislike, have an extraordinary impact on our self-perceptions, worldviews, opinions, and behavior.

A fascinating dimension of social life is that we don't always know or understand people's intentions. This uncertainty can create challenges for us because, as social psychologist Leon Festinger (1954) argues, we all have this fundamental "need to know" or need to understand the world around us. Because human behavior is such a complex process, we are often left with questions about who people are as well as why they act the way they do.[1]

Typically, a common way to "figure people out" is to take bits and pieces of information that we see or learn about others and, when enough cues emerge, separate them into categories—which is a rather superficial way of grouping people. This form of labeling allows us to attribute a wide range of attitudes, values, and beliefs to the people we meet.

This isn't necessarily a bad thing: we engage in all types of labeling of the things around us, and much of our understanding of the world comes as a result of these types of assessments. As Festinger (1954) points out, the value in putting people and groups into categories is that it defines for us to which category or group we belong. Where the labeling tends to become problematic or even dangerous is when we rely on stereotypes or sweeping generalizations to predict and explain the behavior and beliefs of others.[2]

In practice, this quick and simple type of profiling is plagued with inaccuracies or inconsistencies, and the labels we assign to others are often negative—unless they are members of our own ingroup. In that case, there is a tendency to find a much greater level of support, loyalty, grace, and mercy for those whom we identify as belonging to our tribe. We are much more likely to overlook the inappropriate and inconsistent behavior of people we know or those with whom we affiliate than that of those who are different from us.

This labeling is an important feature of social life because it allows us to differentiate between the types of people we align ourselves with and the ones we oppose or gain distance from. As French (2020) point outs, this tendency is called *sorting*, where people organize themselves into certain groups.[3] This notion of sorting is important because, at an extreme, it is one of the main reasons people in the United States are becoming increasingly polarized from one another.[4] In fact, French (2020) argues, our tendency to affiliate with one another often occurs not so much as a result of an affinity toward a particular group of people, a cause, or an ideology but out of *dislike for other groups*.[5]

This point is underscored by Klein (2020) in his book *Why We're Polarized*, where he argues there is a growing physical and social distance between groups and an increased level of hostility and tension between them. Klein also points out that while we may be members of multiple groups that shape our identities—such as religious groups, professional associations, hobbies, and so on—increasingly in the United States, the political groups we belong to have come to dominate all other forms of identity. That is, *identity politics* is a term that is used to portray an extreme form of sorting, where whether one is a Democrat or a Republican determines almost every other dimension of one's identity. Perhaps most importantly, political identity is also how we react to each other.[6]

And because the two main political parties in this country have intentionally tried to separate themselves from one another since the 1990s, with a goal of attracting voters to a distinct set of principles and values, an unintended consequence of that difference has been an increased level of hostility between political groups.[7] While in the past differences of opinion on various topics were based on ideological positions, there was space in which to broker compromises and accomplish goals on a larger scale.

Today the tensions and hostilities between political parties have increased so dramatically that some politicians oppose a bill or policy change simply *because* it is endorsed by those in another party. In short, not only is there a growing trend toward aligning oneself with a particular political group but also that such an alignment requires one to dislike those with different affiliations. This type of animosity not only intensifies our loyalty and solidarity to the groups with whom we choose to affiliate, it limits the amount and type of interaction across groups. A potential consequence of such a trend is that the American experiment could splinter into pockets of people who have no real interest in a unifying structure that makes a democracy possible.[8]

What is fascinating about this form of sorting is there are consistent patterns that translate into other features of social life. Not only is there evidence that people are deciding to live in certain regions of the country where they are more likely to be surrounded by like-minded people, the research tends to show that such physical or geographic sorting also influences voting patterns. In fact, researchers compared voting patterns to residential clustering and found that people who lean conservative in their political views and voting patterns tend to live in states that are dominated by Republicans, while those who lean liberal tend to live in Democrat-dominated states.[9]

Similarly, if one were to link religious views with political party affiliation, one would see a similar pattern; that conservative voters tend to live in certain regions of the country and they also tend to reflect certain religious ideologies. This is particularly true in states like California and regions of the South, where, as politically blue and red states, respectively, the data clearly reflect patterns of religious affiliation.

These geographic, religious, and political patterns also shape our willingness and ability to consider alternative views on topics including what types of information we are willing to consider. This includes the sources of information to keep us informed about what is happening in the world (e.g., Fox News for conservatives and CNN for liberals), as well as the unwillingness to grant consideration to those sources of information that do not confirm what we think we already know or present an opposing viewpoint.

The obvious implication of these patterns is that as we continually surround ourselves only with people that see and understand the world as we do, it creates a strong inclination that the way we live our lives is the most appropriate. Furthermore, such a trend not only creates an environment where we tend to, with little resistance from our surroundings, dislike those who think, act, and believe differently from us but also fosters a belief that these "others" somehow pose a threat to our way of life.

It is here that the arrogance of ethnocentrism begins to emerge and the misguided conclusions that stem from it—if people do not live, believe, or act as we do, they must be wrong. And if they are wrong, we can try to convince them to change their views, vilify them for their beliefs, or simply distance ourselves from them and align ourselves with others who think like we do. While there is some optimism for the former, as they may become potential converts, we have this tendency to see alternative points of view as threats and those who espouse them as the "enemy."[10]

This process of sorting can become a self-fulfilling prophecy, where people surround themselves with people who see and understand the world as they do and, by demonstrating one's loyalty toward their particular party, their allegiance to the tribe or group is secured. And because politics has increasingly become an effective identifier/label to determine the position of others and to assess their suitability as friends and colleagues, it simplifies the process.

By itself, there isn't anything wrong with like-minded people getting together, living near one another, or having similar ideas about how to live life. But when people feel as though they have to identify their tribe and, once in it, they become more extreme in their views, particularly if there is a rival group, they also become unable (and unwilling) to make objective decisions. It is what Sunstein (1999) and others refer to as a "predeliberation tendency," or a bias in decision-making.[11]

Sunstein (1999) has found that as like-minded people get together, they tend to become more extreme in their views and beliefs and often sway those in the group who might not initially feel the same way. Sunstein isn't the only researcher to discover this type of bias. There is a wealth of social psychology literature that suggests people are often willing to ignore or change their beliefs to align them with those of a group, even in those instances where the individual feels strongly about a given topic. In other words, in certain situations, group pressure influences individuals to such a degree that they would rather be wrong than alone.

Additionally, Sunstein (1999) concludes that if enough people in the group believe a certain way, the members will quickly develop strong and similar opinions, even if the position is inaccurate or based on false information. All that seems to be needed is enough people claiming something to be true for other members to go along with that perspective.[12]

This trend results in what French (2020) calls "negative polarization," the movement of people toward opposite views and greater levels of social distancing based on political views. In an interesting development, people's tendency toward negative polarization occurs even with people we know, like, and respect.[13] That is, our need to remain loyal to our tribe is more important than our desire to respect our friends and family members' opinions—and we often feel the need to attack them and question their sense of integrity or morality for choosing the "wrong" side.

In other words, our tribal branding requires us to view certain issues and topics from a particular lens and to engage in a regular pattern of confirmation bias, where we seek out and believe information that confirms what we think we already know and to dismiss any data that contradicts that belief or raises questions about its accuracy. To borrow a popular phrase, information that disagrees with our tribe's point of view is seen as "fake news." Further, when objective data is presented that obviously and clearly contradicts our worldview, we either attack the messenger's moral character or motives, we dismiss the accuracy of the claim, or "prove" our perspective is the correct one based on the use of "alternative facts."

Most disturbing is how all of this is being exploited by today's media and politicians, who have learned that there is tremendous value in promoting controversy, stoking divisions between groups, and keeping people outraged and angry about any number of topics. Clearly social media has made this much easier, with the ability to spread information quickly with little accountability; but by creating a climate of fear and anger, it minimizes the public's ability to see the warning signs of deception that are right in front of them.

Not only is making and keeping people angry a profitable business but it requires an ongoing escalation of situations and circumstances, often creating conflict or controversy where none exist, to feed the emotional addiction it profits from. This is not a new phenomenon, but social media and technology have elevated this trend in unprecedented ways. As Klein (2020) points out, the most effective politicians are those who thrill their supporters. The way this is accomplished is by casting his or her opponent as a threat to his or her supporters' way of life. Klein writes, "The lesson is known by politicians the world over. You don't just need support. You need anger."[14]

What is also fascinating about this tendency to choose party over principle is that, under normal circumstances, people are generally capable of being convinced about a point of view by the best available evidence. That is, in general, people can be very reasonable in weighing evidence on topics or issues that don't have a political dimension.

As critics of Trumpsters point out, the blind allegiance to Trump and Trumpism is often seen as a lack of intelligence or education, but in reality, many Trump supporters are educated and are more than capable of evaluating the available data on a given topic—and in their minds they are offering a well-reasoned, if not impassioned, explanation of events.

However, Klein (2020) points out that these logical, thoughtful, and rational people don't realize that the emotional dependency of being a part of a tribe often requires flawed thinking; that to remain in good standing in the group, particularly if the group casts the issue as a dangerous threat, logical and rational thinking is replaced by a form of cognitive dissonance, where the members recast the issue in such a way that flawed and extreme behavior is acceptable and even appropriate. This is why people will accept false narratives even when they know they are not true and defend those positions, including attacking those who disagree with them.[15]

WHY WE'RE SO ANGRY, HATEFUL, AND POLARIZED

The evidence, then, suggests we are becoming more polarized from each other, living, working, praying, thinking, and acting only as the group's ideology dictates, with such extremist views inevitably leading to intolerance, inflexibility, and leaning into hostility, tension, and even hatred for others that are different from us.

As was discussed in chapter 4, how do we make sense of the seemingly irrational way evangelical Christians endorse and remain loyal to Trump despite the fact that his perspective and actions run counter to much of what it means to be a Christian? What makes Trumpsters so unfailingly loyal to Trump and to so intensely dislike President Biden? What explanations exist that provide an understanding of why so many Republican-controlled legislatures are attempting to change the protocols on elections under the purported cloud of fraud (but only if a Republican loses) when there isn't any evidence that widespread fraud actually exists?

Similarly, what do we make of states passing laws limiting what teachers can share with students about the legacy of slavery and the role of race in American history? Some states, such as Florida, even passed legislation in 2022 that limits the discussion of race in the workplace. What is the reasoning behind the weaponization of woke culture (discussed at length later in the chapter) which, by definition, suggests a willingness to consider points of view on topics that may have gone unnoticed before? How did cancel culture become such a common reaction to a litany of mistakes, misunderstandings, mild transgressions, or oversights?

As we try to gain insight into Trumpsters and the popularity of Trump, along with the need to be a part of a group, we should consider how fear drives much of the discussion and understanding: a fear of being alone, a fear of losing one's cultural, economic, and political status and standing, which drives the need for some type of protection or protector; and a fear of doing the difficult work of carefully considering our own sense of entitlement and unwillingness to take responsibility for misguided actions of the past.

In short, much of what we see in the narrow-minded thinking, the passionate, if not violent opinions and perceptions of others, and the unwillingness to find and broker reasonable compromises stems from the fear of being alone, the fear of losing out, and the fear of accepting responsibility for our poor choices. Many scoff at the media and dishonest and corrupt politicians, and think if we simply removed those people from their positions of authority, the problems would be solved. They won't be. If we are really honest with ourselves, the media and politicians, even the extremists, aren't really to blame either—they are simply giving us what they think we want. And as any good psychologist would assert, rewarded behavior gets repeated.

The Fear of Being Alone: Loneliness in the United States

In trying to make sense of Trump and Trumpsters, we need to expand our lens of understanding beyond individual groups and take a more macro-level view of what is occurring in American society. As we do so, we begin to see there are several factors influencing our thoughts and actions that result in people's decision to join a group like Trumpsters.

Most experts consistently argue that as humans, we are born to be in connection with others. Our sense of well-being, happiness, and even our health are tied to the relationships we form with other people. There is ample evidence that loneliness affects our brains and bodies in significant ways. For example, some data indicates that lonely people get sick more often, take longer to recover from illness, and are at higher risk of heart attacks than those who are connected to others. There is some research that also shows that chronically lonely people are more prone to Alzheimer's disease and dementia. In fact, some studies estimate that one lonely day has the same effect on the body as smoking a pack of cigarettes.[16]

There is also evidence that lonely, isolated people have shorter life expectancies; they are about 25 percent more likely to die prematurely. This includes suicides, but it also includes a host of health-related problems. In fact, persistent loneliness has a greater impact on a person's life span than obesity, heavy drinking, or smoking. There is actually evidence that loneliness reduces a person's longevity twice as much as heavy drinking and three times as much as obesity alone.[17]

Many researchers are also beginning to conclude that perhaps the link between obesity and loneliness is inverted; where loneliness is actually driving much of the obesity problem in this country, not the other way around. Loneliness is also seen as a significant factor in depression among many Americans. In fact, some researchers argue that much of what we are calling depression is actually chronic loneliness. While the social stigma associated with depression and its treatment have lessened considerably in recent times, many people are either unable or unwilling to recognize they are suffering from it. Instead, they report they are lonely.[18] Loneliness is also a significant contributing factor to the opioid crisis in the United States. As with the diagnosis and treatment of depression, this is a complex issue, but many clinicians and researchers are noting that an important reason this country is the biggest consumer of hydrocodone and oxycodone relates to loneliness. They argue that the relationship between loneliness and drug use is actually the lack of oxytocin that comes as a result of feeling love, friendship, and a general sense of well-being that is created when we have connection to others. Unfortunately, as people become more isolated and disconnected from that sense of community, the need to replicate that chemical response with artificial replacements like drugs becomes more attractive.[19]

Sadly, as we have seen, the trend in American society is not toward a greater connectedness between people, but a consistent movement away from it. In sociologist Robert Putnam's 2001 book, *Bowling Alone*, his initial research question centered on the factors that create and sustain emotional and social ties to others in the United States, a topic that naturally lends itself to sociological analysis. What he found, however, is people are increasingly not becoming a part of a larger community and this is seen in all sorts of activities that normally create attachments between people.[20]

Putnam found that the activities that normally serve as anchors of attachment and community were declining, both in frequency and in the significance people attached to them. As the title of the book suggests, Putnam noticed that in the early 1990s, while there were more people who participated in bowling than in the past, fewer of them were joining bowling leagues. He also discovered that people were engaging in lots of other recreational activities, but they weren't doing it together. From participation in bridge clubs, alumni groups, the PTA, to going to the movies, church attendance, youth sports, and a host of other events that normally brought people together, all were being replaced with individually focused activities or the activities were not being performed in a group context.[21]

Even our friendship patterns have changed. Along with a lack of participation in community events, Putnam (2001) found that the number of people who had friends over for dinner showed significant decreases over time. Within families, Putnam found that the number and type of activities people engaged in with family members, such as vacations, watching television or movies, or simply spending time together, have witnessed a considerable decline over the past thirty years.[22]

In light of the declining opportunities for connectedness to one another, it should not be at all surprising to learn that the number of close friends Americans have is also declining, as has our sense of trust in the government and its officials. To illustrate, Putnam (2001) points out that the average American has gone from more than three intimate and close personal friends over the last thirty years to less than two; often this consists of one's spouse.[23]

Most significant is the number of people in this country who have no friends; opinion poll data suggests that by the mid-2000s about 25 percent of people said they had no one with whom to talk about things that mattered to them, a threefold increase since 1980. In short, Putnam's (2001) main conclusion is that we are growing increasingly isolated from one another, there lacks a strong sense of community in the United States, and Americans are increasingly feeling isolated and alone.[24]

Other scholars point to a similar trend and raise the same concerns, such as in Timothy Carney's *Alienated America* (2019) or Jonah Goldberg's *Suicide of the West* (2018). Similarly, Charles Murray points out in his book *Coming Apart*, there are economic factors that are separating people in the United States. Murray argues that these experiences are increasingly separating people into "haves" and "have nots," who have very different life experiences, opportunities, live in very different neighborhoods, and have separate social networks. These twin factors, loneliness and separation/polarization, have a host of consequences for people and the country as a whole, but they are also self-fulfilling—meaning the more it occurs, the greater its effect and intensity. Murray contends that the problems aren't going to improve as the size of the elderly population expands, which increases the sense of isolation and economic dependence.[25]

In addition to the macro-level impact that loneliness can have on social institutions, the sense of disconnectedness can lead some people to feel an increased sense of urgency to become a part of something larger, which allows them to restore their sense of belonging and well-being.[26] This is true even where such an affiliation may not be in what the person actually wants in a tribe or it results in embracing ideas and actions that aren't necessarily in alignment with their worldview.

However, once a decision is made to become a member of such a group, cognitive dissonance offers insight into the ways people allow the group's ideas to have an extraordinary influence on how they see the world as well as the need to defend the group and its members from all types of real and perceived threats.[27]

This dependency can explain why something as mild as an intellectual disagreement or dispute about a proposed policy change can result in extreme responses; people aren't defending their point of view as much as they are responding to a perceived threat about the group's existence. An example of this are those Trumpsters who threaten, intimidate, and engage in hateful speech and behavior to any disagreement with or perceived slight of former president Trump and his agenda. In short, our sense of loneliness is a significant and growing problem, and for some people, the longing that comes from the need to connect to others often results in fears of the future, a heightened perception of threats to the group, and an unrealistic reliance on the group for one's social identity.

The Fear of Losing What We Have

The impact of loneliness is felt at many levels and, as was mentioned in chapter 2, one of the reasons for the wide base of loyal Trump followers stems from a fear that people are losing their place or position in society. In the case of Trumpsters, most of whom are White, there is a deep-seated fear that the way of life that Whites have enjoyed for generations may be changing as more minorities become a significant part of the political, economic, and social landscape in the United States. This fear has been a central theme of the propaganda machine that has been a part of the Republican Party's efforts for some time, but Trump escalated it to the extent that people see diversity and change as a crisis that needs immediate action. In fact, an argument can be made that panic, anger, and fear are key features of Trump's platform.

These two emotions feed off each other; the more afraid we become, anger serves as a useful tool since it gives people something to focus on to alleviate the fear and can even be seen as a socially acceptable response, particularly when a situation requires us to come together against a "common" enemy. Trump is popular because like many charismatic leaders, he promised to protect people from the carefully crafted threat that is being presented to the American public, who want a protector and someone who understands their concerns. It is not necessarily Trump that people wanted, but most of his followers were driven to become Trumpsters out of a sense of fear of losing their way of life.

The Fear of Acknowledging Our Mistakes

As was mentioned, political parties offer people the benefit of a simple and easy way to understand complex issues. Knowing a party's ideology allows a rather simple framework for discussions and debates on issues as well as direction on how to vote on them. As was mentioned in chapter 1, many people voted for Trump not because they admired him or even agreed with the way he acted but simply because he was a Republican, which carried with it an understanding of a perspective on a host of issues.

While there were and are many things people did not and do not like about Trump, many voters felt and feel that he was and is still a better alternative than a Democrat. While this has been a common way for people to understand issues in the past, today's evidence indicates that people are increasingly simplifying how one defines "us" versus "them" groupings and we are using political party affiliation as the primary vehicle. The result is that we then view rival parties with disdain, mistrust, and suspicion and see their perspective as a threat to our way of life. It is a neat and tidy, if uninformed, way of dividing the world and this perspective changes the way we see ourselves and others.[28]

What is fascinating about this tendency is that if we examined the data on how people perceive members of other groups, we see another illustration of how our labeling often reflects inaccurate information that leads to flawed conclusions about others. For example, the images Republicans have about Democrats is often exceptionally inaccurate, as is the way Democrats perceive and understand Republicans. Research shows that Republicans see Democrats as comprised primarily of Blacks, LGBTQIAs, and pro-union members.

In fact, the research shows that while Republicans generally think almost half of Democrats are Black, in fact that number is approximately 24 percent. Similarly, Republicans estimate that close to 50 percent of Democrats are members of the LGBTQIA community, when the actual number is closer to 6 percent. Republicans also tend to think that most Democrats are union members, but the data indicates that it is closer to 11 percent.[29]

Similarly, Democrats' perceptions of Republicans also tend to be equally skewed, thinking they are old, White, Christian, rich people. As the data shows, while Democrats tend to think that nearly half of Republicans are age sixty-five or older, that number is approximately 21 percent. The evidence indicates that Democrats think Republicans are evangelical Christians and Southern. In reality, evangelicals make up an estimated 34 percent of Republicans and 36 percent of Southerners. Democrats also tend to think of Republicans as the party of the wealthy, where almost half earn $250,000 or more per year. In reality, that number is closer to 2 percent.[30] In short, both groups hold unrealistic and rather inaccurate assessments of the other, but these perceptions shape their interactions as well as how each group understands a given issue.

This inaccurate portrayal of others is something the nonprofit group More in Common refers to as a *perception gap*.[31] The gap represents the extent to which a group, in this case Republicans and Democrats, *thinks* they disagree with the other party compared to the level they *actually* disagree with each other. The perception gap also examines how personal attributes, such as education level and behaviors, including the extent and type of media consumption, can narrow or expand the gap.

As part of their Hidden Tribes project, the More in Common organization attempts to document and understand the extent to which these misunderstandings and inaccurate perceptions contribute to the polarization that exists in the United States.[32] For example, some of the most important findings of the study include:

- Both Democrats and Republicans imagine that almost twice as many people in the other party hold extreme views than is really the case.
- On average, Democrats and Republicans believe that more than half of their opponents' views are extreme, but, in reality, the number is closer to 30 percent.
- In general, those Americans in either primary party who hold strong partisan views tend to hold more exaggerated views of their opponents.[33]

Interestingly, those who claim to consume multiple forms of information, including social media, local news, newspapers, and talk radio, tend to experience a wider perception gap than those who only view the media occasionally. Similarly, those who post political views on their social media platforms tend to have a wider perception gap than those who do not. Yudkin, Hawkins, and Dixon (2019) also found that the wider a person's perception gap, the more likely they are to attribute negative personal qualities to their opponents.[34]

Interestingly, educational achievement is related to the perception gap, but in an inverted way. While conventional thinking might assume that those with less education would tend to be more likely to inaccurately assess a person and their party's views, the evidence suggests the opposite. That is, people with higher levels of education actually tend to have more inaccurate assessments of their opponents. Ultimately, Yudkin et al. (2019) found that there is consistent evidence that Americans' views are more similar to their political opponents than they realize, despite the intentional efforts by political parties and candidates to highlight their differing ideologies.[35]

It is this type of fear-based thinking that allows us to put party over principle, tribe over topic, and remain loyal to groups that would not normally gain such a strong and dedicated following. This type of thinking is also what allows politicians and policymakers to manipulate and exploit the public with fear-infused narratives that are then used to anger segments of the population and distract them from what is actually happening. It is this vilification of others that continues to result in disparaging views and comments about outgroups—and to believe the lies and distorted truths presented by politicians, who want to be portrayed as advocates and protectors but are, it seems, really only interested in gaining more power.

While we may recognize and understand this about all politicians to some degree, our fears continue to allow mainstream media and politicians to operate with relative impunity—we don't hold them accountable, we don't call them out when they lie and distort the truth, and then we act surprised when the truth actually comes out and is often different from what we initially thought (assuming we are willing to consider that possibility). In short, we get the kinds of politicians and media sources we deserve. Until we begin to demand more (and better) from politicians and the news media, and to side-line or muffle those who promote misinformation/lies, and distract people from the important issues by keeping them angry, we will continue to find ourselves in the situation we are in now—or worse.

In sum, Trump and Trumpsters aren't the problem; they are a symptom of a much larger one. We are the problem. Our sense of entitlement, our unwill-ingness to accept and admit the wrongdoings of past generations, and our irrational fears about changes that could impact our way of life results in a host of extraordinary rationalizations and justifications that deflect account-ability or allow us to skirt responsibility for what has occurred. It's wrong; it's misguided; it's lazy thinking; and it's a terrible lesson to teach our children.

There are several important illustrations of this type of intellectual and social complacency, such as the aforementioned debate about teaching criti-cal race theory in schools; legislation about "divisive" thinking; controversies about white privilege; and the weaponization of woke culture. Each of these are worthy of some explanation and description.

Illustrations of Misdirected Fear and Anger: Critical Race Theory

As was mentioned in a previous chapter, the controversy surrounding teach-ing critical race theory (CRT) in public schools, as well as other efforts to limit what teachers discuss in the classroom, remains demonstrative of how fear is used to distract the public from important issues. In 2022, for example, the Florida legislature passed a "Stop WOKE (wrongs to our kids and employees) Act" bill that limits how discussions of race are handled in classrooms and in the workplace.[36] This is true despite the fact that there is no evidence that critical race theory is taught in K–12 schools in the state.

The bill limits how teachers and other educators teach public school stu-dents about race, privilege, and oppression in relation to the founding of America. The governor of Florida, Ron DeSantis, had this to say about the legislation in the following combined quotes taken from a CBS News report:

"In Florida we are taking a stand against the state-sanctioned racism that is criti-cal race theory," DeSantis said when he supported the bill in December. "We won't allow Florida tax dollars to be spent teaching kids to hate our country or to hate each other. We also have a responsibility to ensure that parents have the means to vindicate their rights when it comes to enforcing state standards. Finally, we must protect Florida workers against the hostile work environ-ment that is created when large corporations force their employees to endure CRT-inspired 'training' and indoctrination."[37]

As it relates to discussions about race in the workplace, the legislation limits employers who include training on critical race theory or racism, and bans any training or credentials course that tries to offer commentary on whether one group has had a privileged or oppressed status, as determined by their race, sex, or national origin.[38]

The problem is not that this legislation has passed in Florida, but that other states are entertaining similar discussions and passing laws that reflect the same idea. As we allow ourselves to become victims of our own fears, leaders continually promote ideas that escalate unsubstantiated issues or urge us to see the danger in accurately describing the sins of the past. Instead of upholding our sense of decency and integrity, along with taking responsibility for our current and past actions as a nation, we allow ourselves to be convinced we are facing an epic and unfair battle over our way of life—one that requires us to fight, deny, attack, and learn to hate those who call attention to the issues. To highlight the inflammatory nature of the debate about critical race theory and its impact, former president Trump was recently quoted as saying:

> Getting critical race theory out of our schools is not just a matter of values, it's also a matter of national survival. We have no choice, the fate of any nation ultimately depends upon the willingness of its citizens to lay down and they must do this, lay down their very lives to defend their country. If we allow the Marxists and Communists and Socialists to teach our children to hate America, there will be no one left to defend our flag or to protect our great country or its freedom.[39]

The debate about critical race theory has extended beyond public schools, however. Some states, such as South Dakota, are also passing laws prohibiting colleges and universities from teaching it there as well. In March 2022, governor Kristi Noem signed a bill designed to "protect students and employees at institutions of higher education from divisive concepts." Specifically, the new law prohibits colleges from requiring students and teachers to attend trainings or orientations based on critical race theory.[40] Governor Noem stated: "No student or teacher should have to endorse critical race theory in order to attend, graduate from, or teach at our public universities. . . . College should remain a place where freedom of thought and expression are encouraged, not stifled by political agendas."[41]

A similar bill is being considered in Tennessee, where the discussion of critical race theory and other topics related to race are seen as "divisive" in nature; this particular bill would allow people the opportunity to seek damages if they felt they were harmed or punished in some way for not accepting "divisive concepts."[42]

The language contained in these bills is vague and often does not mention critical race theory in particular, but notice how the sentiment behind the bills and laws has been transformed into a discussion about freedom and autonomy. The Tennessee bill tries to punish educators for even discussing these topics, lest someone make a claim that they have been harmed or unfairly punished by being a part of a debate about them. The goal seems to be to limit the discussion; that way people don't have to feel harmed or somehow inadequate for events of the past. This is the danger in allowing such revisionism to occur; there is no end to the extent to which people will gaslight history or limit what children learn about what has actually occurred in our past.

More Fear and Anger: Rejecting White Privilege

The debate about critical race theory is really an attempt to limit the discussion about a larger issue, one that also generates considerable fear and anger: white privilege. That is, many people don't want to talk about systemic racism or even have an accurate portrayal of American history because it reveals an unflattering portrayal of how Whites have mistreated others and taken considerable advantage of marginalized groups. White privilege occurs because people have been convinced that they should expect certain benefits simply because they are White.

Many White politicians and others who deny the existence of white privilege offer two key arguments. They claim either that white privilege does not exist at all, or that it applies only to certain segments of the White population—primarily the wealthy and powerful. The white privilege argument also includes the notion of *white fragility*, which refers to that state of denial that leads some White people to outrage when their privilege is called out.[43]

In response to the first argument, sociologist Joe Feagin argues that American culture has socialized Whites to think they should view their dominant status as natural. Feagin also argues that racial inequalities should be viewed not as a product of Whites' privileged position, but as something for which they hold no responsibility or obligation to remedy.[44]

With regard to the second point, as was discussed in chapter 1, sociologist Arlie Hochschild interviewed working-class White people in Louisiana and discovered a level of discouragement for many residents who feel that the government caters to other groups such as immigrants and Blacks. The implication is that these working-class Whites should be designated as a protected class.[45]

Critics of white privilege argue that working-class Whites should not be expected to acknowledge their favored position in society. After all, Whites who experience poverty and hardship, especially in times of severe economic downturn (such as the COVID-19 pandemic), will indeed have difficulty appreciating their enhanced societal position.

Whites in such circumstances neither see nor accept the argument that they are benefitting from an enhanced position based on race. Instead, the narrative they believe becomes one in which minorities blame all Whites for their circumstances and do not take responsibility for their own behavior.[46] In fact, some evidence indicates the development of *black privilege*, where Whites complain of being accused of racism for the same celebration and identification of their race.[47]

This weaponization of white despair has been a common assertion by politicians who claim that the problem is really about poor choices by Blacks who commit crimes, resist commands by the police, and face the consequences of their actions. This, they say, explains the high number of deaths of Black Americans. In July 2020, when asked in an interview with CBS News about why so many Blacks are killed by the police, President Donald Trump's response was, "So are White people! What a terrible question to ask." He added that "more White people by the way, are killed by police than Black people." Consistent with an unwillingness to recognize the problem, what President Trump failed to acknowledge is that Blacks are killed by the police at a far higher rate than Whites.[48]

One of the greatest challenges to white privilege is convincing Whites that there are systemic obstacles and strategies that inhibit Blacks in ways that Whites have never experienced, considered, or encountered. For example, social policies of the past, such as the G. I. Bill for soldiers after World War II that provided funds for education and home purchases that were not made available for Blacks. This meant that Black soldiers who fought were not eligible for the same benefits as White soldiers. Such strategies created and perpetuated a form of privilege for Whites that has been denied Blacks.[49] Discussions of critical race theory and white privilege are byproducts of the fear and anger that has been fed to the American people, the same people who allow such extraordinary claims to gain legitimacy by being repeated until they gain credibility. Instead of examining the issues with a critical and empirical point of view, what politicians have done, and many Whites have endorsed, is the creation of more fear, more anger, and more lazy thinking by Whites, who do not realize the advantages they have been given at the expense of others.[50]

Weaponizing Fear and Anger: Woke Culture

Another tactic practiced by those who attempt to make and keep people afraid and angry is the notion of woke culture. By itself, there is nothing particularly offensive about acting "woke." This term, which was originally defined as the process of becoming more aware (or awake), carries with it an implication that greater awareness of the nuances of social issues results in a higher level of accountability. That is, as someone becomes more "woke," they are better able to identify problems and issues that stem from the mistreatment of others, miscarriages of social justice, or structural problems that need remedying.

Merriam-Webster defines "woke" as an adjective meaning "aware of and actively attentive to important facts and issues (especially issues of racial and social justice)."[51] Woke first reached mainstream popularity when the Black Lives Matter movement used the hashtag #staywoke following the murder of Michael Brown in Ferguson, Missouri, by police in 2014. Today, the term also carries with it implications of activism, where it includes not only becoming more aware of injustice or social tensions but also being called to action, where people should take steps to remedy problems—that is, it is a form of informal social control to hold someone accountable for their words or behavior on a particular issue or topic.

Like critical race theory, woke culture, discussed earlier in the chapter, has become weaponized as a rallying point for political and social conflict because holding someone accountable for their words or deeds has taken an extreme viewpoint, where people are vilified and despised for seemingly any type of transgression or mistake. These calls against political correctness lie at the heart of the populist movement, which endorses the notion that "woke" people are extremists and their voices need to be quelled.[52]

Of course, these are overly simplistic and distorted versions of what the concept represents or how it is used. Yet, for a large segment of the population, such extremist positions seem to be a reasonable response, particularly for those who understand the process of becoming woke in a pejorative sense—that is, as a process that threatens the "unwoke" way of life. There is nothing wrong with people waking up to the issues and challenges we face in this country, but with that awareness comes a responsibility to identify and address the issues in a thoughtful and reasonable way. For many Americans, such responsibility is replaced with angry rhetoric, which reinforces the narrative of those who foment hate and distracts us all from productively addressing the issues of importance.

In the end, the reason we see the rise in the popularity of Trumpsters, particularly on such a wide scale, is that we are arrogant in our ethnocentric beliefs about the superiority of the groups we belong to and we are imposing a form of self-isolation on one another, despite the fact that we are hardwired for social connection. The tendency toward ethnocentrism and isolation is both a cause and a consequence of heightened levels of fear and anger, encouraged by people and groups who stand to gain from the distraction that these emotions generate.

Our misguided sense of loyalty toward our tribes provides a backstop against accountability for leaders who misinform, misdirect, and distort the truth and allows us to disconnect from our common sense about people, events, and issues. The reason for this is likely that we are afraid of what we might learn about ourselves if we took the time to recognize that much of what we are afraid of and angry about has been fabricated, and we are too lazy to give it much thought.

Many of the problems and issues in this country are complex and the answers are not readily apparent, but the solutions require a willingness to compromise, to consider alternative views as legitimate, and to be willing to extend grace when it is warranted. Regrettably, many Americans prefer to vilify and demonize others rather than "own" our historical and current mistakes. In the end, we have more in common with each other than actual differences, but we allow our insecurities to drive much of our thinking and actions.

Chapter 8

Epilogue

As the 2022 midterm elections loomed, many observers predicted that the Democrats could lose their majority in both the House and the Senate, in part because of historical trends but also due to the state of the economy, with high inflation and rising gas prices on the minds of many voters as they headed to the polling booth. With a mandate to complete its work by the end of 2022, the January 6 committee on the violence at the US Capitol continued to interview witnesses, subpoena and collect documents, and make referrals to the US Department of Justice (DOJ) for contempt of Congress violations by Trump supporters who refused to cooperate.

In April 2022, subpoenas were issued to several Republican members of Congress, including House Minority Leader Kevin McCarthy and judiciary committee chairman Jim Jordan, along with House Republicans Andy Biggs, Scott Perry, and Mo Brooks. The subpoenas came after these leaders refused to voluntarily cooperate with the committee, and they have detailed knowledge of the events surrounding the insurrection at the US Capitol along with having communication with Trump before, during, and after the events on January 6, 2021.[1]

It is expected that all of the subpoenas will be ignored, forcing the committee to recommend contempt of Congress charges to the DOJ. In an extraordinary move, in October 2022, at the conclusion of one of its last public hearings, the committee voted unanimously to subpoena former president Trump to produce documents and appear before the committee to answer questions about his involvement in the events leading up to and including the violence at the US Capitol.[2] While Trump's attorneys accepted the subpoena, the committee, recognizing the end of its charter with the Republican takeover of the House at the end of 2022, withdrew its demand that Trump testify.

This chapter offers an update on the findings by the congressional committee, as well as other related events involving Trump's actions, such as the withholding and concealing of classified documents at his home at the Mar-a-Lago resort in Florida. This chapter will also offer insight into the implications of this case, with most observers concluding that a criminal indictment of Trump is inevitable. Given his actions in the documents case as well as the events on January 6, it is worth considering the potential consequences for Trump (and the rest of the country) should the DOJ decide to prosecute him. This chapter concludes with some observations about the future of Trumpism and how Trump supporters continue to have a cultural, social, and political influence on the United States regardless of whether or not Trump decides to seek re-election in 2024.

UPDATE ON THE JANUARY 6 COMMITTEE

As the committee continued to collect evidence from testimony and other documents in early 2022 there remained questions about whether or not Trump, as president, committed criminal acts in his efforts to overturn the 2020 election. The committee members believe they obtained sufficient evidence that Trump might have committed multiple felonies and sought a ruling on the evidence at the time from a federal judge.[3]

In March 2022, a federal judge ruled that Trump "more likely than not" committed a felony by trying to pressure his vice president to obstruct Congress and overturn the election loss. Judge David Carter said that Trump's alleged plan to overturn his defeat to President Joe Biden amounted to a "coup." Carter also said that "the Court finds it more likely than not that President Trump corruptly attempted to obstruct the Joint Session of Congress on January 6, 2021," and that "the illegality of the plan was obvious."[4]

The judge also ruled that the congressional committee had the right to review emails written to Trump by John Eastman, who was serving as one of Trump's attorneys at the time. Eastman attempted to prevent the review of some emails he sent to Trump, claiming attorney-client privilege. However, the judge ruled that because Eastman was actively involved in the planning of a crime, the attorney-client privilege did not apply. In his ruling, the judge also stated: "Dr. Eastman and President Trump launched a campaign to overturn a democratic election, an action unprecedented in American history. Their campaign was not confined to the ivory tower—it was a coup in search of a legal theory."[5]

More damning evidence emerged in late April 2022 as text messages from House Minority Leader McCarthy, as well as those from Republicans in the House and Senate, suggest that a far more elaborate plot had been developed to overturn the election than what had previously been thought. While McCarthy and others have denied their involvement in or knowledge of the events surrounding the January 6 violence, in their 2022 book, *This Will Not Pass: Trump, Biden, and the Battle for America's Future*, Jonathan Martin and Alexander Burns provide evidence in the form of audiotapes and texts that directly contradict these denials. It also elevates the concerns about what former president Trump as well as members of his inner circle knew, planned, and participated in before, during, and after the violence at the Capitol.[6]

In an extraordinary moment, Jamie Raskin, a Democratic member of the House committee on the events at the US Capitol, recounts events during the violence when Secret Service agents attempted to remove former vice president Pence from the Capitol. After being secured in a portion of the Capitol during the riot, Pence's Secret Service agents, whom Raskin suspected were working in collaboration with Trump's team, asked him to enter an armored limousine, ostensibly to take him to safety. However, others suspect that the real motive was to take Pence away from the building and thereby prevent him from certifying the election results, particularly after Pence stated he was unwilling to violate his oath of office to keep Trump in power.[7]

Raskin argues that Pence knew that leaving the building was part of a larger plot to overthrow the results. "[Pence] uttered what I think are the six most chilling words of this entire thing I've seen so far: 'I'm not getting in that car,'" Raskin said. "He knew exactly what this inside coup they had planned for was going to do."[8] This information came as part of an interview for a book by Philip Rucker and Carol Leonnig titled *I Alone Can Fix It: Donald J. Trump's Catastrophic Final Year* (2021). According to Tim Giebels, the lead agent of Pence's security team on January 6, Pence repeatedly refused to be evacuated from the Capitol until the election results were certified. Pence is reported to have said to Giebels: "I'm not getting in the car, Tim. I trust you, Tim, but you're not driving the car. If I get in that vehicle, you guys are taking off. I'm not getting in the car."[9] Such extraordinary stories not only seem larger than fiction, but they call attention to just how close this country came to experiencing a coup.

Perhaps the most dramatic testimony offered about Trump's role in the January 6 violence came from an aide to Chief of Staff Mark Meadows, Cassidy Hutchinson. During the summer of 2022, Hutchinson, who gave four closed-door depositions, revealed how Trump and his closest advisors were warned about the potential for violence prior to January 6 and that Trump tried desperately to be a part of the US Capitol events. This testimony continues to underscore the narrative that Trump incited and supported the insurrection as part of an attempt to steal a second presidential term. It also highlighted the fact that many of his top advisors believe his efforts to do so were illegal.[10]

For instance, Hutchinson told the committee that Trump was aware that supporters were bringing weapons to the rally on January 6 and that, when the weapons were being confiscated, Trump told staffers to remove the metal detectors at the Ellipse, where the rally was being held. This is telling because after the rally, where Trump urged his supporters to march to the Capitol, he knew or suspected they were armed. Later it was confirmed that many of the rioters had various weapons when they stormed the building.[11]

Hutchinson also testified that people around Trump had advance knowledge of this plan to march with supporters to the Capitol. She informed the committee that Trump lawyer Rudy Giuliani told her on January 2 that Trump was planning to go to the Capitol. Hutchinson also testified that she heard a secondhand account of how Trump was so enraged at his Secret Service detail for blocking him from going to the Capitol on January 6 that he lunged to the front of his presidential limo and tried to turn the wheel. She testified that Tony Ornato, the White House deputy chief of staff at the time, said that Robert Engel, who was the Secret Service agent in charge on January 6, repeatedly told Trump on their way back to the White House after Trump's Ellipse speech that it wasn't safe to go to the Capitol.[12]

According to Hutchinson, Ornato recounted Trump screaming, "I'm the f**king President. Take me up to the Capitol now." Trump then "reached up toward the front of the vehicle to grab at the steering wheel," Hutchinson stated. She added that, according to Ornato, Trump used his other hand to "lunge" at Engel.[13] Ornato and others have argued that Hutchinson's story is inaccurate and they are currently testifying before the committee.[14]

In October 2022, at the conclusion of its last public hearing on the matter, given all that has been learned about the events before, during, and after the January 6 violence, and given the nearly overwhelming evidence of Trump's knowledge about the events, as well as his potential participation in the events leading up to the attack on the US Capitol, the committee voted unanimously to subpoena Trump to produce documents related to the events and to appear before the committee to answer questions.[15]

TRUMP AND WITHHOLDING SENSITIVE
DOCUMENTS AT MAR-A-LAGO

As with much of Trump's behavior, many of his actions are not surprising if one considers his general approach to being president of the United States. While experts offered commentary on his motives, the allegations surrounding Trump illegally retaining and concealing sensitive government documents, even those that put the country's national security at risk, are not that surprising. This is especially true given that Trump has not been held accountable for much of his behavior. Still, the implications of Trump's actions in this instance have had a rather chilling effect on members of the intelligence community.

While this case began shortly after Trump left the White House, the issues surrounding Trump's actions culminated in August 2022 when the FBI raided Trump's property at the Mar-a-Lago resort in Florida. Critics, including Trump himself, called the raid politically motivated, while Trump made baseless claims that the FBI planted evidence of wrongdoing.[16] However, as the case continues to unfold, it is becoming more apparent that Trump's general dismissive approach to sensitive government documents as president carried over into his actions after he left the White House—and he may have committed several crimes in the process.

As others have noted, Trump's handling of classified information as president drew significant attention and concern from federal intelligence officials. In fact, his dismissive approach to the security of information created a climate of mistrust from law enforcement and intelligence agencies about Trump's inability to protect national secrets.[17] These concerns were underscored in 2019 when Trump showed journalist Bob Woodward letters that North Korean dictator Kim Jong-un had written to him, documents he knew were classified.[18]

In addition, it was commonly known among Trump's advisors that he regularly shredded sensitive documents while at the White House, at his Mar-a-Lago resort, and even aboard Air Force One. This was true despite repeated attempts by his chiefs of staff, White House counsel, and other aides to refrain from doing so. Trump's aides routinely attempted to piece together torn documents, and on at least two occasions, Trump was said to have flushed shredded documents down the toilet inside the White House.[19]

So alarming was Trump's behavior regarding classified information that, upon his election to the White House, President Joe Biden barred Trump from receiving the courtesy intelligence briefings traditionally given to former presidents, citing Trump's "erratic behavior." This is the first time a former president's access to classified briefings has been denied.[20]

Background to the Case

Months after leaving the White House, the National Archives and Records Administration (NARA), the federal agency that preserves governmental records and presidential files, realized they were missing documents that Trump should have handed over to them once his presidency ended. Specifically, NARA did not have the correspondence sent from North Korean leader Kim Jong-un and other documents, such as the famously altered Hurricane Dorian map, which Trump modified with a black Sharpie pen to show that the hurricane's path was inaccurate. As per normal protocol, NARA contacted Trump's representatives for the missing information.[21] In May 2021, NARA emailed Trump's lawyers again with the request for their "immediate assistance" to return the Kim letters, along with multiple files in numerous boxes that were in Trump's White House residence during the final days of his presidency. Instead of being sent to NARA, these boxes were sent to Mar-a-Lago.[22]

In June 2021, NARA again instructed a former lawyer in Trump's White House counsel's office to send them the Kim letters.[23] In January 2022, NARA received fifteen boxes of documents, gifts, and other government property from Mar-a-Lago that should have been transferred to NARA during the administration transition.[24] The boxes included documents from the CIA, the FBI, and the National Security Agency on a variety of topics of national security interest. Archivists and federal agents determined that 184 unique documents (totaling seven hundred pages) had classification markings, of which twenty-five documents were marked "top secret," ninety-two "secret," and sixty-seven were identified as "confidential."[25]

In an extraordinary moment, Trump dictated a statement, which he wanted to be released and sent to NARA, stating that everything requested by NARA had been returned. One of Trump's attorneys declined because he was not sure all requested material had been returned. In place of Trump's statement, a different one was released three days later, saying that "[t]he papers were given easily and without conflict and on a very friendly basis."[26]

In February 2022, because they did not believe all the documents had been returned, NARA sent a criminal referral to the DOJ. Following an initial review, in April 2022, the DOJ opened a criminal investigation and initiated a grand jury process.[27] The FBI interviewed Trump administration officials and aides at Mar-a-Lago about the handling of presidential records, including former White House Counsel Pat Cipollone and his former deputy, Patrick Philbin.[28]

During this time, NARA said it would let the FBI access the documents retrieved from Mar-a-Lago. Trump's lawyers continued to delay the retrieval of the documents, citing executive privilege. In May 2022, the acting archivist of the United States wrote a letter to Trump's attorney, M. Evan Corcoran, to reiterate that Trump had taken hundreds of pages of classified materials with him, including highly classified materials, and that their extended negotiations over alleged executive privilege was delaying investigations and threat assessments already underway. As a result, further requests for delays by Trump officials would not be accepted.[29] As part of the assessment of the risks resulting from the missing information, the FBI collaborated with intelligence agencies to determine if the missing information created any risks to the nation or intelligence personnel.[30]

As far back as May 2021, the DOJ subpoenaed Trump for all documents in his custody bearing any classification markings. Trump's advisers repeatedly urged him to fully comply with the subpoena, despite his desire to retain possession of some documents. Trump told his advisers that he had returned all government records.[31] After the subpoena was issued, Walt Nauta, who served as a White House valet and personal aide to Trump at Mar-a-Lago, was recorded on Mar-a-Lago security cameras moving boxes from a storage room at the resort to Trump's private residence, claiming it was at Trump's request.[32]

In early June 2021, investigators from the DOJ and the FBI met with Trump's attorneys at Mar-a-Lago about the classified material that was subpoenaed on May 11. In that meeting, a Trump lawyer gave the agents thirty-eight classified documents with specific sensitivity markings in "a single Redweld envelope, double-wrapped in tape."[33] During this visit, FBI agents noticed more than fifty boxes in the storage room designated for sensitive information, but were prohibited from looking inside them. With the help of an informant, the DOJ came to believe that more classified documents remained on the premises. The culmination of these events led the DOJ to seek a search warrant for the materials.[34]

The search warrant showed that the FBI was investigating Trump for suspected violations of a portion of the Espionage Act of 1917 and the Sarbanes-Oxley Act. In general, the Espionage Act of 1917 makes it a crime for anyone who engages in the unauthorized retention or disclosure of documents related to national defense, which could be used to harm the United States. The maximum penalty is ten years in prison.[35]

As part of the Sarbanes-Oxley Act, destroying or concealing documents or records, regardless of their relevance to national security, "with the intent to impede, obstruct or influence the investigation or proper administration of any matter" within the jurisdiction of any federal department or agency is a criminal offense, with a maximum penalty of twenty years in prison. This would likely address Trump's attempt to prevent NARA from recovering the documents as well as hide them from the FBI.[36]

There is another section of federal law, Section 2071 of Title 18, that makes it a crime to steal or destroy government documents, which also has a maximum penalty of ten years in prison. Ostensibly, this federal law would target the allegations that Trump flushed government documents down the toilet or shredded them. It would also include the intentional effort of keeping documents that belonged to the government and NARA.[37]

Federal Judge Bruce Reinhart of the US District Court for the Southern District of Florida approved the warrant on August 5, 2022. On August 8, 2022, FBI agents searched Trump's residence at Mar-a-Lago for the material specified in the warrant, including classified material. FBI agents conducted the search using "taint teams," to ensure that no privileged correspondence between Trump and his lawyers was removed. They further searched what was called Trump's "45 Office," and Trump's residence. Classified documents were recovered from unsecured places in both locations and many were found outside of a locked storage room at Mar-a-Lago. The FBI then issued another subpoena for Mar-a-Lago surveillance video footage for the weeks leading up to the search, suggesting Trump might have additional government documents.[38]

In total, FBI agents have seized more than thirteen thousand government documents, 103 of which were classified. Documents and empty folders with classified markings were found both in the basement storage room and in Trump's 45 Office. Two weeks after the search, Trump filed a motion in the Southern District of Florida asking for the appointment of a special master to review all material seized, material not covered by the warrant, potentially privileged information under attorney-client confidentiality, or excluded under executive privilege. The case was assigned to District Judge Aileen Cannon, a Trump appointee.[39]

Judge Cannon asked the DOJ to provide the detailed property receipt Trump had requested as well as a status of any and all DOJ review of that material, including whether DOJ had filtered the documents for potentially privileged information. The Justice Department explained that the review of seized materials had already been completed and the FBI investigators had finished their examination of documents and could identify a small set of files that might fall under attorney-client privilege. The DOJ stated they were taking steps to resolve those questions.[40]

The DOJ also stated that the US intelligence agencies were engaged in a classification review and damage assessment of this information. The DOJ court filing also revealed that some of the recovered materials were so sensitive in nature that the FBI and DOJ personnel involved in reviewing the information needed additional security clearances to examine the documents.[41]

While Trump initially stated that he had declassified the documents—later boasting that he could do so simply by thinking about it[42]—the DOJ argued that neither his counsel nor custodian ever asserted that Trump declassified the documents or asserted executive privilege over them but, rather, that he actually treated them as if they were classified. The DOJ also highlighted the fact that Trump's lawyers prohibited federal officials from opening or examining any other boxes held in the storage room to confirm whether classified documents remained there. Though Trump's lawyers certified they had conducted a thorough search following the subpoena from May 11, the FBI's search and discovery of material on August 8 demonstrated that this was not the case.[43]

A related argument offered by the DOJ was that Trump lacked standing over presidential records since they are considered government property under the Presidential Records Act. They urged the judge to reject Trump's executive privilege claims, arguing that Trump cited no case in which executive privilege had been used to prohibit the sharing of documents by the government.[44] To underscore the extreme negligence with which these documents had been handled and stored, in their court filing, when they discovered the documents at Trump's residence, the DOJ attached a photo of a spread of classified documents laid out on the floor as evidence. Multiple red and yellow cover sheets bore classified markings of "Top Secret," "Secret," and "Sensitive Compartmented Information."[45]

In response, Trump's lawyers argued the discovery of the information was part of the very nature of presidential records and that the location where they were stored at Mar-a-Lago was a secure one. Trump's attorneys also argued that if NARA did not secure the cooperation necessary to retrieve the information from Trump, they should have asked for it again instead of referring the matter to the DOJ. Trump's attorneys also rejected the DOJ's assertion that it had screened out any attorney-client privileged records, arguing that their filter team had nearly complete discretion in addressing potential privilege disputes.[46]

Judge Cannon ordered the DOJ to halt its review of the materials while allowing the intelligence community to continue its assessment of the potential harm caused to national security. She granted Trump's request for a special master to review the seized documents for attorney-client and executive privilege and ordered the DOJ and Trump to file a joint list of candidates to serve in that role.[47]

Legal experts called the judgment deeply flawed and said it gave special treatment to Trump. Other experts said that the judge did not seem to understand the nature of executive privilege and that there was no basis for her to give a special master authority to review sensitive material that could be covered by executive privilege.[48] Others found contradictions in Cannon's ruling, questioning how the executive branch could use the files to assess the risk to national security but not as part of an active criminal investigation.[49]

In September 2022, Cannon appointed Raymond Dearie, a former federal judge with years of experience in handling sensitive documents and hearing cases involving intelligence topics, to the special master position and tasked him to review all documents seized in the Mar-a-Lago search. She upheld her initial ruling, refusing to grant the DOJ's request to allow them to again access the approximately one hundred documents bearing classification markings.[50]

In response, the DOJ appealed Cannon's ruling, and asked the Eleventh Circuit Court of Appeals to immediately allow the criminal investigation to proceed and grant them the right to resume review of the classified documents in question.[51] The DOJ also requested that classified documents be exempt from review by the special master and that Trump or his attorneys be given access to the documents since these individuals could potentially become witnesses to the events under investigation. The federal appeals court granted the DOJ's request, with the three-judge panel unanimously declaring it was in the public interest for the DOJ to determine if any of the records were handled in a way that threatened national security.[52]

In October 2022, Trump appealed to the US Supreme Court and asked it to vacate the Eleventh Circuit's decision that allowed the special master to review the classified documents seized at Mar-a-Lago, arguing that the appeals court had lacked jurisdiction to review it in the first place. On October 13, 2022, the Supreme Court denied Trump's request, without offering details.[53]

At the first hearing about the special master's review, Judge Dearie began the process of unpacking the disputes between the DOJ and Trump as well as to get both parties to articulate their reasoning for their respective positions. This included requiring Trump to decide if he was going to go on the record that he declassified documents before taking them to Mar-a-Lago. The special master also wanted clarity on the specifics of Trump's claims about the seized documents.

The DOJ was also instructed to submit electronic copies of all unclassified documents to both Dearie and the Trump legal team. Trump's team objected and Judge Cannon blocked several of Dearie's orders.[54] In response to Judge Cannon's restraint of Dearie's requests, the DOJ filed an appeal to eliminate the use of a special master in the case altogether. While the DOJ's initial appeal focused on the one hundred sensitive documents taken during the raid on Mar-a-Lago, Judge Cannon's rulings suggested to the DOJ that her involvement in the case from the outset was misguided and inappropriate.[55] The DOJ requested that the Eleventh Circuit Court of Appeals fast-track their request for review. In December 2022, the court ruled in favor of the DOJ request to remove the special master to oversee the seized documents. Trump appealed to the US Supreme Court, who supported the Appeals Court ruling that the judge in the case, Aileen Cannon, had overstepped her authority in authorizing a special master and prohibited the DOJ from examining the documents in question.[56]

With all of the disputes and motions filed in court, it is easy to lose track of what's actually happened in the case. The upshot is that Trump took sensitive documents, some of which had the highest security classifications, which are critical to the country's national security interests, and did not store them according to standard protocols that have been used by intelligence officials and former presidents.

Moreover, Trump's team continued to withhold this information despite repeated requests from NARA and a subpoena from the DOJ to comply with federal law. Not only was the keeping of these documents in violation of federal laws, regardless of whether they were declassified or not, but the extremely sensitive nature of this information and the circumspect security related to their storage, coupled with the willful disregard to comply with federal agencies, resulted in the only viable option: an FBI raid. That questions remain about whether Trump has continued to hide documents in other locations suggests an intentional disregard for the rule of law. As more evidence emerges about what happened and as information about Trump's actions has become clearer, most experts note that it is very likely Trump will be criminally indicted for his actions in this case.[57]

Such a decision is not one to be made lightly, as the criminal prosecution of a former president—whether because he withheld documents that belong to the government, he incited an insurrection at the US Capitol, or both—has a host of serious consequences. As more information continues to become available, it becomes increasingly disturbing to learn how elected political leaders could be so careless with the responsibilities of their oath of office and to their constituents. While the documents case is the latest in a long line of actions that should be alarming to the public, public opinion polls continue to show support for Trump, along with an overwhelming majority of members of the Republican Party.

SHOULD THE DOJ PROSECUTE TRUMP IF THE EVIDENCE SUPPORTS AN INDICTMENT?

The problem with the ruling that Trump more than likely committed felonies in his efforts to overturn the election are legal and political. From a legal standpoint, Judge Carter had a lower standard of proof to meet in rendering his decision—a preponderance of evidence is much easier to meet than proof beyond a reasonable doubt. This is important since, if prosecutors from the DOJ decide to bring criminal charges against Trump, they would have to prove intent and do so to a jury that requires a unanimous vote to convict. This does not mean they shouldn't consider bringing charges, but it does mean that there are many layers to consider in such a decision.

On one hand, there are those who argue that the government has no choice but to bring charges against Trump, particularly since there is ample evidence by Trump's words and actions that he knew what he was doing. As Atkins (2022) points out, the politics and challenges related to prosecuting Trump have been seen from his candidacy and throughout his presidency. Republicans have threatened repercussions if Democrats prosecute Trump, as it will be portrayed as a political act—putting future Democratic leaders in jeopardy of similar treatment.[58]

Given that Republicans have not been willing to hold Trump accountable for any of his actions, including the evidence and details surrounding his first impeachment trial, which seem clearer now that the war between Russia and Ukraine continues to escalate, one has to wonder if the initial accusations had merit. Reluctance from the GOP to hold Trump accountable was also seen during his second impeachment trial, where Republicans refused to convict Trump for his attempt to overturn the election that led to violence at the US Capitol. Had Republicans found Trump guilty, it would have prevented him from ever holding office again—yet, as they had throughout Trump's presidency, they chose political party over principle and refused to even censure him for his actions.

In the larger sense, though, there are philosophical reasons why prosecuting Trump is a complicated and serious issue. Most experts note that democracy can't survive if crimes go unpunished or if the public believes that leaders are above the law. More importantly, without any meaningful accountability, elected officials in the future are likely to commit far more serious acts in order to win elections and hold on to power, knowing that their opponents are unable to stop them.

Perhaps, as Atkins (2022) points out, there isn't sufficient evidence to prosecute Trump. However, there are reasons to consider that Trump has committed crimes for which he should be held accountable. There is some indication that Trump obstructed the Mueller investigation—more than one thousand former prosecutors signed a letter stating that if any other person acted as Trump did, he or she would be charged with obstructing justice and prosecuted. There also appears growing evidence that Trump interfered with the election and may even be guilty of conspiring to overthrow its results.[59]

Another consideration in prosecuting Trump is the potential outcome of doing so. Given his popularity, questions remain about whether a fair and impartial jury could ever be constructed and, if so, would they actually vote to convict him? Given that criminal trials require unanimous votes to convict, is it possible that jurors could impede the process, resulting in either a hung jury or an outright exoneration? This is particularly true given how frequently Trump has clung to the idea that he has been the victim of multiple political attacks in the form of "witch hunts" and other forms of persecution.

More disturbing would be the possibility of Trump being found not guilty; if that were to occur, it would be a clear message to the American people that there are different rules of accountability for leaders, which could have a devastating impact on people's trust in government and democracy. However, none of these reasons, as Atkins (2022) argues, justify not prosecuting Trump and/or members of his inner circle. To voluntarily avoid a trial, despite all the difficulties and challenges presented, would reward the very behavior the country is trying to avoid. Similarly, failing to prosecute Trump out of a fear of civil unrest is equally misguided. If the decision was made to not prosecute or if Trump was not convicted, would any reasonable person think that he (were he to be reelected) or any future leader would have any reason to be concerned about accountability?[60]

These difficult decisions come at a time when the DOJ, under Attorney General Merrick Garland, has had to reform the office, as many have perceived the DOJ as having been weaponized by Trump for his own political gain. From the outset of his time in office, Garland has pledged to be deliberate in his prosecution of those who were involved in the January 6 attacks on the US Capitol and to "do the right thing," which means "following the facts and the law wherever they may lead." This promise to restore the independence and reputation of the Justice Department has produced more than 925 people charged with a crime, including charges of seditious conspiracy against the leader of a far-right militia, with 417 pleading guilty.[61]

EFFORTS CONTINUE TO PROMOTE THE BIG LIE

Despite the lack of evidence about election fraud and the efforts of several Republican candidates, worried about the upcoming midterm elections in November 2022, to distance themselves from the "stolen" election claims, there remained a group of Trump supporters who continued to argue that not only was the election stolen from Trump but that there was a remedy to reinstate him as president. In fact, days before the 2022 midterm elections, approximately 60 percent of Republican candidates for governor, Congress, and other elected official positions, said they still believed the 2020 election was compromised.[62] In the aftermath of those elections, where Republicans expected a landslide victory in both the House and the Senate, voters clearly sent a message to Republican candidates about the credibility of such a position by giving a majority to Democrats in the Senate and only a very slim majority to Republicans in the House.

As Haberman, Berzon, and Schmidt (2022) point out, many states attempted to pass resolutions rescinding the Electoral College votes for President Biden as well as bring lawsuits in a continued effort to overturn the election. Legal experts noted, as with the claims of voter fraud, there was no basis to these claims and there was no plausible way, according to the Constitution, for Trump to be reinstated as president. The justification for the decertification efforts, led by John Eastman, a former law professor and attorney for Trump, was based on a fringe legal theory, one that has been criticized by legal experts, which contends that state lawmakers have the power to choose how electors are selected, and they can change them long after the Electoral College has certified votes if they find fraud and illegality sufficiently altered the outcome.[63]

Evidence of support for Eastman's claims were seen during fall 2021, where 186 state legislators from thirty-nine states signed a letter written by Wendy Rogers, a Republican state senator from Arizona, calling on "each state to decertify its electors where it has been shown the elections were certified prematurely and inaccurately."[64]

The real problem with these claims was not that they had any legal standing or even any reasonable chance of changing the 2020 election. Even among Trump's staunchest supporters, there was disagreement about whether such an approach was viable or an appropriate use of time, energy, and resources. Still, as Trump continued to claim election illegitimacy and maintained a vindictive response to those who disagreed with him, Republicans had to at least appear to agree with him. Rather, the real problem centered on how many Republican-controlled state legislatures were modifying the election protocols so that disputes in the future were more likely to be handled in a way that reflected favorably on Republican candidates.[65]

While some of these laws may be challenged in court, there is considerable concern that changes in the way voters are allowed to vote, discussed in the previous chapter, as well as allowing states to invalidate the votes if they are not favorable to Republican candidates, posed serious risks to people's trust in the entire process. That is, if people feel their votes don't matter or will not be accurately counted, they may fail to vote at all. The irony of this development should not be overlooked—many states are engaging in the construction of the very problem they are disputing: the widespread fraudulence and corruption of elections.

TRUMP IS FIRMLY IN CONTROL OF
THE REPUBLICAN PARTY

Whether one accepts the fact that the 2020 election was fair or not, the reality is that Trump is no longer president. While this may change if he decides to seek reelection in 2024 and actually wins, what is not in question is Trump's firm hold over control of the Republican Party.

As Smith (2022) points out, Republicans wanting to be elected realize that if they are to have any chance of success, either in the form of the party's nomination or the election, they will have to demonstrate loyalty to Trump. That situation has emerged largely because the Republican Party gave enormous and unfettered power to Trump in the first place. While the merits of such a decision can be debated at length, with many unanswered questions regarding the wisdom of such a decision, the reality is that Trump's hold on the party is extraordinary. If January 6 has shown us anything, it is that there is virtually nothing Trump can do to cause the party to rebel against him.[66]

This is true even in those moments when the violence at the Capitol and Trump's role in it caused some Republicans moral pause. Even after the moment of honesty and integrity, where Trump loyalists like Senator Lindsey Graham proclaimed, "Today, all I can say is: count me out. Enough is enough." Similarly, House Minority Leader Kevin McCarthy called on Trump to "accept his share of responsibility" for the violence at the Capitol. Calling Trump's actions on January 6 "atrocious and totally wrong" and saying that Trump "incited people" to attack the Capitol, McCarthy also stated to Republican leaders, "I've had it with this guy" and that Trump's remarks were "not right by any shape or any form."[67] After considering the use of the Twenty-Fifth Amendment, McCarthy told his colleagues on January 10 that he had personally recommended Trump resign before his term ended. McCarthy stated:

> What he did is unacceptable. Nobody can defend that and nobody should defend it, he told his fellow Republicans. Later McCarthy is quoted as saying: I mean, you guys all know him, too—do you think he'd ever back away? But what I think I'm going to do is I'm going to call him. . . . The only discussion I would have with him is that I think this [impeachment resolution] will pass and it would be my recommendation you should resign.[68]

However, when McConnell and McCarthy realized that the GOP was likely to continue supporting Trump despite the overwhelming evidence that he participated in one of the most extraordinary events in US history, they backpedaled, realigned their positions on Trump, and bent to his will. McConnell was recently quoted as saying, "I didn't get to be the leader of this party by siding with only 15 percent of the caucus." McConnell's position seems to be that were he not to side with the majority of Republicans, his ability to lead the party would be negated, regardless of his own feelings on Trump's actions. McCarthy, who aspired to be Speaker of the House should the Republicans take over the majority in the next election, made sure that he and Trump were on good terms after the statements from the audiotapes were revealed.[69]

If such realignment with Trump in the face of his party's support were not enough, recall that even as the events of January 6 were unfolding, 147 Republicans still voted to overturn the election results based on Trump's claims of fraud, a claim that no one really takes seriously. Add to this the unwillingness of Republicans to vote to convict him during the second impeachment trial, a vote in which only ten Republicans joined Democrats in the House and fell ten votes shy of the two-thirds majority in the Senate. Thus, it seems painfully obvious that Republicans are either afraid to disagree with Trump, or worse, actually believe the rhetoric he presents.[70]

Additionally, one must consider the fact that so many Republican-controlled state legislatures have changed voting laws that not only make it more difficult for people to cast their votes (affecting more people of color, who tend to lean and vote Democratic) as well as the appointment of election officials who will oversee the process of certification, which raises questions of whether or not Republicans are gaming the system in such a way to ensure future Republican candidates have a decided advantage, should there be any question about the outcome of the election. Part of the reason for all these efforts, critics claim, is that Republicans know that when the playing field is level and everybody can participate in the democratic process, they cannot win, so the only recourse is to obtain power by throwing out democratic norms and overthrowing elections, even if that means using instruments of violence, fear, and terror to do so.[71]

THE REPUBLICAN BACKPEDAL

As Republicans in Congress continue to criticize and oppose the congressional committee's investigation of the events leading up to and including the violence at the US Capitol, routinely arguing that the committee's work is partisan and political, that events have been overblown, and that participants were patriots protesting a great injustice, in late April 2022, explosive evidence was uncovered that raised a host of new questions about their own roles, as well as Trump's, in the attacks.

After a judge ruled that Mark Meadows, former White House chief of staff, was required to turn over 2,139 text messages to the committee, the evidence revealed startling and disturbing revelations about what happened prior to the end of the election and through the early days of the Biden administration.[72] It portrays accounts that Trump's inner circle were intentionally searching for ways to declare the election invalid or to circumvent the results to keep Trump in power.

In one of the texts, House Representative Marjorie Taylor Greene suggested to Meadows that some Republicans wanted Trump to declare martial law and invalidate the election. In April 2022, Greene stated under oath that she could not recall making such statements or texts, a claim that many of her Republican colleagues question. The texts also show that Greene was among several Republican members of Congress who attempted to get Trump to end the violence at the Capitol on January 6 despite the recent claims by Greene that the insurrection was little more than a demonstration by patriots and the violence has been overblown in scope.[73]

Another group of texts shows former secretary of energy Rick Perry and Donald Trump Jr. suggesting that the violence at the Capitol should be attributed to Antifa activists and that Trump should find ways to invalidate or overturn the election results. These texts also provide evidence of Meadows's role in coordinating efforts in several states to overturn the election results as well. What these disturbing texts reveal is not an ad hoc, unplanned, or spurious reaction to the outcome of the 2020 election but, rather, a much more sophisticated, thoughtful, and chilling effort to keep Trump in office.[74]

In addition to the text messages, a new book, complete with audiotape transcriptions of conversations between congressional leaders, sheds light on their initial and subsequent reactions and positions on the violence at the Capitol and the election. In their 2022 book, *This Will Not Pass: Trump, Biden, and the Battle for America's Future*, Alex Burns and Jonathan Martin point to private conversations congressional leaders had regarding Trump's role in the January 6 insurrection. The most damaging comments were made by House Minority Leader Kevin McCarthy, who stated he would recommend to Trump that he resign in the face of a second impeachment trial. Senate Majority Leader Mitch McConnell privately told colleagues that he felt there were enough GOP votes after the events on January 6 to impeach Trump.[75]

As McCarthy denied making these statements, claiming the story was "totally false and wrong," arguing he never advised Trump to resign, Burns and Martin offered audiotaped evidence that McCarthy lied to the public about his role in the insurrection as well as about the conversations he had with and about Trump. While the explosive nature of these tapes should raise important questions about what congressional leaders knew, felt, and said during the aftermath of the January 6 events as well as the legitimacy of the "Big Lie" as a strategy to keep Republicans in power, many observers note that these inconsistencies are part of a new normal, where lies, misinformation, distortions, and deceptions are simply a part of politics-as-usual in today's government.

In fact, there are some observers who wonder if the findings of the congressional committee and the damning evidence of Trump's role and that of his followers in the events will move the needle of public opinion sufficiently to garner meaningful accountability of those involved. This is a lamentable prediction, but it is not without any basis. It may very well be that the public, distracted by high inflation, rising gas prices, mass shootings, and other matters, may simply ignore or minimize these developments despite the seriousness of what Trump's administration attempted to do (and will likely try to do again in the future).

For some, it may be that they have made up their minds about who Trump is and what he is about, and have little concern about the impact his actions have on the country. For others, the outrage may be short-lived and still not sufficient enough to change their vote or to demand any meaningful responsibility from those involved. They may not realize the impact of what's happening because they have so bought into the rhetoric and Trump's narrative that they can't conceptualize the possibility that he may not be telling them all that is going on—they are so focused on their own fears and anger about certain people and certain topics that they ignore the truth. As the old African proverb states, "The sheep will spend its entire life fearing the wolf, only to be eaten by the shepherd."

LESSONS LEARNED FROM THE TRUMP PRESIDENCY

What did a Trump presidency teach us? What does the visible and vocal presence of Trumpsters, who comprise millions of voters, who seem less concerned with the methods used by Republicans to lie, cheat, and steal crucial elements of a democracy in order to retain power, tell us about the future of democracy in this country? What do we learn from the increased division and polarization that seems to be a visible and concerning feature of American culture? It is easy to dismiss Trumpsters as extremists or as uneducated, backward-thinking people who are simply afraid of losing their dominant position in society. This was part of the discussion in chapter 7 and should be a part of any thoughtful understanding of how and why people have pursued Trumpism in all its forms. Fear is a powerful motivator and most people will do almost anything to anyone in order to avoid being afraid.

As pointed out by Sandel (2018), part of the challenge is to reconsider how and why Trump's brand of politics has become such a popular position for many people in the United States and why the counterarguments by Democrats continue to fail. It is a mistake to think of Trump's election in 2016 as an aberration or an unlikely event in American politics. Trump's rise to power comes at a time when many people are angry and afraid about their lives and have an increasingly common perception that the government, the economy, and the culture have ignored and failed them.

The rise of Trumpism may be more than people's propensity for ethnocentrism, more than a mere tendency toward entitlement, more than a protest against globalization and technological advances. Sandel (2018) argues that what we are seeing in the rise of right-wing extremism is a symptom of a much larger problem—the failure of progressive politics to understand the needs of everyday people. The Democratic Party, he argues, has become more focused on issues relating to the elite than the working classes. Starting in the 1990s, when the Clinton administration began to align with Republicans on globalization and deregulation of certain industries, with a goal of stimulating the economy, the result was a far more damaging increase in inequality among people.[76]

Even President Obama, who erected a campaign on the moral and spiritual purpose of the party, found himself as a newly elected president in the dilemma of appeasing the corporate elite through a financial crisis that was years in the making. He bailed out the banks in an effort to restore the economy with measures that held none of them accountable for the behavior that led to the problem in the first place and he did not offer help to the ordinary Americans who lost their homes and faced financial ruin. It was this approach that fueled the anger toward corporate greed, as evidenced by the Occupy movement and the popularity of Bernie Sanders on one hand, and the rise of the Tea Party and leaders like Newt Gingrich and eventually Donald Trump on the other.[77]

The problem isn't just about jobs or racism or xenophobic tendencies of one group or the other. The problem is also recognizing that people are angry because they have not been heard on the things that matter most to them. For example, the typical response to inequality is to raise the issue of equality of opportunity. It is based on the idea that those who work hard should be able to go as far as their talents will take them. Culturally, the idea of upward mobility is part of what makes the United States so special.

However, it has never really been the case that upward mobility occurs on a grand scale and that possibility for most people has become more difficult than ever before, making people doubt if moving up is really possible. Americans born to poor parents tend to stay poor as adults and it is now easier to rise out of poverty in countries other than the United States (Sandel 2018). Adding to this is the idea that there is a growing perception that hard work and talent isn't enough; that those people who have those traits and still don't succeed begin to believe that the system is rigged and the people at the top cheated to get there.[78]

This comes at a time when the dignity of work is threatened through the loss of jobs due to technological advances and outsourcing. The development of artificial intelligence and robotics will allow machines to perform much of the work currently performed by humans. At the same time that the number of jobs for those in the working classes continue to shrink, those at the top benefit from huge bonuses, salaries, and severance packages and serve as reminders that the chances of success for most people continues to decline. Many Democrats have responded to the loss of jobs and even the dignity of work with proposals of universal or basic income. Such ideas may appear to be reasonable and even viable options, but at the same time it fuels populist anger because it sounds like a handout, not a solution.[79]

In addition, while free trade agreements and immigration are presented as a threat to local jobs and wages, these are not the core issues for most people. What many observers note is that, for most people, these discussions seem to convey the idea that the country cares more about cheap products and cheap labor than its citizens, a sentiment that makes them feel betrayed by the government and corporate America. The result is a strong and ugly backlash against immigrants and a dedicated and intense focus on nationalism and, as discussed in previous chapters, a need to "take back" what is rightfully theirs.[80]

Sandel (2018) argues that it is a mistake to ignore these feelings of betrayal, identity, and purpose and to instead focus only on issues of fairness. What makes Trump and Trumpism so popular is that it not only calls attention to these emotions, the message Trump continued to promote was that he was the protector of the people—the little guys who were losing a battle against the elite. Forgetting for the moment that many of his decisions would have actually hurt more people than helped—or that they occurred as a result of legislation from a Republican-controlled Congress—to most people, that matters less than the belief that there was someone fighting for them.[81]

This is why Trump has so many followers and believers—who think he understands them and their concerns. What we see in Trump supporters, then, is a group of people who likely view liberals, Democrats, and progressives as completely out of touch with what most people need or are concerned about. This means that Trumpsters aren't a group that is going away anytime soon; if anything, as more people become affected by these changes and become more disenchanted with their lives, they may become more amenable to Trump's messages and begin to accept the rhetoric. Equally dangerous is ignoring or minimizing Trumpsters as a small minority of people who hold extremist views: a failure to recognize this group as a determined and viable influence in American politics only provides more space for more authoritarian and angry messages from them.

****

In the end we have to make something of the Trump presidency, his actions, particularly as they relate to the 2020 election and its aftermath. We also need to offer some observations about the reactions and responses by Trumpsters, including members of the Republican Party, who seem determined to continue to embrace the trends that began in 2016 with Trump's candidacy. Despite all the rhetoric and posturing by those who have been and are being implicated in the efforts to overturn the election, as well as the recognition of those who participated in some way in the violence at the US Capitol in 2021, on balance it seems reasonable to conclude that they were involved, they were intentional about their efforts on a much wider scale than anyone imagined, and it almost worked.

Whether or not the Justice Department decides to prosecute Trump or anyone inside his circle of influence for attempting to interfere with the election certification, the fact remains that they tried to overthrow a legitimate election. Regardless of the claims that there was widespread fraud or nefarious activity that would question the results, something no investigative agency or court has found evidence to support, the reality is these people knew what they were doing. The recent audiotapes, along with the text messages from the Burns and Martin (2022) book, testimonies from witnesses, and other evidence demonstrate that many in the Republican Party and Trump's inner circle tried to play fast and loose with the rules in the hopes of staying in office.

In the final analysis, we also need to offer some sort of concluding commentary on Trumpsters and why they continue to cling to misinformation, espouse conspiracy theories, and remain loyal to the former president and his narrative despite more than enough evidence to convince them otherwise. One can only imagine their reaction were a president or candidate from another party to have engaged in similar conduct—would there be any need for arm-twisting to convince them this person should be held accountable?

More importantly, as was discussed in chapter 7, the reasons for such divisions and polarization are likely related to fear—but what is missing from that analysis is the reason for the fear. Yes, some people are dissatisfied and are not getting what they want out of life, but that isn't because democracy isn't working. Perhaps the anger, bitterness, resentment, hatred, and division that we see is, as Nichols (2021) points out, because we have turned into selfish, entitled, self-centered, spoiled children who think that the world and the government should focus on meeting our every need and desire. Failing that, we feel entitled to engage in escalated and violent temper tantrums about how we are being slighted and our country is in danger of falling apart.[82]

Is it really the case that Americans have become so self-absorbed and shallow that we do not feel any measure of responsibility for others or for the greater good? There have been moments in the past when Americans have risen to the occasion of doing what's right, what's good for the country, and putting our individual needs aside. Examples include the country's response to the attack on Pearl Harbor during World War II or the sense of compassion for fellow Americans and first responders in the aftermath of the 9/11 tragedy. We have recognized the need to help the less fortunate during natural disasters, both at home and abroad, and our level of compassion has been a beacon for others who see the United States as a world leader and example of what could happen if we allow ourselves the space and willingness to understand, sympathize, and empathize with others.

Unfortunately, lately those sentiments and sense of responsibility toward the greater good seem to have been replaced with a fiery and intolerant embracing of selfishness and victimhood, and the suspension of common sense and good judgment. As Nichols (2021) points out, good people can become poor citizens, and when they are afraid, those same people can do terrible things to each other. This is particularly true when political leaders attempt to exploit and capitalize on those vulnerabilities and construct narratives that massage those fears. It should not be surprising, then, to see how easily we become discouraged and disappointed in our friends, neighbors, family, and leaders who don't see the world the same way.[83]

American culture has always placed an emphasis on individualism, freedom, and autonomy, but it has also promoted the idea of kindness, compassion, integrity, and trustworthiness. Regrettably, today it seems that many people equate kindness with weakness, think that compassion and concern for others is for suckers, and that cheating, lying, and stealing to get what you want is rewarded and valued. Ultimately, we are responsible for our actions, and we will pay a steep price for our insecurities. And while we might try to assign blame to Democrats or Republicans, or Fox News or CNN, we will have no one to blame for what we have constructed but ourselves. As was mentioned in the previous chapter, in the end, we get the kinds of politicians, mass media sources, leaders, and society we deserve.

Notes

CHAPTER 1

1. Rybicki, Elizabeth, and Whitaker, L. Paige. (2020). "Counting Electoral Votes: An Overview of Procedures at the Joint Session, Including Objections by Members of Congress." Congressional Research Service. Available at: https://sgp.fas.org/crs/misc/RL32717.pdf.

2. Ibid.

3. Ibid.

4. Ibid.

5. Ibid.

6. Ibid.

7. Ibid.

8. Kiely, Eugene, and Rieder, Rem. (2020). "Trump's Repeated False Attacks on Mail-in Ballots." Factcheck.org, September 25. Available at: https://www.factcheck.org/2020/09/trumps-repeated-false-attacks-on-mail-in-ballots/.

9. Yen, Hope; Swenson, Ali; and Seitz, Amanda. (2020). "AP Fact Check: Trump's Claims of Voter Rigging Are All Wrong." Associated Press, December 3. Available at: https://apnews.com/article/election-2020-ap-fact-check-joe-biden-donald-trump-technology-49a24edd6d10888dbad61689c24b05a5.

10. Yen, Swenson, and Seitz (2020).

11. Ibid.

12. Ibid.

13. Ibid.

14. Ibid.

15. Ibid.

16. Ibid.

17. Kiely and Rieder (2020).

18. Riccardi, Nicholas. (2020). "Here's the Reality Behind Trump's Claims About Mail Voting." Associated Press, September 30. Available at: https://apnews.com/article/virus-outbreak-joe-biden-election-2020-donald-trump-elections-3e8170c3348ce3719d4bc7182146b582.

19. Ibid.

20. Kiely and Rieder (2020).

21. Ibid.

22. Ibid.

23. Ibid.

24. Ibid.

25. Ibid.

26. Ibid.

27. Ibid.

28. Cummings, William; Garrison, Joey; and Sargent, Jim. (2021). "By the Numbers: President Donald Trump's Failed Efforts to Overturn the Election." *USA Today*, January 6. Available at: https://www.usatoday.com/in-depth/news/politics/elections/2021/01/06/trumps-failed-efforts-overturn-election-numbers/4130307001/.

29. Ibid.

30. A Pennsylvania judge ruled that Pennsylvania voters could not go back and "cure" their ballots if they failed to provide proper identification three days after the election. This was a minor procedural point and had no real impact on the outcome of voting for the state (Cummings, Garrison, and Sargent, 2021).

31. Ibid.

32. Ibid.

33. Shear, Michael D., and Saul, Stephanie. (2021). "Trump, in Taped Call, Pressured Georgia Official to 'Find' Votes to Overturn Election." *New York Times*, January 3. Available at: https://www.nytimes.com/2021/01/03/us/politics/trump-raffensperger-call-georgia.html.

34. Ibid.

35. Ibid.

36. Cummings, Garrison, and Sargent (2021).

37. Ibid.

38. Ibid.

39. Balsamo, Michael. (2020). "Attorney General Bill Barr Says No Evidence of Widespread Fraud in 2020 Election." Fox 13 Tampa Bay, December 1. Available at: https://www.fox13news.com/news/barr-no-evidence-of-fraud-thatd-change-election-outcome.

40. Karl, Jonathan. (2021). "Inside Bill Barr's Breakup With Trump." *The Atlantic*, June 27. Available at: https://www.theatlantic.com/politics/archive/2021/06/william-barrs-trump-administration-attorney-general/619298/.

41. Tan, Shelly; Shin, Youjin; and Danielle Rindler. (2021). "How One of America's Ugliest Days Unraveled Inside and Outside the Capitol." *Washington Post*, January 9. Available at: https://www.washingtonpost.com/nation/interactive/2021/capitol-insurrection-visual-timeline/.

42. Ibid.

43. Ibid.

44. In August 2021, the officer responsible for shooting Babbitt, Lt. Byrd, was cleared of any wrongdoing. The officer stated in an interview that he and other members of Congress were trapped and yelled repeatedly for the rioters to get back. As the mob broke through, Byrd fired a single shot, killing Babbitt. "I know that day

I saved countless lives," Byrd said. "I know members of Congress, as well as my fellow officers and staff, were in jeopardy and in serious danger. And that's my job" (Long and Balsamo, 2021).

45. Turner-Cohen, Alex. (2021). "Capitol Riot Mob Wanted to Kill Mike Pence and Run Pelosi Over with a Car." News.com, January 11. Available at: https://www.news.com.au/world/north-america/us-politics/us-capitol-riot-mob-wanted-to-kill-mike-pence-run-pelosi-over-with-a-car/news-story/ab3277f484a9d04c162dc1c985aa4edc.

46. Schmidt, Michael S., and Broadwater, Luke. (2021). "Officers' Injuries, Including Concussions, Show Scope of Violence at Capitol Riot." *New York Times*, July 11. Available at: https://www.nytimes.com/2021/02/11/us/politics/capitol-riot-police-officer-injuries.html.

47. Ibid.

48. Ibid.

49. Ibid.

50. Ibid.

51. Ibid.

52. Quoted in Tan, Shin, and Rindler (2021).

53. Castronuovo, Celine. (2021). "Capitol Police Told Not to Use Most Aggressive Tactics in Riot Response, Report Finds." *The Hill*, April 13. Available at: https://thehill.com/policy/national-security/548104-capitol-police-told-not-to-use-most-aggressive-tactics-in-riot-response.

54. Dilanian, Ken; Winter, Tom; Dienst, Jonathan; and Blankstein, Andrew. (2021). "FBI, NYPD Told Capitol Police about Possibility of Violence Before Riot, Senior Officials Say." NBC News, January 10. Available at: https://www.nbcnews.com/news/crime-courts/fbi-nypd-told-capitol-police-about-possibility-violence-riot-senior-n1253646.

55. Ibid.

56. Ibid.

57. Tan, Shin, and Rindler (2021).

58. Ibid.

59. Ibid.

60. Ibid.

61. Ibid.

62. Ibid.

63. Chappell, Bill. (2021). "Architect of the Capitol Outlines $30 Million in Damages From Pro-Trump Riot." NPR, February 24. Available at: https://www.npr.org/sections/insurrection-at-the-capitol/2021/02/24/970977612/architect-of-the-capitol-outlines-30-million-in-damages-from-pro-trump-riot.

64. Cai, Weiyi. (2021). "A Step-by-Step Guide to the Second Impeachment Trial of Donald J. Trump." *New York Times*, February 13. Available at: https://www.nytimes.com/interactive/2021/02/08/us/politics/trump-second-impeachment-timeline.html.

65. Ibid.

66. Ibid.

67. Foran, Claire. (2021). "GOP Sen. Collins: Trump Incited an Insurrection to Prevent Peaceful Transfer of Authority." CNN, February 13. Available at: https://edition.cnn.com/politics/live-news/trump-impeachment-trial-02-13-2021/index.html.

68. Vogt, Adrienne. (2021). "McConnell: Trump Is Practically and Morally Responsible for Provoking Capitol Riot." CNN, February 13. Available at: https://edition.cnn.com/politics/live-news/trump-impeachment-trial-02-13-2021/index.html.

69. Jenkins, Brian. (2021). "Why We Need a January 6 Commission to Investigate the Attack on the Capitol." Rand Corporation, January 20. Available at: https://www.rand.org/blog/2021/01/why-we-need-a-january-6-commission-to-investigate-the.html.

70. Ibid.

71. Naylor, Brian. (2021). "Senate Republicans Block a Plan for an Independent Commission on January 6th Capitol Riot." NPR, May 28. Available at: https://www.npr.org/2021/05/28/1000524897/senate-republicans-block-plan-for-independent-commission-on-jan-6-capitol-riot.

72. Zanotti, Emily. (2021). "House Dems Plot Own Investigation of Capitol Riot After Senate Votes Down January 6th Commission." *The Daily Wire*, May 30. Available at: https://www.dailywire.com/news/house-dems-plot-own-investigation-of-capitol-riot-after-senate-votes-down-january-6-commission.

73. Walsh, Deirdre. (2021). "4 Takeaways From the Emotional First Select Committee Hearing on the Capitol Attack." NPR, July 28. Available at: https://www.npr.org/2021/07/28/1021113538/4-takeaways-from-the-emotional-1st-select-committee-hearing-on-the-capitol-attack.

74. Metzger, Bryan. (2021). "FBI Finds No Evidence That Trump and His Allies Were Directly Involved With Organizing the Violence of the Capitol Riot: Report." *Business Insider*, August 20. Available at: https://www.businessinsider.com/trump-not-directly-involved-in-organizing-capitol-riot-violence-report-2021-8.

75. Ibid.

76. Hall, Madison; Gould, Skye; Harrington, Rebecca; Shamsian, Jacob; Haroun, Azmi; Ardrey, Taylor; and Snodgrass, Erin. (2021). "615 People Have Been Charged in the Capitol Insurrection So Far. This Searchable Table Shows Them All." *Insider*, August 18. Available at: https://www.insider.com/all-the-us-capitol-pro-trump-riot-arrests-charges-names-2021-1.

77. Billeaud, Jacques, and Tarm, Michael. (2021). "As Prospect of Jail Looms, Capitol Riot Suspects Express Regret." *Christian Science Monitor*, March 31. Available at: https://www.csmonitor.com/USA/Politics/2021/0331/As-prospect-of-jail-looms-Capitol-riot-suspects-express-regret.

78. Ibid.

79. Rubin, Olivia, and Mallin, Alexander. (2021). "Because President Trump Said So: Over a Dozen Capitol Rioters Say They Were Following Trump's Guidance." ABC News, February 9. Available at: https://abcnews.go.com/US/president-trump-dozen-capitol-rioters-trumps-guidance/story?id=75757601.

80. Ibid.

81. Ibid.

82. Ibid.

83. Long, Colleen, and Balsamo, Michael. (2021). "Capitol Police Officers Sue Trump, Allies Over Insurrection." Associated Press, August 26. Available at: https://apnews.com/article/capitol-siege-michael-pence-4cd64aab06e0f943ca8f83fd0b65 037d.

84. Kennedy, Brigid. (2021). "The Thousands of Hours of Jan. 6 Footage the Government Wants to Keep Private." Yahoo.com, August 30. Available at: https://www.yahoo.com/now/thousands-hours-jan-6-footage-205934034.html.

85. Conerly, Tonja R.; Holmes, Kathleen; and Tamang, Asha Lal. (2021). *Introduction to Sociology 3e.* Openstax.org. Available at: https://openstax.org/books/introduction-sociology-3e/pages/21-introduction-to-social-movements-and-social-change.

86. Ibid.
87. Ibid.
88. Ibid.
89. Ibid.
90. Ibid.

CHAPTER 2

1. Gould, Lewis. (2003). *Grand Old Party: A History of Republicans.* New York: Random House.

2. Richardson, Heather Cox. (2014). *To Make Men Free: A History of the Republican Party.* New York: Basic Books.

3. Gould (2003).
4. Ibid.
5. Quince, Annabelle, and Phillips, Keri. (2016). "The Grand Old Party." ABC.net. July 10. Available at: https://www.abc.net.au/radionational/programs/rearvision/grand-old-party/7550832.
6. Gould (2003).
7. Richardson (2014).
8. Gould (2003).
9. Cobb (2021).
10. Richardson (2014).
11. Cobb (2021).
12. Rose (2017).
13. Gould (2003).
14. Rose (2017).
15. Gould (2003).
16. Rose (2017).
17. Richardson (2014).
18. Rose (2017).
19. Ibid.
20. Cobb (2021).

21. Riguer, Leah Wright. (2016). *The Loneliness of the Black Republican: Pragmatic Politics and the Pursuit of Power*. Princeton, NJ: Princeton University Press.

22. Balakian, Peter. (2020). "President Lincoln's Republican Party Was the Original Party of Big Government." *Literary Hub*, September 17. Available at: https://lithub.com/president-lincolns-republican-party-was-the-original-party-of-big-government/.

23. Balakian (2020).

24. Ibid.

25. Krugman (2021).

26. Cobb (2021).

27. McNamara, Robert H. (2020). *The Criminalization of Immigration*. Westport, CT: ABC-CLIO.

28. The Skimm. (2020). "The History of the GOP and How the Party Changed." February 23. Available at: https://www.theskimm.com/news/history-of-gop-4z2tVlvLHXAcnRIEDPzj9Y.

29. Ibid.

30. Mounk, Yaschi. (2021). "After Trump, Is American Democracy Doomed by Populism?" Council on Foreign Relations, January 14. Available at: https://www.cfr.org/in-brief/after-trump-american-democracy-doomed-populism.

31. Kimmel, Michael. (2018). *Healing From Hate: How Young Men Get Into—and Out of—Violent Extremism*. Berkeley, CA: University of California Press.

32. Bolton, John. (2020). *The Room Where It Happened: A White House Memoir*. New York: Simon & Schuster.

33. Lowndes, Joseph. (2019). "Populism and Race in the United States from George Wallace to Donald Trump." In de la Torre, Carlos (ed.), *Routledge Handbook of Global Populism*, pp. 197–200. London/New York: Routledge.

34. Main, Thomas J. (2021). *The Rise of Illiberalism*. Washington, DC: The Brookings Institution.

35. Foster, John Bellamy. (2017). "This Is Not Populism." *Monthly Review*, June 1. Available at: https://monthlyreview.org/2017/06/01/this-is-not-populism/.

36. Saldana (2021).

37. Mounk, Yaschi. (2019). *The People vs. Democracy*. Boston, MA: Harvard University Press.

38. Jupskas, Andres. (n.d.). "What Is Populism?" Center for Research on Extremism. Available at: https://www.sv.uio.no/c-rex/english/groups/compendium/what-is-populism.html.

39. Mounk (2019).

40. Ibid.

41. Applebaum, Yoni. (2016). "Trump Claims 'I Alone Can Fix It' During Republican National Convention." *The Atlantic*, July 21. Available at: https://www.theatlantic.com/politics/archive/2016/07/trump-rnc-speech-alone-fix-it/492557/.

42. Mounk (2019).

43. Stanley, Jason. (2020). *How Fascism Works*. New York: Random House.

44. Ibid.

45. Ibid.

46. Ibid.

47. Ibid.

48. Ibid.

49. Ibid.

50. Lati, Marisa. (2021). "What Is Critical Race Theory and Why Do Republicans Want to Ban It?" *Washington Post*, May 29. Available at: https://www.washingtonpost .com/education/2021/05/29/critical-race-theory-bans-schools/.

51. Mascaro, Lisa. (2021). "Capitol Rally Seeks to Rewrite January 6th by Exalting Rioters." Associated Press, September 13. Available at: https://apnews.com/article/joe -biden-donald-trump-capitol-siege-d2fb23af3f01387412a1a00b4eac531c.

52. Stanley (2020).

53. Ibid.

54. Polychroniou, C. J. (2017). "The Difference Between Fascism and Trumpism." CommonDreams, July 10. Available at: https://www.commondreams.org/views/2021 /07/10/differences-between-fascism-and-trumpism.

55. Ibid.

56. Ibid.

57. Ibid.

58. Ibid.

59. Kilgore, Ed. (2021). "The Chilling Message of Trump's Embrace of Ashli Babbitt." *New York Magazine*, July 7. Available at: https://nymag.com/intelligencer/2021 /07/trump-who-shot-ashli-babbitt-january-6-insurrection-riot.html.

60. Ibid.

61. Polychroniou (2017).

62. Jupskas (n.d.).

63. Aguirre, Mariano. (2020). "Trumpism, an Ideology for the Extreme Far-Right Globally." Open Democracy.net, December 14. Available at: https://www .opendemocracy.net/en/trumpism-ideology-extreme-far-right-globally/.

64. Ibid.

65. Ibid.

66. Ibid.

67. Ibid.

68. Fitzduff, Mari, ed. (2017). *Why Irrational Politics Appeals*. Westport, CT: Praeger.

69. Ibid.

70. Dean, John W., and Altemeyer, Bob. (2020). *Authoritarian Nightmare: The Ongoing Threat of Trump's Followers*. Brooklyn, NY: Melville House.

71. Azarian, Robert. (2018). "A Complete Psychological Analysis of Trump's Support." *Psychology Today*, December 27. Available at: https://www.psychologytoday .com/us/blog/mind-in-the-machine/201812/complete-psychological-analysis-trumps -support.

72. Milligan, Susan. (2021). "Republicans Flee the GOP After Capitol Riots." *US News*, April 7. Available at: https://www.usnews.com/news/politics/articles/2021-04 -07/republicans-flee-the-gop-after-capitol-riots.

73. Azarian (2017).

74. Ibid.

75. Dean and Altemeyer (2020).

76. Brookings Institution. (2021). *New 2020 Voter Data: How Biden Won, How Trump Kept the Race Close and What It Tells Us About the Future*. Available at: https://www.brookings.edu/blog/fixgov/2021/07/06/new-2020-voter-data-how-biden-won-how-trump-kept-the-race-close-and-what-it-tells-us-about-the-future/.

77. Cherlin, Andrew J. (2020). "Why Did So Many Urban Working-Class Whites Support President Trump?" Contexts.org, October 1. Available at: https://contexts.org/articles/why-did-so-many-urban-working-class-whites-support-president-trump/.

78. Hochschild, Arlie Russell. (2018). *Strangers in Their Own Land: Anger and Mourning on the American Right*. New York: The New Press.

79. Ibid.

80. Ibid.

81. Dean and Altemeyer (2020).

82. Smith, David Norman, and Hanley, Eric. (2018). "The Anger Games: Who Voted for Donald Trump in the 2016 Election and Why?" *Critical Sociology*, 44(2): 195–212. Available at: https://doi.org/10.1177/089692051774065.

83. Haltiwanger, John. (2020). "Trump Has Repeatedly Been Endorsed by White Supremacist Groups and Other Far-Right Extremists and They've Looked to Him as a Source of Encouragement." *Business Insider*, September 30. Available at: https://www.businessinsider.com/trumps-history-of-support-from-white-supremacist-far-right-groups-2020-9.

84. Ibid.

85. Ibid.

86. Ibid.

87. Rose, Joel. (2021). "Dangerous and More Widespread: Conspiracy Theories Spread Faster than Ever." NPR, March 2. Available at: https://www.npr.org/2021/03/02/971289977/through-the-looking-glass-conspiracy-theories-spread-faster-and-wider-than-ever.

88. Ibid.

89. Ibid.

90. Ibid.

91. Ibid.

92. Jacobs, Tom. (2018). "Inside the Minds of Hardcore Trump Supporters." *Pacific Standard*, February 15. Available at: https://psmag.com/news/inside-the-minds-of-hardcore-trump-supporters.

93. Ibid.

94. Dean and Altemeyer (2020).

95. Ibid.

96. Jacobs (2018).

97. Adams, Rebecca. (2000). *Deadhead Social Science: You Ain't Gonna Learn What You Don't Wanna Know*. Boston, MA: Rowman & Littlefield.

98. Divola, Barry. (2017). "Bruce Springsteen and the Mega Fans Who Tour the World to See Him." *Sydney Morning Herald*, January 20. Available at: https://www.smh.com.au/entertainment/music/bruce-springsteen-and-the-megafans-who-tour-the-world-to-see-him-20170119-gturo2.html.

99. Bender, Michael, C. (2021). *Frankly, We Did Win This Election: The Definitive Account of Trump's Final Year in Office*. New York: Twelve Publishing.

CHAPTER 3

1. Lalich, Janja. (2004). *Bounded Choice: True Believers and Charismatic Cults*. Berkeley, CA: University of California Press.

2. Dawson, Lorne. (2013). *Comprehending Cults: The Sociology of New Religious Movements*. New York: Oxford University Press.

3. Lalich (2004).

4. Dawson (2013).

5. Lifton, Robert Jay. (2019). *Losing Reality: On Cults, Cultism, and the Mindset of Political and Religious Zealotry*. New York: The New Press.

6. Lifton (2019).

7. Ibid.

8. Ross, Rick Alan. (2014). *Cults Inside Out*. North Charleston, SC: CreateSpace Independent Publishing Platform.

9. Ibid.

10. Singer, Margaret Thaler. (2003). *Cults in Our Midst: The Continuing Fight Against the Hidden Menace*. San Francisco, CA: Jossey-Bass.

11. Ibid.

12. Hassan, Steven. (2020). *The Cult of Trump*. New York: Basic Books.

13. Ibid.

14. Lalich (2004).

15. Ibid.

16. Ibid.

17. Ibid.

18. Ibid.

19. Hassan (2020).

20. Ibid.

21. Ibid.

22. Singer (2003).

23. Ibid.

24. Ibid.

25. Ibid.

26. Naftulin, Julia. (2020). "3 Reasons Why People Join Cults, According to a Cult Recovery Therapist." *Insider*, September 23. Available at: https://www.insider.com/why-people-join-cults-according-to-therapist-who-treats-survivors-2020-9.

27. Gurgel, Barbara. (2021). "How Do Normal, Successful, Smart People End Up Joining a Cult?" *The Daily Beast*, May 12. Available at: https://www.thedailybeast.com/why-do-people-join-cults.

28. Ibid.

29. Ibid.

30. Ross (2014).

31. Singer (2003).

32. Lalich (n.d.).

33. Gurgel (2021).

34. Dawson (2013).

35. Ibid.

36. Lee, Bandy X. (2017). *The Dangerous Case of Donald Trump*. New York: Thomas Dunne Books.

37. Ibid.

38. Hassan (2020).

39. Ibid.

40. Ibid.

41. Ibid.

42. Ibid.

43. Ibid.

44. Ibid.

45. Kessler, Glenn; Rizzo, Salvador; and Kelly, Meg. (2021). "Trump's False and Misleading Claims Total 30,573 Over Four Years." *Washington Post*, January 24. Available at: https://www.washingtonpost.com/politics/2021/01/24/trumps-false-or-misleading-claims-total-30573-over-four-years/.

46. Pottratz, Robert. (2021). "Donald Trump and Gaslighting." *SC Times*, January 15. Available at: https://www.sctimes.com/story/opinion/2021/01/15/donald-trump-and-gaslighting/4167553001/.

47. Lee (2017).

48. Ibid.

49. Egawa (2021).

50. Rothschild, Michael. (2021). *The Storm Is Upon Us: How QAnon Became a Movement, Cult, and Conspiracy Theory of Everything*. New York: Melville House.

51. LaFrance, Adrienne. (2020). "The Prophesies of Q." *The Atlantic*, June. Available at: https://www.theatlantic.com/magazine/archive/2020/06/qanon-nothing-can-stop-what-is-coming/610567.

52. Rothschild (2021).

53. Heller, Zoey. (2021). "What Makes a Cult a Cult?" *The New Yorker*, July 12. Available at: https://www.newyorker.com/magazine/2021/07/12/what-makes-a-cult-a-cult.

54. Ibid.

55. Rothschild (2021).

56. Ibid.

57. LaFrance (2021).

58. Rothschild (2021).

59. Schulson (2021).

60. LaFrance (2021).

61. Hassan (2020).

62. Ibid.

63. Ibid.

64. Rhodes, Ben. (2020). "The Path to Autocracy." *The Atlantic*, June 15. Available at: https://www.theatlantic.com/ideas/archive/2020/06/american-orbanism/612658/.

65. Ibid.

66. Ibid.

67. Ibid.

68. Williams, Aimee, and Hopkins, Valerie. (2019). "Trump Praises Hungary's Orbán in White House Visit." *Financial Times*, May 13. Available at: https://www.ft.com/content/06f69c6c-75a8-11e9-bbad-7c18c0ea0201.

69. Hubbard, Kaia. (2021). "Far-Right Extremism Echoes Across Europe." *US News*, February 18. Available at: https://www.usnews.com/news/best-countries/articles/2021-02-18/far-right-extremism-growing-across-europe-survey-finds.

70. Ibid.

71. Ibid.

72. Moens, Barbara, and Hirsch, Cornelius. (2022). "How the Far Right Got Out of the Doghouse." *Politico*, October 3. Available at: https://www.politico.eu/article/the-far-right-is-out-of-the-doghouse/.

73. Martin, Michel. (2022). "What Recent Wins for Far-Right Parties in Europe Could Mean for the Region." NPR, October 1. Available at: https://www.npr.org/2022/10/01/1126419403/what-the-recent-wins-for-far-right-parties-in-europe-could-mean-for-the-region.

74. Rhodes (2020).

75. LaFrance (2021).

76. Ross (2014).

77. Rothschild (2021).

78. Juergensmeyer, Mark. (2000). *Terrorism in the Mind of God: The Global Rise of Religious Violence*. Berkeley, CA: University of California Press.

79. Stein, Alexandra. (2016). *Terror, Love, and Brainwashing: Attachment in Cults and Totalitarian Systems*. New York: Routledge.

80. Rothschild (2021).

CHAPTER 4

1. Mulligan, Katrina; Steele, Brette; Clark, Simon; Padmanabhan, Asha; and Hinkler, Rachel. (2021). "A National Policy Blueprint to End White Supremacist Violence." Center for American Progress, March 21. Available at: https://www.americanprogress.org/issues/security/reports/2021/04/21/498156/national-policy-blueprint-end-white-supremacist-violence/.

2. Ibid.

3. Ibid.

4. Ibid.

5. Ibid.

6. Ibid.

7. Ibid.

8. Ibid.

9. Stewart, Emily. (2018). "Trump Again Says He's the Least Racist Person There Is." *Vox*, January 15. Available at: https://www.vox.com/policy-and-politics/2018/1/15/16891996/trump-least-racist.

10. Zeitz, Joshua. (2017). "The Real History of American Immigration." *Politico*, August 6. Available at https://www.politico.com/magazine/story/2017/08/06/trump-history-of-american-immigration-215464.

11. Serwer, Adam. (2018). "White Nationalism's Deep American Roots." *The Atlantic*, April. Available at: https://www.theatlantic.com/magazine/archive/2019/04/adam-serwer-madison-grant-white-nationalism/583258.

12. Taub, Amanda. (2016). "White Nationalism, Explained." *New York Times*, November 21. Available at: https://www.nytimes.com/2016/11/22/world/americas/white-nationalism-explained.html.

13. Serwer (2018).

14. Taub (2016).

15. Southern Poverty Law Center. (n.d.). "Alt-Right." Available at: https://www.splcenter.org/fighting-hate/extremist-files/ideology/alt-right.

16. Anti-Defamation League. (n.d.). "Alt Right: A Primer on the New White Supremacy." Available at: https://www.adl.org/resources/backgrounders/alt-right-a-primer-on-the-new-white-supremacy.

17. Southern Poverty Law Center (n.d.).

18. National Public Radio. (2016). "What You Need to Know About the Alt-Right." NPR, August 26. Available at: https://www.npr.org/2016/08/26/491452721/the-history-of-the-alt-right.

19. Ibid.

20. Ibid.

21. Hemmer, Nicole. (2016). *Messengers of the Right: Conservative Media and the Transformation of American Politics*. Philadelphia, PA: University of Pennsylvania Press.

22. Ibid.

23. Taub (2016).

24. Srikantiah, Jayashri, and Sinnar, Shirin. (2019). "White Nationalism as Immigration Policy." *Stanford Law Review*, 71 (March). Available at: https://www.stanfordlawreview.org/online/white-nationalism-as-immigration-policy.

25. Ibid.

26. Ibid.

27. Ibid.

28. Ibid.

29. Anti-Defamation League. (n.d.). "Alt-Right: A Primer on the New White Supremacy." Available at: https://www.adl.org/resources/backgrounders/alt-right-a-primer-about-the-new-white-supremacy.

30. Neuman, Scott. (2020). "Trump Now Says He Condemns 'All White Supremacists,' After Declining to at Debate." NPR, October 1. Available at: https://www.npr.org/sections/live-updates-protests-for-racial-justice/2020/10/01/919375470/trump-now-says-he-condemns-all-white-supremacists-after-declining-to-at-debate.

31. Haltiwanger, John. (2020). "Trump Has Repeatedly Been Endorsed by White Supremacist Groups and Other Far-Right Extremists, and They've Looked to Him as a Source of Encouragement." *Business Insider*, September 30. Available at: https://www.businessinsider.com/trumps-history-of-support-from-white-supremacist-far-right-groups-2020-9.

32. Ibid.

33. Ibid.

34. Ibid.

35. Kriner, Matthew, and Lewis, Jon. (2021). "Pride and Prejudice: The Violent Evolution of the Proud Boys." *Combatting Terrorism Center*, 14(6), July/August. Available at: https://ctc.usma.edu/pride-prejudice-the-violent-evolution-of-the-proud-boys/.

36. Ibid.

37. Wolfson, Aaron. (2021). "Actor Profile: Proud Boys." The Armed Conflict Location and Event Data Project (ACLED). April 22. Available at: http://acleddata.com/2021/04/22/actor-profile-proud-boys/.

38. Kriner and Lewis (2021).

39. Wolfson (2021).

40. Ibid.

41. Ibid.

42. Ibid.

43. Kriner and Lewis (2021).

44. Wolfson (2021).

45. Kriner and Lewis (2021).

46. Ibid.

47. Ibid.

48. Ibid.

49. Pineda, Khrysgiana. (2020). "The Boogaloo Movement Is Gaining Momentum. Who Are the Boogaloo Bois and What Do They Want?" *USA Today*, June 19. Available at: https://www.usatoday.com/story/news/nation/2020/06/19/what-is-boogaloo-movement/3204899001/.

50. Ibid.

51. Ibid.

52. Ibid.

53. Ibid.

54. Ibid.

55. Ibid.

56. McQueen, Eric. (2021). "Examining Extremism: Oath Keepers." Center for Strategic and International Studies, June 17. Available at: https://www.csis.org/blogs/examining-extremism/examining-extremism-oath-keepers.

57. Giglio. Mike. (2020). "A Pro-Trump Militant Group Has Recruited Thousands of Police, Soldiers, and Veterans." *The Atlantic*, November. Available at: https://www.theatlantic.com/magazine/archive/2020/11/right-wing-militias-civil-war/616473/.

58. Ibid.

59. Dickinson, Tim. (2021). "Oath Keepers Use a Dystopian Fever Dream to Snare Police Forces, Military Vets." *Rolling Stone*, October 28. Available at: https://www.yahoo.com/entertainment/oath-keepers-dystopian-fever-dream-120024425.html.

60. Ibid.

61. Ibid.

62. Ibid.

63. Bray, Mark. (2017). *Antifa: The Anti-Fascist Handbook*. New York: Melville House.

64. Reyes, Lorenzo, and Stanglin, Doug. (2017). "What Is Antifa and What Does the Movement Want?" *USA Today*, August 23. Available at: https://www.usatoday.com/story/news/2017/08/23/what-antifa-and-what-does-movement-want/593867001/.

65. Wendling, Mike. (2020). "US Election 2020: Who Are the Proud Boys and Who Are Antifa?" BBC, September 30. Available at: https://www.bbc.com/news/election-us-2020-54352635.

66. Reyes and Stanglin (2017).

67. Wendling (2020).

68. Kunzelman, Michael. (2021). "Feds Seek Tougher Sentences for Veterans Who Stormed the Capitol." Yahoo News, November 3. Available at: https://www.yahoo.com/news/feds-seek-tougher-sentences-veterans-041514021.html.

69. Scott, Eugene. (2021). "Data About the Capitol Rioters Serves Another Blow to the White, Working-Class Trump Supporter Narrative." *Washington Post*, April 12. Available at: https://www.washingtonpost.com/politics/2021/04/12/data-about-capitol-rioters-serves-another-blow-white-working-class-trump-supporter-narrative/.

70. Wade, Peter. (2021). "Dozens of Oregon Cops Have Paid Dues to the Oath Keepers Militia Group: Report." *Rolling Stone*, October 15. Available at: https://www.rollingstone.com/politics/politics-news/oregon-cops-oath-keepers-members-1243194/.

71. Anti-Defamation League. (n.d.). "The Great Replacement: An Explainer." Available at: https://www.adl.org/resources/backgrounders/the-great-replacment-an-explainer.

72. Ibid.

73. Ibid.

74. Byman, Daniel L. (2021). "White Supremacist Terrorism: Key Trends to Watch in 2021." *Brookings Institution*, January 15. Available at: https://www.brookings.edu/blog/order-from-chaos/2021/01/15/white-supremacist-terrorism-key-trends-to-watch-in-2021/.

75. Dickinson, Caitlin. (2021). "Alarming Finding: 30 Percent of Republicans Say Violence May Be Needed to Save US, Poll Shows." Yahoo News, November 1. Available at: https://news.yahoo.com/prri-poll-republicans-violence-040144322.html.

76. Byman (2021).

77. Martin, Bradley; Koblentz-Stenzler, Liram; and Pack, Alexander. (2021). "Trump Supporters Face White Supremacist Radicalization on Social Media."

Newsweek, January 25. Available at: https://www.newsweek.com/trump-supporters -face-white-supremacist-radicalization-social-media-opinion-1563813.

78. Klein, Ezra. (2020). *Why We Are Polarized.* New York: Avid Reader Press.

CHAPTER 5

1. Graham, David. A. (2020). "Jeff Sessions Explains Why Christians Support Donald Trump." *The Atlantic*, June. Available at: https://www.theatlantic.com/ideas/ archive/2020/06/why-christians-support-trump/613669/.

2. Gerson, Michael. (2018). "Trump and the Evangelical Temptation." *The Atlantic*, April 15. Available at: https://www.theatlantic.com/magazine/archive/2018/04/the -last-temptation/554066/.

3. Wacker, Grant. (n.d.). "The Christian Right." National Humanities Center. Available at: http://nationalhumanitiescenter.org/tserve/twenty/tkeyinfo/chr_rght.htm.

4. Ibid.

5. McVicar, Michael J. (2018). "The Religious Right in America." *Oxford Research Encyclopedia*. Available at: https://oxfordre.com/religion/view/10.1093/ acrefore/9780199340378.001.0001/acrefore-9780199340378-e-97; Stewart, Katherine. (2020). *The Power Worshippers: Inside the Dangerous Rise of Religious Nationalism*. London: Bloomsbury.

6. Stewart, Katherine. (2020). *The Power Worshippers: Inside the Dangerous Rise of Religious Nationalism*. London: Bloomsbury; Little, David. (n.d.). "Religious Freedom and Christianity, an Overview." Berkley Center for Religion, Peace and World Affairs, Georgetown University. Available at: https://berkleycenter.georgetown .edu/essays/religious-freedom-and-christianity-an-overview.

7. McVicar (2018).

8. Stewart (2020); Little (n.d.).

9. McVicar (2018).

10. Ibid.

11. Stewart (2020).

12. Ibid.; McVicar (2018).

13. Stewart (2020); Little (n.d.).

14. McVicar (2018).

15. Stewart (2020); McVicar (2018).

16. McVicar (2018).

17. Kohls, Ryan. (2018). "Explained: Evangelicals, the Religious Right and Trump." Aljazeera, November 6. Available at: https://www.aljazeera.com/news/2018 /11/6/explained-evangelicals-the-religious-right-and-trump; Stewart (2020); McVicar (2018).

18. Kohls (2018); Little (n.d.).

19. McVicar (2018).

20. Kohls (2018); McVicar (2018).

21. Ibid.

22. Du Mez, Kristen Kobes. (2020). *Jesus and John Wayne: How White Evangelicals Corrupted a Faith and Fractured a Nation*. London: Liveright.

23. Ibid.

24. Ibid.

25. Mahdawi, Arwa. (2019). "Brett Kavanaugh Shows True Colours in Supreme Court Abortion Dissent." *The Guardian*, February 9. Available at: https://www.theguardian.com/commentisfree/2019/feb/09/brett-kavanaugh-shows-true-colours-in-supreme-court-abortion-dissent.

26. Millhiser, Ian. (2020). "What Trump Has Done to the Courts, Explained." *Vox*, September 29. Available at: https://www.vox.com/policy-and-politics/2019/12/9/20962980/trump-supreme-court-federal-judges.

27. Ballotpedia. (2021). "Federal Judges Nominated by President Trump." Available at: https://ballotpedia.org/Federal_judges_nominated_by_Donald_Trump.

28. Elving, Ron. (2018). "What Happened With Merrick Garland in 2016 and Why It Matters Now." NPR, June 29. Available at: https://www.npr.org/2018/06/29/624467256/what-happened-with-merrick-garland-in-2016-and-why-it-matters-now.

29. Levine, Marianne. (2021). "McConnell: I'd Block Biden SCOTUS Nominee in 2024." *Politico*, June 14. Available at: https://www.politico.com/news/2021/06/14/mcconnell-biden-scotus-494340.

30. Ibid.

31. Breuninger, Kevin. (2022). "Senate Confirms Ketanji Brown Jackson to the Supreme Court, Making Her the First Black Woman to Serve as a Justice." CNBC, April 7. Available at: https://www.cnbc.com/2022/04/07/ketanji-brown-jackson-confirmed-to-supreme-court-first-black-woman-justice.html.

32. Liptak, Adam. (2018). "Supreme Court Sides With Baker Who Turned Away Gay Couple." *New York Times*, June 4. Available at: https://www.nytimes.com/2018/06/04/us/politics/supreme-court-sides-with-baker-who-turned-away-gay-couple.html.

33. Perry, Samuel; Whitehead, Andrew; and Grubbs, Joshua B. (2020). "Culture Wars and COVID-19 Conduct: Christian Nationalism, Religiosity, and Americans' Behavior During the Coronavirus Pandemic." *Journal for the Scientific Study of Religion*, July 26. Available at: https://onlinelibrary.wiley.com/doi/full/10.1111/jssr.12677.

34. Little (n.d.).

35. LeBlanc, Paul. (2021). "Ex-Trump Advisor Michael Flynn's Call for 'One Religion' in the US Garners Swift Condemnation." CNN, November 15. Available at: https://www.cnn.com/2021/11/15/politics/michael-flynn-one-religion/index.html.

36. LeBlanc (2021).

37. Haynes, Jeffrey. (2021). *Trump and the Politics of Neo-Nationalism: The Christian Right and Secular Nationalism in America*. London: Routledge.

38. Ibid.; Stewart (2020).

39. Perry et al. (2020).

40. Wise, Alana. (2021). "The Political Fight Over Vaccine Mandates Deepens Despite Their Effectiveness." NPR, October 17. Available at: https://www.npr.org

/2021/10/17/1046598351/the-political-fight-over-vaccine-mandates-deepens-despite
-their-effectiveness.

41. Liptak, Adam. (2021). "Supreme Court Allows Challenge to Texas Abortion Law but Leaves It in Effect." *New York Times*, December 10. Available at: https://www.nytimes.com/2021/12/10/us/politics/texas-abortion-supreme-court.html.

42. Ibid.

43. Ibid.

44. Ibid.

45. Ibid.

46. Kinery, Emma. (2022). "Biden Promises to Codify Roe if Two More Democrats Are Elected to the Senate." CNBC, September 23. Available at: https://www.cnbc.com/2022/09/23/biden-promises-to-codify-roe-if-two-more-democrats-are-elected-to-the-senate.html.

47. Lee, Morgan. (2021). "Critical Race Theory: What Christians Need to Know." *Christianity Today*, July 2. Available at: https://www.christianitytoday.com/ct/podcasts/quick-to-listen/critical-race-theory-racism-evangelicals-divided-podcast.html.

48. Ibid.

49. Ibid.

50. Sawchuck, Stephen. (2021). "What Is Critical Race Theory and Why Is It Under Attack?" *Education Week*, May 18. Available at: https://www.edweek.org/leadership/what-is-critical-race-theory-and-why-is-it-under-attack/2021/05.

51. Ibid.

52. Ibid.

53. Ibid.

54. Ibid.

55. Ibid.

56. Ibid.

57. Ibid.

58. Ibid.

59. Ibid.

60. Valverde, Miriam. (2017). "Trump Claims He Got Rid of the Johnson Amendment. Is That True?" PolitiFact, July 18. Available at: https://www.politifact.com/factchecks/2017/jul/18/donald-trump/trump-claims-he-got-rid-johnson-amendment-true/.

61. Ibid.

62. Kohls (2018); Valderde (2017).

63. Terry, Ruth. (2019). "The Christian Right and Left Share the Same Faith but Couldn't Be More Different." *Yes Magazine*, December 24. Available at: https://www.yesmagazine.org/social-justice/2019/12/24/political-christian-belief.

64. Posner, Sarah. (2021). "How the Christian Right Embraced Voter Suppression." *Vox*, September 28. Available at: https://www.vox.com/22696286/evangelicals-texas-georgia-voting-law-trump.

65. Ibid.

66. Ibid.

67. Public Religion Research Institute. (2020). "The American Religious Land-scape in 2020." Available at: https://www.prri.org/research/2020-census-of-american-religion/.

68. Igielnik, Ruth; Keeter, Scott; and Hartig, Hannah. (2021). "Behind Biden's 2020 Victory." Pew Research Center, June 30. Available at: https://www.pewresearch.org/politics/2021/06/30/behind-bidens-2020-victory/.

69. Posner (2021).

70. Ibid.

71. Brennan Center for Justice. (2021). *Voting Laws Roundup: May 2021.* Available at: https://www.brennancenter.org/our-work/research-reports/voting-laws-roundup-may-2021.

72. Terry (2019).

73. Ibid.

74. Ibid.

75. Kohls (2018).

CHAPTER 6

1. Sumner, William G. (1940). *Folkways: A Study of the Sociological Importance of Usages, Manners, Customs, Mores and Morals.* Boston: Ginn & Company.

2. Ibid.

3. Brewer, Marilynn. (2016). "Ethnocentrism and the Theory of Social Identity." In Sternberg, Robert J.; Fiske, Susan T.; and Foss, Donald J. (eds.), *Scientists Making a Difference*, pp. 360–64. New York: Cambridge University Press.

4. Ferraro, Gary P.; Andreatta, Susan; and Holdsworth, Chris. (2017). *Cultural Anthropology: An Applied Perspective.* Toronto: Nelson.

5. Howard, Michael. (2007). *The First World War.* New York: Oxford University Press.

6. Keegan, John. (2000). *The First World War.* New York: Knopf Doubleday.

7. Gilbert, Martin. (2004). *The First World War: A Complete History* (second edition). New York: Holt; Strachan, Hew. (2001). *The First World War.* Vol. 1, *To Arms.* New York: Oxford University Press.

8. Keegan (2004).

9. Gilbert (2004); Keegan (2000); Howard (2007).

10. Ibid.

11. Ibid.

12. Ibid.

13. Ibid.

14. Ibid.

15. Ibid.

16. PBS. (n.d.). "WWI Casualty and Death Tables." Available at: https://web.archive.org/web/20150307054112/http://www.pbs.org/greatwar/resources/casdeath_pop.html.

17. Gilbert (2004); Keegan (2000); Strachan (2000).

18. Gilbert (2004).

19. Gilbert (2004); Keegan (2000); Strachan (2000).

20. MacMillan, Margaret. (2003). *Paris 1919*. New York: Random House; Churchill, Winston. (2015). *The World Crisis: 1911–1919*. London: Bloomsbury Academic.

21. MacMillan (2003); Keegan (2000); Strachan (2000).

22. MacMillan (2003): Strachan (2000); Howard (2007).

23. Gilbert (2004); Howard (2007).

24. Ibid.

25. Ibid.

26. Ibid.

27. Ibid.

28. Ullrich, Volker. (2016). *Hitler: Ascent:1939–1945*. New York: Knopf.

29. Stoltzfus, Nathan. (2016). *Hitler's Compromises: Coercion and Consensus in Nazi Germany*. New Haven, CT: Yale University Press.

30. Shirer, William, L. (2010). *The Rise and Fall of the Third Reich: A History of Nazi Germany*. New York: Blackstone; Spielvogel, Jackson J., and Redles, David. (2009). *Hitler and Nazi Germany* (sixth edition). New York: Pearson.

31. Hett, Benjamin Carter. (2020). *The Nazi Menace: Hitler, Churchill, Roosevelt, Stalin and the Road to War*. New York: Henry Holt and Company.

32. Ibid.

33. Ullrich (2016); Hett (2020).

34. Ibid.

35. Shirer (2010); Stoltzfus (2016).

36. Spielvogel and Redles (2009).

37. Ibid.

38. Ullrich (2016); Shirer (2010).

39. Ibid.

40. Hett (2020).

41. Ullrich (2016); Stoltzfus (2016).

42. Ibid.

43. Stoltzfus (2016); Spielvogel and Redles (2009); Hett (2019); Hett (2020).

44. Ibid.

45. Ibid.

46. Ullrich (2016); Shirer (2010); Stoltzfus (2016); Hett (2019); Hett (2020).

47. The National World War II Museum. (n.d.). "Research Starters: Worldwide Deaths in World War II." Available at: https://www.nationalww2museum.org/students-teachers/student-resources/research-starters/research-starters-worldwide-deaths-world-war.

48. Ullrich (2016); Hett (2020).

49. Rosenfeld, Gavriel D. (2019). "An American Fuhrer? Nazi Analogies and the Struggle to Explain Donald Trump." *Cambridge Core*, December 4. Available at: https://www.cambridge.org/core/journals/central-european-history/article/an-american-fuhrer-nazi-analogies-and-the-struggle-to-explain-donald-trump/25CBE639F23D2D80870EA4D3F1E6D566.

50. Ibid.

51. Ibid.

52. Bender, Michael. (2021). *Frankly, We Did Win This Election*. New York: Twelve Publishing.

53. Kelly, John. (2021). *Betrayal: The Final Act of the Trump Show*. New York: Dutton.

54. Bender (2021).

55. Ullrich (2016).

56. Rosenfeld (2019).

57. Ibid.

58. Snyder, Timothy. (2017). *On Tyranny: Twenty Lessons from the Twentieth Century*. New York: Crown.

59. Stanley, Jason. (2020). *How Fascism Works*. New York: Random House; Albright, Madeleine. (2018). *Fascism: A Warning*. New York: Harper Collins.

60. Rosenfeld (2019).

61. Ibid.

62. Ibid.

63. Ibid.

CHAPTER 7

1. Festinger, Leon. (1954). "A Theory of Social Comparison Processes." *Human Relations*, 7(2): 117–40.

2. Ibid.

3. French, David. (2020). *Divided We Fall: America's Secession Threat and How to Restore Our Nation*. New York: St. Martin's Press.

4. Klein, Ezra. (2020). *Why We're Polarized*. New York: Avid Reader Press.

5. Ibid.

6. Klein (2020).

7. French (2020).

8. Sasse, Ben. (2018). *Them: Why We Hate Each Other and How to Heal.* New York: St. Martin's Press. See also French (2020); Klein (2020).

9. French (2020).

10. Sasse (2018).

11. Sunstein, Cass. (1999). "The Law of Group Polarization." University of Chicago Law School. December. Working Paper No. 92. Available at: https://ssrn.com/abstract=199668.

12. Ibid.

13. French (2020).

14. Klein (2020), 64.

15. Kahan, Dan M.; Peters, Ellen; Wittlin, Maggie; Slovic, Paul; Ouellette, Lisa Larrimore; Braman, Donald; and Mandel, Gregory. (2012). "The Polarizing Impact of Science Literacy and Numeracy on Perceived Climate Change Risks." *Nature Climate Change*, 2: 732–35.

16. Cacioppo, John, and Patrick, William. (2008). *Loneliness: Human Nature and the Need for Social Connection.* New York: W.W. Norton. See also Olds, Jacqueline, and Schwartz, Richard S. (2009). *The Lonely American: Drifting Apart in the Twenty-first Century.* Boston, MA: Beacon Books.

17. Pressman, Sarah. (2020). "COVID-19 Blew Up the Epidemic of Loneliness." *Psychology Today*, September 2.

18. Cacioppo and Patrick (2008).

19. Sasse (2018); Cacioppo and Patrick (2009); Pressman (2020).

20. Putnam, Robert. (2001). *Bowling Alone: The Collapse and Revival of American Community.* New York: Simon & Schuster.

21. Ibid.

22. Ibid.

23. Ibid.

24. Ibid.

25. Murray, Charles. (2012). *Coming Apart: The State of White America 1960–2010.* New York: Crown.

26. Sasse (2018).

27. Festinger, Leon. (1957). *A Theory of Cognitive Dissonance.* Stanford, CA: Stanford University Press. See also Sasse (2018).

28. Mason, Lilliana. (2018). *Uncivil Agreement: How Politics Became Our Identity.* Chicago: University of Chicago Press.

29. Burnett, John. (2022). "Americans Are Fleeing to Places Where Political Views Match Their Own." NPR, February 18. Available at: https://www.npr.org/2022/02/18/1081295373/the-big-sort-americans-move-to-areas-political-alignment; French (2020).

30. Ibid.

31. Yudkin, Daniel; Hawkins, Stephen; and Dixon, Tim. (2019). "The Perception Gap: How False Impressions Are Pulling Americans Apart." More in Common. Download of the report available at: https://perceptiongap.us/.

32. Ibid.

33. Ibid.

34. Ibid.

35. Ibid.

36. Jones, Zoe Christien. (2022). "Florida Legislature Passes 'Stop WOKE Act,' Second Controversial Education Bill This Week." CBSNews, March 10. Available at: https://www.cbsnews.com/news/florida-critical-race-theory-education-stop-woke-act/.

37. Ibid.

38. Ibid.

39. Levin, Bess. (2022). "Trump Tells Supporters They Must Fight to the Death to Stop Schools from Teaching Kids About Systemic Racism." *Vanity Fair*, March 14. Available at: https://www.vanityfair.com/news/2022/03/donald-trump-critical-race-theory-lay-down-lives.

40. Matzen, Morgan. (2022). "Gov. Kristi Noem Signs Bill Limiting 'Divisive Comments' and Critical Race Theory from Colleges." Yahoo News, March 21.

Available at: https://www.yahoo.com/news/gov-kristi-noem-signs-bill-175316757 .html.

41. As quoted in ibid.

42. Kruesi, Kimberlee. (2022). "Tenn. 'Divisive Concept' Bill Targeting Colleges Advances." Yahoo News, March 21. Available at: https://www.yahoo.com/news/tenn -divisive-concept-bill-targeting-233636647.html.

43. DiAngelo, Robin. (2018). *White Fragility: Why It's So Hard for White People to Talk About Racism*. Boston, MA: Beacon Press.

44. Feagin, Joe R. (2006). *Systematic Racism: A Theory of Oppression*. New York: Routledge.

45. Hochschild, Arlie R. (2018). *Strangers in Their Own Land*. New York: The New Press.

46. Starkey, Brandon. (2017). "Why Do So Many White People Deny the Existence of White Privilege?" *The Undefeated*, March 1. Available at: https://theundefeated .com/features/why-do-so-many-white-people-deny-the-existence-of-white-privilege/.

47. Ibid.

48. Bowden, Ebony. (2020). "Trump Says 'More White People' Are Killed by Police Than African Americans." *New York Post*, July 14. Available at: https:// nypost.com/2020/07/14/trump-more-white-people-are-killed-by-police-than-african -americans/.

49. Starkey (2017).

50. Delgado, Richard, and Stefancic, Jean. (2012). *Critical Race Theory: An Intro-duction* (second edition). New York: New York University Press.

51. *Merriam-Webster*, s.v. "woke," last modified February 2, 2023, https://www .merriam-webster.com/dictionary/woke.

52. Sherman, Rhona. (2022). "What Does Woke Mean? Definition of Woke Cul-ture in 2021—and What Critics Mean by 'Woke Police.'" NationalWorld, January 31. Available at: https://www.nationalworld.com/whats-on/arts-and-entertainment /what-does-woke-mean-definition-of-woke-culture-in-2021-and-what-critics-mean -by-woke-police-3215758.

CHAPTER 8

1. Treene, Alayna; Solender, Andrew; and Cai, Sophia. (2022). "Jan. 6 Committee Opens a Pandora's Box of Retaliation." *Axios*, May 13. Available at: https://www .axios.com/2022/05/13/jan-6-committee-opens-a-pandoras-box-of-retaliation.

2. Walsh, Deirdre; Mohammad, Linah; Kenin, Justine; Campbell, Barbara; and Pfeiffer, Sacha. (2022). "Jan. 6 Committee Issues Subpoena on Trump and Wants Him to Testify Mid-November." NPR, October 21. Available at: https://www.npr.org/2022 /10/21/1130644852/jan-6-committee-issues-a-subpoena-on-trump-and-wants-him-to -testify-mid-november.

3. Wolfe, Jan. (2022). "Trump Likely Committed Crime with Plan to Obstruct Congress, US Judge Rules." Reuters, March 28. Available at: https://www.yahoo.com /news/trump-likely-committed-felony-obstructing-160842714.html.

4. Ibid.

5. Ibid.

6. Martin, Jonathan, and Burns, Alexander. (2022). *This Will Not Pass: Trump, Biden, and the Battle for America's Future.* New York: Simon & Schuster.

7. Kika, Thomas. (2022). "Pence Refusing to Get in Secret Service Car on Jan. 6 'Chilling': Raskin." *Newsweek*, April 23. Available at: https://www.newsweek.com/pence-refusing-get-secret-service-car-jan-6-chilling-raskin-1700341.

8. Ibid.

9. Ibid.

10. Cohen, Marshall; Cohen, Zachary; and Rogers, Alex. (2022). "7 Takeaways from Tuesday's Shocking January 6 Hearing." CNN, June 29. Available at: https://www.cnn.com/2022/06/28/politics/january-6-hearing-day-6-takeaways-hutchinson/index.html.

11. Ibid.

12. Ibid.

13. Ibid.

14. Ibid.

15. Walsh, Deirdre; Mohammad, Linah; Kenin, Justine; Campbell, Barbara; and Pfeiffer, Sacha. (2022). "Jan. 6 Committee Issues Subpoena on Trump and Wants Him to Testify Mid-November." NPR, October 21. Available at: https://www.npr.org/2022/10/21/1130644852/jan-6-committee-issues-a-subpoena-on-trump-and-wants-him-to-testify-mid-november.

16. Durkee, Allison. (2022). "Special Master Demands Trump Prove Claims FBI Planted Evidence at Mar-a-Lago." *Forbes*, September 22. Available at: https://www.forbes.com/sites/alisondurkee/2022/09/22/special-master-demands-trump-prove-claims-fbi-planted-evidence-at-mar-a-lago/?sh=598a943f6e22.

17. Liptak, Kevin. (2022). "Mar-a-Lago—and Its Owner—Have Long Caused Concerns for US Intelligence." CNN, August 14. Available at: https://www.cnn.com/2022/08/14/politics/trump-documents-mar-a-lago/index.html.

18. Stein, Chris. (2022). "Trump Admitted Letters to Kim Jong-Un Were Secret, Audio Reveals." *The Guardian*, October 19. Available at: https://www.theguardian.com/us-news/2022/oct/19/trump-north-korea-kim-jong-un-letters-bob-woodward-audio.

19. Shelton, Shania. (2022). "Photos Show Handwritten Notes that Trump Apparently Ripped Up and Attempted to Flush Down the Toilet." CNN, August 8. Available at: https://www.cnn.com/2022/08/08/politics/trump-white-house-notes-toilet-photos-cnntv.

20. Sanger, David E. (2021). "Biden Bars Trump from Receiving Intelligence Briefings, Citing 'Erratic Behavior.'" *New York Times*, February 6. Available at: https://www.nytimes.com/2021/02/05/us/politics/biden-trump-intelligence-briefings.html.

21. Orr, Gabby; Brown, Pamela; and Reid, Paula. (2022). "Archives Threatened to Go to Congress and Justice Department to Get Trump to Turn Over Records." *The Mercury News*, February 13. Available at: https://www.mercurynews.com/?returnUrl=https%3A%2F%2Fwww.mercurynews.com%2F2022%2F02%2F11%2Farchives-threatened-to-go-to-congress-over-trump-records%2F%3FclearUserState%3Dtrue.

22. Feuer, Alan, and Haberman, Maggie. (2022). "Email Shows Early Tension Between Trump and National Archives." *The New York Times*, August 24. Available at: https://www.nytimes.com/2022/08/24/us/politics/national-archives-letter-trump.html.

23. Montague, Zach, and McCarthy, Lauren (2022). "The Timeline Related to the FBI's Search of Mar-a-Lago." *New York Times*, August 12. Available at: https://www.nytimes.com/2022/08/12/us/politics/trump-classified-records-timeline.html.

24. Ibid.

25. Barrett, Devlin, and Stein, Perry. (2022). "Affidavit to Search Trump's Mar-a-Lago Says 184 Classified Files Found in January." *Washington Post*, August 26. Available at: https://www.washingtonpost.com/national-security/2022/08/26/trump-affidavit-released/.

26. Dawsey, Josh, and Alemany, Jacqueline. (2022). "Trump's Lawyer Refused His Request in February to Say All Documents Returned." *Washington Post*, October 3. Available at: https://www.washingtonpost.com/national-security/2022/10/03/trump-alex-cannon-documents/.

27. Perez, Evan; Orr, Gabby; and Brown, Pamela. (2022). "Feds Removed Documents from Mar-a-Lago in June with Grand Jury Subpoena." CNN, August 11. Available at: https://www.abc57.com/news/feds-seized-documents-from-mar-a-lago-in-june-with-grand-jury-subpoena.

28. Haberman, Maggie. (2022). "FBI Interviewed Top White House Lawyers About Missing Trump Documents." *New York Times*, August 16. Available at: https://www.nytimes.com/2022/08/16/us/politics/trump-cipollone-philbin-interviews-fbi.html.

29. Feuer, Alan. (2022). "Trump Kept More than 700 Pages of Classified Documents, Letter from National Archives Says." *New York Times*, August 23. Available at: https://www.nytimes.com/2022/08/23/us/politics/trump-classified-documents-fbi-letter.html/.

30. Ibid.

31. Broadwater, Luke; Brenner, Katie; and Haberman, Maggie. (2022). "Inside the 20-Month Fight to Get Trump to Return Presidential Material." *New York Times*, August 26. Available at: https://www.nytimes.com/2022/08/26/us/politics/trump-documents-search-timeline.html.

32. Pengelly, Martin. (2022). "Trump Ordered Records Moved After Subpoena, Mar-a-Lago Staffer Said—Reports." *The Guardian*, October 13. Available at: https://www.theguardian.com/us-news/2022/oct/12/donald-trump-mar-a-lago-documents.

33. Cohen, Marshall. (2022). "Judge Unseals Less Redacted Version of Affidavit Used for Mar-a-Lago Search Warrant." CNN, September 13. Available at: https://ksltv.com/505584/judge-unseals-less-redacted-version-of-affidavit-used-for-mar-a-lago-search-warrant/.

34. Palmer, Ewan. (2022). "Trump Lawyers Stopped FBI Agents Checking Storage Room Boxes." *Newsweek*, August 31. Available at: https://www.newsweek.com/trump-search-documents-fbi-maralago-lawyers-june-1738370.

35. Woodruff Swan, Betsy; Cheney, Kyle; and Wu, Nicholas. (2022). "FBI Search Warrant Shows Trump Under Investigation for Potential Obstruction of

Justice, Espionage Act Violations." *Politico*, August 12. Available at: https://www
.politico.com/news/2022/08/12/search-warrant-shows-trump-under-investigation-for
-potential-obstruction-of-justice-espionage-act-violations-00051507.

36. Ibid.

37. Ibid.

38. Barrett and Dawsey (2022).

39. Ibid.

40. Shivaram, Deepa, and Lucas, Ryan. (2022). "Trump Says FBI Agents Searched
His Mar-a-Lago Home in Florida." NPR, August 9. Available at: https://www.npr
.org/2022/08/08/1116427430/trump-says-fbi-agents-raided-his-mar-a-lago-home-in
-florida.

41. Ibid.

42. Olander, Olivia. (2022). "Trump: I Could Declassify Documents by Thinking
About It." *Politico*, September 21. Available at: https://www.politico.com/news/2022
/09/21/trump-i-could-declassify-documents-by-thinking-about-it-00058212.

43. Lynch, Sarah N. (2022). "Trump's Lawyers Downplay Discovery of Classified
Documents at His Florida Home." Reuters, September 1. Available at: https://www
.reuters.com/world/us/media-outlets-ask-court-unseal-more-records-tied-fbi-search
-trumps-homes-2022-08-31/.

44. Sherman, Mark, and Tucker, Eric. (2022). "Justice Department Asks Court to
Deny Donald Trump Plea Over FBI Search." PBS, October 11. Available at: https://
www.pbs.org/newshour/politics/justice-department-asks-court-to-deny-donald-trump
-plea-over-fbi-search.

45. Wolfe, Jan. (2022). "Trump Likely Committed Crime With Plan to Obstruct
Congress, US Judge Rules." Reuters, March 28. Available at: https://www.yahoo.com
/news/trump-likely-committed-felony-obstructing-160842714.html.

46. Sherman and Tucker (2022).

47. Cheney, Kyle. (2022). "Judge Appoints Special Master, Rejects DOJ Bid
to Delay Mar-a-Lago Ruling." *Politico*, September 15. Available at: https://www
.politico.com/news/2022/09/15/judge-rejects-doj-bid-to-delay-mar-a-lago-ruling
-appoints-special-master-00057123.

48. Thomas, Jake. (2022). "Judge Cannon's Ruling on Classified Documents
Ripped by Legal Experts." *Newsweek*, September 29. Available at: https://www
.newsweek.com/judge-cannons-ruling-classified-documents-claim-ripped-legal
-experts-1747727.

49. Ibid.

50. Tucker, Eric. (2022). "Veteran Judge Named Special Master in Trump Documents Search." Associated Press, September 16. Available at: https://apnews.com/
article/new-york-donald-trump-brooklyn-mar-a-lago-government-and-politics-4a620
0ebc4fe6418c25ca380a43a6338.

51. Thomsen, Jacqueline. (2022). "Justice Department Asks Appeals Court to
Allow Review of Classified Documents in Trump Probe." Reuters, September
17. Available at: https://www.reuters.com/legal/us-justice-department-appeals-court
-ruling-seized-trump-documents-2022-09-17/.

52. Ibid.

53. Hurley, Lawrence. (2022). "Supreme Court Rejects Trump's Request in Dispute Over Mar-a-Lago Documents." NBC News, October 13. Available at: https://www.nbcnews.com/politics/supreme-court/supreme-court-rejects-trump-request-dispute-mar-lago-documents-rcna51775.

54. Mallin, Alexander. (2022). "DOJ Asks Appeals Court to Shut Down Special Master's Case in Trump Dispute." ABC News, October 14. Available at: https://abcnews.go.com/Politics/doj-asks-appeals-court-shut-special-masters-review/story?id=91528237.

55. Ibid.

56. Thomasen, Jacquline. (2022). "US Appeals Court Rules Against Trump in Documents Fight, Ends Arbiter." Reuters, December 1. Available at: https://www.reuters.com/world/us/us-appeals-court-reverses-appointment-special-master-trump-documents-probe-2022-12-01/.

57. Foer, Franklin. (2022). "The Inevitable Indictment of Donald Trump." *The Atlantic*, October. Available at: https://www.theatlantic.com/politics/archive/2022/10/merrick-garland-donald-trump-investigation-indictment/671683/.

58. Atkins, David. (2022). "Refusing to Prosecute Trump Is a Political Act." *Washington Monthly*, March 23. Available at: https://washingtonmonthly.com/2022/03/23/refusing-to-prosecute-trump-is-a-political-act/.

59. Ibid.

60. Ibid.

61. Hall, Madison. (2022). "417 Rioters Have Pleaded Guilty for Their Role in the Capitol Insurrection So Far. This Table Is Tracking Them All." *Insider*, October 17. Available at: https://www.insider.com/capitol-rioters-who-pleaded-guilty-updated-list-2021-5.

62. FiveThirtyEight. (2022). "60 Percent of Americans Will Have an Election Denier on the Ballot This Fall." FiveThirtyEight, November 2. Available at: https://projects.fivethirtyeight.com/republicans-trump-election-fraud/.

63. Haberman, Maggie; Berzon, Alexandra; and Schmidt, Michael S. (2022). "Trump Allies Continue Legal Drive to Erase His Loss, Stoking Election Doubts." *New York Times*, April 18. Available at: https://www.nytimes.com/2022/04/18/us/politics/trump-allies-election-decertify.html.

64. Ibid.

65. Ibid.

66. Smith, David. (2022). "Trump's 'Cult-Like Control' of Republican Party Grows Stronger Since Insurrection." *The Guardian*, January 5. Available at: https://www.theguardian.com/us-news/2022/jan/05/donald-trump-republican-party-capitol-attack-insurrection.

67. Ibid.

68. Ibid.

69. Ibid.

70. Atkins (2022); Smith (2022).

71. Atkins (2022).

72. Collinson, Stephen. (2022). "The Lies and Delusions Revealed in Mark Meadows' Texts Are Already Poisoning the Next Election." CNN, April 26. Available at:

https://www.cnn.com/2022/04/26/politics/meadows-texts-trump-lies-2022-election
-analysis/index.html.

73. Cillizza, Chris. (2022). "Why It Matters that Kevin McCarthy Lied." CNN,
April 22. Available at: https://www.cnn.com/2022/04/22/politics/mccarthy-trump-jan
-6-lie/index.html.

74. Ibid.

75. Martin and Burns (2022).

76. Sandel, Michael J. (2018). "Populism, Trump, and the Future of Democracy."
openDemocracy, May 9. Available at: https://www.opendemocracy.net/en/populism
-trump-and-future-of-democracy/.

77. Ibid.

78. Ibid.

79. Ibid.

80. Ibid.

81. Ibid.

82. Nichols, Tom. (2021). *Our Own Worst Enemy: The Assault from Within on
Modern Democracy*. New York: Oxford University Press.

83. Ibid.

References

Adams, Rebecca. (2000). *Deadhead Social Science: You Ain't Gonna Learn What You Don't Wanna Know.* Boston, MA: Rowman & Littlefield.

Aguirre, Mariano. (2020). "Trumpism, an Ideology for the Extreme Far-Right Globally." Open Democracy.net, December 14. Available at: https://www.opendemocracy.net/en/trumpism-ideology-extreme-far-right-globally/.

Albright, Madeleine. (2018). *Fascism: A Warning.* New York: Harper Collins.

Anti-Defamation League. (n.d.). "Alt-Right: A Primer About the New White Supremacy." Available at https://www.adl.org/resources/backgrounders/alt-right-a-primer-about-the-new-white-supremacy.

Anti-Defamation League. (n.d.) "The Great Replacement: An Explainer." Available at: https://www.adl.org/resources/backgrounders/the-great-replacment-an-explainer.

Applebaum, Yoni. (2016). "Trump Claims 'I Alone Can Fix It' During Republican National Convention," *The Atlantic*, July 21. Available at: https://www.theatlantic.com/politics/archive/2016/07/trump-rnc-speech-alone-fix-it/492557/.

Atkins, David. (2022). "Refusing to Prosecute Trump Is a Political Act." *Washington Monthly*, March 23. Available at: https://washingtonmonthly.com/2022/03/23/refusing-to-prosecute-trump-is-a-political-act/.

Azarian, Robert. (2018). "A Complete Psychological Analysis of Trump's Support." *Psychology Today*, December 27. Available at: https://www.psychologytoday.com/us/blog/mind-in-the-machine/201812/complete-psychological-analysis-trumps-support.

Balakian, Peter. (2020). "President Lincoln's Republican Party Was the Original Party of Big Government." *Literary Hub*, September 17. Available at: https://lithub.com/president-lincolns-republican-party-was-the-original-party-of-big-government/.

Ballotpedia. (2021). "Federal Judges Nominated by President Trump." Available at: https://ballotpedia.org/Federal_judges_nominated_by_Donald_Trump.

Balsamo, Michael. (2020). "Attorney General Bill Barr Says No Evidence of Widespread Fraud in 2020 Election." Fox 13 Tampa Bay, December 1. Available at: https://www.fox13news.com/news/barr-no-evidence-of-fraud-thatd-change-election-outcome.

Banco, Erin. (2021). "Emails Reveal New Details of Trump White House Interference in CDC COVID Planning." *Politico*, November 12. Available at: https://www.politico.com/news/2021/11/12/trump-cdc-covid-521128.

Barrett, Devlin, and Dawsey, Josh. (2022). "Agents at Trump's Mar-a-Lago Seized 11 Sets of Classified Documents, Court Filing Shows." *Washington Post*, August 12. Available at: https://www.washingtonpost.com/national-security/2022/08/12/trump-warrant-release/.

Barrett, Devlin, and Stein, Perry. (2022). "Affidavit to Search Trump's Mar-a-Lago Says 184 Classified Files Found in January." *Washington Post*, August 26. Available at: https://www.washingtonpost.com/national-security/2022/08/26/trump-affidavit-released/.

Bender, Michael C. (2021). *Frankly, We Did Win This Election: The Definitive Account of Trump's Final Year in Office.* New York: Twelve Publishing.

Benner, Katie; Rogers, Katie; and Schmidt, Michael S. (2022). "Garland Faces Growing Pressure as Jan. 6 Investigation Widens." *New York Times*, April 2. Available at: https://www.nytimes.com/2022/04/02/us/politics/merrick-garland-biden-trump.html.

Billeaud, Jacques, and Tarm, Michael. (2021). "As Prospect of Jail Looms, Capitol Riot Suspects Express Regret." *Christian Science Monitor*, March 31. Available at: https://www.csmonitor.com/USA/Politics/2021/0331/As-prospect-of-jail-looms-Capitol-riot-suspects-express-regret.

Bolton, John. (2020). *The Room Where It Happened: A White House Memoir.* New York: Simon & Schuster.

Boston, Rob. (2006). "The Religious Right and American Freedom." Americans United for Separation of Church and State.org. June. Available at: https://au.org/church-state/june-2006-church-state/featured/the-religious-right-and-american-freedom.

Bradlee, Ben. (2018). *The Forgotten: How the People of One Pennsylvania County Elected Donald Trump and Changed America.* New York: Little, Brown and Co.

Bray, Mark. (2017). *Antifa: The Anti-Fascist Handbook.* New York: Melville House.

Brennan Center for Justice. (2021). *Voting Laws Roundup: May 2021.* Available at: https://www.brennancenter.org/our-work/research-reports/voting-laws-roundup-may-2021.

Brennan Center for Justice. (2021). *Voting Laws Roundup: October 2021.* Available at: https://www.brennancenter.org/our-work/research-reports/voting-laws-roundup-october-2021.

Breuninger, Kevin. (2022). "Senate Confirms Ketanji Brown Jackson to the Supreme Court, Making Her the First Black Woman to Serve as a Justice." CNBC, April 7. Available at: https://www.cnbc.com/2022/04/07/ketanji-brown-jackson-confirmed-to-supreme-court-first-black-woman-justice.html.

Brewer, Marilynn. (2016). "Ethnocentrism and the Theory of Social Identity." In Sternberg, Robert J.; Fiske, Susan T.; and Foss, Donald J. (eds.), *Scientists Making a Difference*, pp. 360–64. New York: Cambridge University Press.

Broadwater, Luke; Brenner, Katie; and Haberman, Maggie. (2022). "Inside the 20-Month Fight to Get Trump to Return Presidential Material." *New York Times*,

August 26. Available at: https://www.nytimes.com/2022/08/26/us/politics/trump -documents-search-timeline.html.

Brookings Institution. (2021). *New 2020 Voter Data: How Biden Won, How Trump Kept the Race Close and What It Tells Us About the Future*. Available at: https: //www.brookings.edu/blog/fixgov/2021/07/06/new-2020-voter-data-how-biden -won-how-trump-kept-the-race-close-and-what-it-tells-us-about-the-future/.

Burnett, John. (2022). "Americans Are Fleeing to Places Where Political Views Match Their Own." NPR, February 18. Available at: https://www.npr.org/2022/02 /18/1081295373/the-big-sort-americans-move-to-areas-political-alignment.

Byman, Daniel L. (2021). "White Supremacist Terrorism: Key Trends to Watch in 2021." Brookings Institution, January 15. Available at: https://www.brookings .edu/blog/order-from-chaos/2021/01/15/white-supremacist-terrorism-key-trends -to-watch-in-2021/.

Cacioppo, John, and Patrick, William. (2008). *Loneliness: Human Nature and the Need for Social Connection*. New York: W.W. Norton.

Cai, Weiyi. (2021). "A Step-by-Step Guide to the Second Impeachment Trial of Donald J. Trump." *New York Times*, February 13. Available at: https://www.nytimes.com/ interactive/2021/02/08/us/politics/trump-second-impeachment-timeline.html.

Cameron, Rob. (2021). "White Supremacy Created the Capitol Assault." *Foreign Policy*, January 11. Available at: https://foreignpolicy.com/2021/01/11/white -supremacy-capitol-assault-trump-supporters/.

Carney, Timothy. (2020). *Alienated America: While Some Places Thrive, Others Collapse*. New York: Harper.

Castronuovo, Celine. (2021). "Capitol Police Told Not to Use Most Aggressive Tactics in Riot Response, Report Finds." *The Hill*, April 13. Available at: https: //thehill.com/policy/national-security/548104-capitol-police-told-not-to-use-most -aggressive-tactics-in-riot-response.

Cavicchi, Daniel. (1998). *Tramps Like Us: Music and Meaning Among Springsteen Fans.* New York: Oxford University Press.

Chappell, Bill. (2021). "Architect of the Capitol Outlines $30 Million in Damages From Pro-Trump Riot." NPR, February 24. Available at: https://www.npr.org/ sections/insurrection-at-the-capitol/2021/02/24/970977612/architect-of-the-capitol -outlines-30-million-in-damages-from-pro-trump-riot.

Cheney, Kyle. (2022). "Judge Appoints Special Master, Rejects DOJ Bid to Delay Mar-a-Lago Ruling." *Politico*, September 15. Available at: https://www.politico .com/news/2022/09/15/judge-rejects-doj-bid-to-delay-mar-a-lago-ruling-appoints -special-master-00057123.

Cherlin, Andrew J. (2020). "Why Did So Many Urban Working-Class Whites Support President Trump?" Contexts.org. October 1. Available at: https://contexts.org/ articles/why-did-so-many-urban-working-class-whites-support-president-trump/.

Chuck, Elizabeth, and Siemaszko, Corky. (2022). "COVID's Toll in the US Reaches a Once Unfathomable Number: 1 Million Deaths." NBCNews.com, May 4. Available at: https://www.nbcnews.com/news/us-news/covids-toll-us-reaches-1 -million-deaths-unfathomable-number-rcna22105.

Churchill, Winston. (2015). *The World Crisis: 1911–1919.* London: Bloomsbury Academic.

Cillizza, Chris. (2022). "Why It Matters That Kevin McCarthy Lied." CNN, April 22. https://www.cnn.com/2022/04/22/politics/mccarthy-trump-jan-6-lie/index.html.

Clark, Simon. (2020). "How White Supremacy Returned to Mainstream Politics." Center for American Progress, July 1. Available at: https://www.americanprogress.org/issues/security/reports/2020/07/01/482414/white-supremacy-returned-mainstream-politics/.

Cobb, Jelani. (2021). "What's Happening to the Republicans?" *New Yorker Magazine*, March 8. Available at: https://www.newyorker.com/magazine/2021/03/15/what-is-happening-to-the-republicans.

Cohen, Marshall. (2022). "Judge Unseals Less Redacted Version of Affidavit Used for Mar-a-Lago Search Warrant." CNN, September 13. Available at: https://ksltv.com/505584/judge-unseals-less-redacted-version-of-affidavit-used-for-mar-a-lago-search-warrant/.

Cohen, Marshall; Cohen, Zachary; and Rogers, Alex. (2022). "7 Takeaways from Tuesday's Shocking January 6 Hearing." CNN, June 29. Available at: https://www.cnn.com/2022/06/28/politics/january-6-hearing-day-6-takeaways-hutchinson/index.html.

Collins, John. (1991). *The Cult Experience: An Overview of Cults, Their Traditions, and Why People Join Them.* Springfield, IL: Charles C. Thomas.

Collinson, Stephen. (2022). "The Lies and Delusions Revealed in Mark Meadows' Texts Are Already Poisoning the Next Election." CNN, April 26. Available at: https://www.cnn.com/2022/04/26/politics/meadows-texts-trump-lies-2022-election-analysis/index.html.

Conerly, Tonja R.; Holmes, Kathleen; and Tamang, Asha Lal. (2021). *Introduction to Sociology 3e.* Openstax.org. Available at: https://openstax.org/books/introduction-sociology-3e/pages/21-introduction-to-social-movements-and-social-change.

Cummings, William; Garrison, Joey; and Sargent, Jim. (2021). "By the Numbers: President Donald Trump's Failed Efforts to Overturn the Election." *USA Today*, January 6. Available at: https://www.usatoday.com/in-depth/news/politics/elections/2021/01/06/trumps-failed-efforts-overturn-election-numbers/4130307001/.

Daley, Beth. (2017). "One Way Trump Is Different from European Nationalists." *The Conversation.* January 18. Available at: https://theconversation.com/one-way-trump-is-different-from-european-nationalists-71259.

Dawsey, Josh, and Alemany, Jacqueline. (2022). "Trump's Lawyer Refused His Request in February to Say All Documents Returned." *Washington Post*, October 3. Available at: https://www.washingtonpost.com/national-security/2022/10/03/trump-alex-cannon-documents/.

Dawson, Lorne. (2013). *Comprehending Cults: The Sociology of New Religious Movements.* New York: Oxford University Press.

Dean, John W., and Altemeyer, Bob. (2020). *Authoritarian Nightmare: The Ongoing Threat of Trump's Followers.* Brooklyn, NY: Melville House.

Delgado, Richard, and Stefancic, Jean. (2012). *Critical Race Theory: An Introduction* (second edition). New York: New York University Press.

DiAngelo, Robin. (2018). *White Fragility: Why It's So Hard for White People to Talk About Racism*. Boston, MA: Beacon Press.

Dickinson, Caitlin. (2021). "Alarming Finding: 30 Percent of Republicans Say Violence May Be Needed to Save US, Poll Shows." Yahoo News, November 1. Available at: https://news.yahoo.com/prri-poll-republicans-violence-040144322 .html.

Dickinson, Tim. (2021). "Oath Keepers Use a Dystopian Fever Dream to Snare Police Forces, Military Vets." *Rolling Stone*, October 28. Available at: https://www.yahoo .com/entertainment/oath-keepers-dystopian-fever-dream-120024425.html.

Dilanian, Ken; Winter, Tom; Dienst, Jonathan; and Blankstein, Andrew. (2021). "FBI, NYPD Told Capitol Police About Possibility of Violence Before Riot, Senior Officials Say." NBC News, January 10. Available at: https://www.nbcnews.com /news/crime-courts/fbi-nypd-told-capitol-police-about-possibility-violence-riot -senior-n1253646.

Divola, Barry. (2017). "Bruce Springsteen and the Mega Fans Who Tour the World to See Him." *Sydney Morning Herald*, January 20. Available at: https://www.smh .com.au/entertainment/music/bruce-springsteen-and-the-megafans-who-tour-the -world-to-see-him-20170119-gturo2.html.

Drezner, Daniel W. (2021). "The Trump Legacy." *Washington Post*, January 30. Available at: https://www.washingtonpost.com/outlook/2021/01/20/trump-legacy/.

Du Mez, Kristen Kobes. (2020). *Jesus and John Wayne: How White Evangelicals Corrupted a Faith and Fractured a Nation*. London: Liveright.

Durkee, Allison. (2022). "Special Master Demands Trump Prove Claims FBI Planted Evidence at Mar-a-Lago." *Forbes*, September 22. Available at: https://www.forbes .com/sites/alisondurkee/2022/09/22/special-master-demands-trump-prove-claims -fbi-planted-evidence-at-mar-a-lago/?sh=598a943f6e22.

Egawa, Shoko. (2021). "US Must Not Underestimate the Risks of the Trump Cult." AsiaNikkei.com, January 19. Available at: https://asia.nikkei.com/Opinion/US -must-not-underestimate-the-risks-of-the-Trump-cult.

Elias, Jennifer, and Breuninger, Kevin. (2021). "More than 50 Police Officers Were Hurt at Pro-Trump Riot at the Capitol That Also Killed Four." CNBC.com, January 7. Available at: https://www.cnbc.com/2021/01/07/four-dead-after-pro -Trump-rioters-storm-capitol.html.

Elving, Ron. (2018). "What Happened With Merrick Garland in 2016 and Why It Matters Now." NPR, June 29. Available at: https://www.npr.org/2018/06/29 /624467256/what-happened-with-merrick-garland-in-2016-and-why-it-matters -now.

Eyre, Anne. (n.d.). "Religious Cults in the Twentieth Century." American Studies Resource Center. Available at: http://www.americansc.org.uk/Online/cults.htm.

Feagin, Joe R. (2006). *Systematic Racism: A Theory of Oppression*. New York: Routledge.

Fenwick, Cody. (2020). "Is Trump's Base of Support a Cult? Ask 3 People Who Left It." Alternet.org, January 23. Available at: https://www.alternet.org/2020/01/is -trumps-base-of-support-a-cult-ask-3-people-who-left-it/.

Ferraro, Gary P.; Andreatta, Susan; and Holdsworth, Chris. (2017). *Cultural Anthropology: An Applied Perspective*. Toronto: Nelson.

Festinger, Leon. (1954). "A Theory of Social Comparison Processes." *Human Relations*, 7(2): 117–40.

Festinger, Leon. (1957). *A Theory of Cognitive Dissonance*. Stanford, CA: Stanford University Press.

Feuer, Alan. (2022). "Trump Kept More than 700 Pages of Classified Documents, Letter from National Archives Says." *New York Times*, August 23. Available at: https://www.nytimes.com/2022/08/23/us/politics/trump-classified-documents-fbi-letter.html/.

Feuer, Alan, and Haberman, Maggie. (2022). "Email Shows Early Tension Between Trump and National Archives." *New York Times*, August 24. Available at: https://www.nytimes.com/2022/08/24/us/politics/national-archives-letter-trump.html.

Fitzduff, Mari, ed. (2017). *Why Irrational Politics Appeals*. Westport, CT: Praeger.

FiveThirtyEight. (2022). "60 Percent of Americans Will Have an Election Denier on the Ballot This Fall." November 2. Available at: https://projects.fivethirtyeight.com/republicans-trump-election-fraud/.

Foer, Franklin. (2022). "The Inevitable Indictment of Donald Trump." *The Atlantic*, October. Available at: https://www.theatlantic.com/politics/archive/2022/10/merrick-garland-donald-trump-investigation-indictment/671683/.

Foran, Claire. (2021). "GOP Sen. Collins: Trump Incited an Insurrection to Prevent Peaceful Transfer of Authority." CNN, February 13. Available at: https://edition.cnn.com/politics/live-news/trump-impeachment-trial-02-13-2021/index.html.

Foster, John Bellamy. (2017). "This Is Not Populism." *Monthly Review*, June 1, Available at: https://monthlyreview.org/2017/06/01/this-is-not-populism/.

French, David. (2020). *Divided We Fall: America's Secession Threat and How to Restore Our Nation.* New York: St. Martin's Press.

FromTPM.org. (2020). "How Cults Function." April 4. Available at: https://www.fromtpm.com/blog/2020/04/04/how-cults-function-a-general-overview/.

Gerson, Michael. (2018). "Trump and the Evangelical Temptation." *The Atlantic*, April. Available at: https://www.theatlantic.com/magazine/archive/2018/04/the-last-temptation/554066/.

Giglio, Mike. (2020). "A Pro-Trump Militant Group Has Recruited Thousands of Police, Soldiers, and Veterans." *The Atlantic*, November. Available at: https://www.theatlantic.com/magazine/archive/2020/11/right-wing-militias-civil-war/616473/.

Gilbert, Martin. (2004). *The First World War: A Complete History* (second edition). New York: Holt.

Goldberg, Jonah. (2018). *Suicide of the West: How the Rebirth of Tribalism, Populism, Nationalism, and Identity Politics Is Destroying American Democracy*. New York: Crown.

Gould, Lewis. (2003). *Grand Old Party: A History of Republicans*. New York: Random House.

Graham, David. A. (2020). "Jeff Sessions Explains Why Christians Support Donald Trump." *The Atlantic*, June. Available at: https://www.theatlantic.com/ideas/archive/2020/06/why-christians-support-trump/613669/.

Gurgel, Barbara. (2021). "How Do Normal, Successful, Smart People End Up Joining a Cult?" *The Daily Beast*, May 12. Available at: https://www.thedailybeast.com/why-do-people-join-cults.

Haberman, Maggie. (2022). "FBI Interviewed Top White House Lawyers About Missing Trump Documents." *New York Times*, August 16. Available at: https://www.nytimes.com/2022/08/16/us/politics/trump-cipollone-philbin-interviews-fbi.html.

Haberman, Maggie; Berzon, Alexandra; and Schmidt, Michael S. (2022). "Trump Allies Continue Legal Drive to Erase His Loss, Stoking Election Doubts." *New York Times*, April 18. Available at: https://www.nytimes.com/2022/04/18/us/politics/trump-allies-election-decertify.html.

Hall, Madison. (2022). "417 Rioters Have Pleaded Guilty for Their Role in the Capitol Insurrection So Far. This Table Is Tracking Them All." *Insider*, October 17. Available at: https://www.insider.com/capitol-rioters-who-pleaded-guilty-updated-list-2021-5.

Hall, Madison; Gould, Skye; Harrington, Rebecca; Shamsian, Jacob; Haroun, Azmi; Ardrey, Taylor; and Snodgrass, Erin. (2021). "615 People Have Been Charged in the Capitol Insurrection So Far. This Searchable Table Shows Them All." *Insider*, August 18. Available at: https://www.insider.com/all-the-us-capitol-pro-trump-riot-arrests-charges-names-2021-1.

Haltiwanger, John. (2020). "Trump Has Repeatedly Been Endorsed by White Supremacist Groups and Other Far-Right Extremists and They've Looked to Him as a Source of Encouragement." *Business Insider*, September 30. Available at: https://www.businessinsider.com/trumps-history-of-support-from-white-supremacist-far-right-groups-2020-9.

Haltiwanger, John. (2021). "Trump's Biggest Accomplishments and Failures from His 1-Term Presidency." *Business Insider*, January 20. Available at: https://www.businessinsider.com/trump-biggest-accomplishments-and-failures-heading-into-2020-2019-12#failure-damaging-democracy-15.

Hassan, Steven. (2020). *The Cult of Trump*. New York: Basic Books.

Haynes, Jeffrey. 2021. *Trump and the Politics of Neo-Nationalism: The Christian Right and Secular Nationalism in America*. London: Routledge.

Heller, Zoey. (2021). "What Makes a Cult a Cult?" *The New Yorker*, July 12. Available at: https://www.newyorker.com/magazine/2021/07/12/what-makes-a-cult-a-cult.

Hemmer, Nicole. (2016). *Messengers of the Right: Conservative Media and the Transformation of American Politics*. Philadelphia, PA: University of Pennsylvania Press.

Hett, Benjamin Carter. (2019). *Death of Democracy: Hitler's Rise to Power and the Downfall of the Weimar Republic*. New York: St. Martin's Press.

Hett, Benjamin Carter. (2020). *The Nazi Menace: Hitler, Churchill, Roosevelt, Stalin and the Road to War*. New York: Henry Holt & Company.

History.com. (n.d.). "This Date in History: World War I Ends." Available at: https://www.history.com/this-day-in-history/world-war-i-ends.

Hochschild, Arlie Russell. (2018). *Strangers in Their Own Land: Anger and Mourning on the American Right*. New York: The New Press.

Howard, Michael. (2007). *The First World War.* New York: Oxford University Press.

Hubbard, Kaia. (2021). "Far-Right Extremism Echoes Across Europe." *US News,* February 18. Available at: https://www.usnews.com/news/best-countries/articles /2021-02-18/far-right-extremism-growing-across-europe-survey-finds.

Hurley, Lawrence. (2022). "Supreme Court Rejects Trump's Request in Dispute Over Mar-a-Lago Documents." NBC News, October 13. Available at: https:// www.nbcnews.com/politics/supreme-court/supreme-court-rejects-trump-request -dispute-mar-lago-documents-rcna51775.

Hutchinson, Earl. (2020). "Trump Voters Are More Than a Bunch of Angry White Guys." *Bay State Banner,* November 19. Available at: https://www.baystatebanner .com/2020/11/19/trumps-voters-are-more-than-a-bunch-of-angry-white-guys/.

Igielnik, Ruth; Keeter, Scott; and Hartig, Hannah. (2021). "Behind Biden's 2020 Victory." Pew Research Center, June 30. Available at: https://www.pewresearch .org/politics/2021/06/30/behind-bidens-2020-victory/.

Jackson, Sam. (2020). *Oath Keepers: Patriotism and the Edge of Violence in a Right-Wing Antigovernment Group.* New York: Columbia University Press.

Jacobs, Tom. (2018). "Inside the Minds of Hardcore Trump Supporters." *Pacific Standard,* February 15. Available at: https://psmag.com/news/inside-the-minds-of -hardcore-trump-supporters.

Jenkins, Brian. (2021). "Why We Need a January 6 Commission to Investigate the Attack on the Capitol." Rand Corporation, January 20. Available at: https://www .rand.org/blog/2021/01/why-we-need-a-january-6-commission-to-investigate-the .html.

Jones, Zoe Christien. (2022). "Florida Legislature Passes 'Stop WOKE Act,' Second Controversial Education Bill This Week." CBSNews, March 10. Available at: https: //www.cbsnews.com/news/florida-critical-race-theory-education-stop-woke-act/.

Juergensmeyer, Mark. (2000). *Terrorism in the Mind of God: The Global Rise of Religious Violence.* Berkeley: University of California Press.

Jupskas, Andres. (n.d.). "What Is Populism?" Center for Research on Extremism. Available at: https://www.sv.uio.no/c-rex/english/groups/compendium/what-is -populism.html.

Kahan, Dan M.; Peters, Ellen; Witlin, Maggie; Slovic, Paul; Ouellette, Lisa Larrimore; Braman, Donald; and Mandel, Gregory. (2012). "The Polarizing Impact of Science Literacy and Numeracy on Perceived Climate Change Risks." *Nature Climate Change,* 2: 732–35.

Karl, Jonathan. (2021). "Inside Bill Barr's Breakup With Trump." *The Atlantic,* June 27. Available at: https://www.theatlantic.com/politics/archive/2021/06/william -barrs-trump-administration-attorney-general/619298/.

Keegan, John. (2000). *The First World War.* New York: Knopf Doubleday.

Kelly, John. (2021). *Betrayal: The Final Act of the Trump Show.* New York: Dutton.

Kennedy, Brigid. (2021). "The Thousands of Hours of Jan. 6 Footage the Government Wants to Keep Private." Yahoo.com, August 30. Available at: https://www.yahoo .com/now/thousands-hours-jan-6-footage-205934034.html.

Kessler, Glenn; Rizzo, Salvador; and Kelly, Meg. (2021). "Trump's False and Misleading Claims Total 30,573 Over Four Years." *Washington Post,* January 24.

Available at: https://www.washingtonpost.com/politics/2021/01/24/trumps-false-or
-misleading-claims-total-30573-over-four-years/.

Kiely, Eugene, and Rieder, Rem. (2020). "Trump's Repeated False Attacks on Mail-in
Ballots." FactCheck.org, September 25. Available at: https://www.factcheck.org
/2020/09/trumps-repeated-false-attacks-on-mail-in-ballots/.

Kika, Thomas. (2022). "Pence Refusing to Get in Secret Service Car on Jan. 6
'Chilling': Raskin." *Newsweek*, April 23. Available at: https://www.newsweek.com
/pence-refusing-get-secret-service-car-jan-6-chilling-raskin-1700341.

Kilgore, Ed. (2021). "The Chilling Message of Trump's Embrace of Ashli Babbitt."
New York Magazine, July 7. Available at: https://nymag.com/intelligencer/2021/07
/trump-who-shot-ashli-babbitt-january-6-insurrection-riot.html.

Kimmel, Michael. (2018). *Healing From Hate: How Young Men Get Into—and Out
of—Violent Extremism*. Berkeley, CA: University of California Press.

Kinery, Emma. (2022). "Biden Promises to Codify Roe if Two More Democrats Are
Elected to the Senate." CNBC, September 23. Available at: https://www.cnbc.com
/2022/09/23/biden-promises-to-codify-roe-if-two-more-democrats-are-elected-to
-the-senate.html.

Klein, Ezra. (2020). *Why We Are Polarized*. New York: Avid Reader Press.

Klinenberg, Eric. (2002). *Heat Wave: A Social Autopsy of Disaster in Chicago*.
Chicago, IL: University of Chicago Press.

Kohls, Ryan. (2018). "Explained: Evangelicals, the Religious Right and Trump."
Aljazeera, November 6. Available at: https://www.aljazeera.com/news/2018/11/6/
explained-evangelicals-the-religious-right-and-trump.

Kriner, Matthew, and Lewis, Jon. (2021). "Pride and Prejudice: The Violent Evolution
of the Proud Boys." *Combatting Terrorism Center*, 14(6), July/August. Available
at: https://ctc.usma.edu/pride-prejudice-the-violent-evolution-of-the-proud-boys/.

Kruesi, Kimberlee. (2022). "Tenn. 'Divisive Concept' Bill Targeting Colleges
Advances." Yahoo News, March 21. Available at: https://www.yahoo.com/news/
tenn-divisive-concept-bill-targeting-233636647.html.

Krugman, Paul. (2021). "How Did We Get Here? What Happened to the Republican
Party?" *Austin American Statesman*, January 9. Available at: https://www.statesman
.com/story/opinion/columns/more-voices/2021/01/09/opinion-how-republican
-party-went-feral/6588613002/.

Kunzelman, Michael. (2021). "Feds Seek Tougher Sentences for Veterans Who
Stormed the Capitol." Yahoo News, November 3. Available at: https://www.yahoo
.com/news/feds-seek-tougher-sentences-veterans-041514021.html.

LaFrance, Adrienne. (2020). "The Prophesies of Q." *The Atlantic*, June. Available at:
https://www.theatlantic.com/magazine/archive/2020/06/qanon-nothing-can-stop
-what-is-coming/610567.

Lalich, Janja. (2004). *Bounded Choice: True Believers and Charismatic Cults*.
Berkeley: University of California Press.

Lalich, Janja. (n.d.). "Dr. Lalich's Theory on Brainwashing." JanjaLalich.com.
Available at: https://janjalalich.com/about/dr-lalichs-theory-on-brainwashing/.

Lati, Marisa. (2021). "What Is Critical Race Theory and Why Do Republicans Want to Ban It?" *Washington Post*, May 29. Available at: https://www.washingtonpost.com/education/2021/05/29/critical-race-theory-bans-schools/.

LeBlanc, Paul. (2021). "Ex-Trump Advisor Michael Flynn's Call for 'One Religion' in the US Garners Swift Condemnation." CNN, November 15. Available at: https://www.cnn.com/2021/11/15/politics/michael-flynn-one-religion/index.html.

Lee, Bandy X. (2017). *The Dangerous Case of Donald Trump*. New York: Thomas Dunne Books.

Lee, Morgan. (2021). "Critical Race Theory: What Christians Need to Know." *Christianity Today*, July 2. Available at: https://www.christianitytoday.com/ct/podcasts/quick-to-listen/critical-race-theory-racism-evangelicals-divided-podcast.html.

Levin, Bess. (2022). "Trump Tells Supporters They Must Fight to the Death to Stop Schools from Teaching Kids About Systemic Racism." *Vanity Fair*, March 14. Available at: https://www.vanityfair.com/news/2022/03/donald-trump-critical-race-theory-lay-down-lives.

Levine, Marianne. (2021). "McConnell: I'd Block Biden SCOTUS Nominee in 2024." *Politico*, June 14. Available at: https://www.politico.com/news/2021/06/14/mcconnell-biden-scotus-494340.

Lifton, Robert Jay. (2019). *Losing Reality: On Cults, Cultism, and the Mindset of Political and Religious Zealotry*. New York: The New Press.

Liptak, Adam. (2018). "Supreme Court Sides With Baker Who Turned Away Gay Couple." *New York Times*, June 4. Available at: https://www.nytimes.com/2018/06/04/us/politics/supreme-court-sides-with-baker-who-turned-away-gay-couple.html.

Liptak, Adam. (2021). "Supreme Court Allows Challenge to Texas Abortion Law but Leaves It in Effect." *New York Times*, December 10. Available at: https://www.nytimes.com/2021/12/10/us/politics/texas-abortion-supreme-court.html.

Liptak, Kevin. (2022). "Mar-a-Lago—and Its Owner—Have Long Caused Concerns for US Intelligence." CNN, August 14. Available at: https://www.cnn.com/2022/08/14/politics/trump-documents-mar-a-lago/index.html.

Little, David. (n.d.). "Religious Freedom and Christianity, an Overview." Berkley Center for Religion, Peace and World Affairs, Georgetown University. Available at: https://berkleycenter.georgetown.edu/essays/religious-freedom-and-christianity-an-overview.

Long, Colleen, and Balsamo, Michael. (2021). "Capitol Police Officers Sue Trump, Allies Over Insurrection." Associated Press, August 26. Available at: https://apnews.com/article/capitol-siege-michael-pence-4cd64aab06e0f943ca8f83fd0b65037d.

Lowndes, Joseph. (2019). "Populism and Race in the United States from George Wallace to Donald Trump." In de la Torre, Carlos (ed.), *Routledge Handbook of Global Populism*, pp. 197–200. London/New York: Routledge.

Lynch, Sarah N. (2022). "Trump's Lawyers Downplay Discovery of Classified Documents at His Florida Home." Reuters, September 1. Available at: https://

www.reuters.com/world/us/media-outlets-ask-court-unseal-more-records-tied-fbi-search-trumps-homes-2022-08-31/.

MacMillan, Margaret. (2003). *Paris 1919*. New York: Random House.

Mahdawi, Arwa. (2019). "Brett Kavanaugh Shows True Colours in Supreme Court Abortion Dissent." *The Guardian*, February 9. Available at: https://www.theguardian.com/commentisfree/2019/feb/09/brett-kavanaugh-shows-true-colours-in-supreme-court-abortion-dissent.

Main, Thomas J. (2021). *The Rise of Illiberalism*. Washington, DC: The Brookings Institution.

Mallin, Alexander. (2022). "DOJ Asks Appeals Court to Shut Down Special Master's Case in Trump Dispute." ABC News, October 14. Available at: https://abcnews.go.com/Politics/doj-asks-appeals-court-shut-special-masters-review/story?id=91528237.

Marcotte, Amanda. (2021). "Why the Panic Over Critical Race Theory Is the Perfect Right-Wing Troll." *Salon*, June 15. Available at: https://www.salon.com/2021/06/15/why-the-panic-over-critical-race-theory-is-the-perfect-right-wing-troll/.

Martin, Bradley; Koblentz-Stenzler, Liram; and Pack, Alexander. (2021). "Trump Supporters Face White Supremacist Radicalization on Social Media." *Newsweek*, January 25. Available at: https://www.newsweek.com/trump-supporters-face-white-supremacist-radicalization-social-media-opinion-1563813.

Martin, Jonathan, and Burns, Alexander. (2022). *This Will Not Pass: Trump, Biden, and the Battle for America's Future.* New York: Simon & Schuster.

Martin, Michel. (2022). "What the Recent Wins for Far-Right Parties in Europe Could Mean for the Region." NPR, October 1. Available at: https://www.npr.org/2022/10/01/1126419403/what-the-recent-wins-for-far-right-parties-in-europe-could-mean-for-the-region.

Mascaro, Lisa. (2021). "Capitol Rally Seeks to Rewrite January 6 by Exalting Rioters." Associated Press, September 13. Available at: https://apnews.com/article/joe-biden-donald-trump-capitol-siege-d2fb23af3f01387412a1a00b4eac531c.

Mason, Lilliana. (2018). *Uncivil Agreement: How Politics Became Our Identity*. Chicago: University of Chicago Press.

Mathis, Joel. (2021). "The Jan. 6 'Plot' That Wasn't." Yahoo News, August 20. Available at: https://www.yahoo.com/news/jan-6-plot-wasnt-172353059.html.

Matzen, Morgan. (2022). "Gov. Kristi Noem Signs Bill Limiting 'Divisive Comments' and Critical Race Theory from Colleges." Yahoo News, March 21. Available at: https://www.yahoo.com/news/gov-kristi-noem-signs-bill-175316757.html.

McQueen, Eric. (2021). "Examining Extremism: Oath Keepers." Center for Strategic and International Studies, June 17. Available at: https://www.csis.org/blogs/examining-extremism/examining-extremism-oath-keepers.

McVicar, Michael J. (2018). "The Religious Right in America." *Oxford Research Encyclopedia*. Available at: https://oxfordre.com/religion/view/10.1093/acrefore/9780199340378.001.0001/acrefore-9780199340378-e-97.

Metzger, Bryan. (2021). "FBI Finds No Evidence that Trump and His Allies Were Directly Involved With Organizing the Violence of the Capitol Riot: Report."

Business Insider, August 20. Available at: https://www.businessinsider.com/trump -not-directly-involved-in-organizing-capitol-riot-violence-report-2021-8.

Milligan, Susan. (2021). "Republicans Flee the GOP After Capitol Riots." *US News*, April 7. Available at: https://www.usnews.com/news/politics/articles/2021-04-07/ republicans-flee-the-gop-after-capitol-riots.

Moens, Barbara, and Hirsch, Cornelius. (2022). "How the Far Right Got Out of the Doghouse." *Politico*, October 3. available at: https://www.politico.eu/article/the-far -right-is-out-of-the-doghouse/.

Montague, Zach, and McCarthy, Lauren (2022). "The Timeline Related to the FBI's Search of Mar-a-Lago." *The New York Times*, August 1. Available at: https://www .nytimes.com/2022/08/12/us/politics/trump-classified-records-timeline.html.

Mounk, Yaschi. (2019). *The People vs. Democracy*. Boston, MA: Harvard University Press.

Mounk, Yaschi. (2021). "After Trump, Is American Democracy Doomed by Populism?" Council on Foreign Relations, January 14. Available at: https://www .cfr.org/in-brief/after-trump-american-democracy-doomed-populism.

Mulligan, Katrina; Steele, Brette; Clark, Simon; Padmanabhan, Asha; and Hinkler, Rachel. (2021). "A National Policy Blueprint to End White Supremacist Violence." Center for American Progress, March 21. Available at: https://www .americanprogress.org/issues/security/reports/2021/04/21/498156/national-policy -blueprint-end-white-supremacist-violence/.

Murray, Charles. (2012). *Coming Apart: The State of White America 1960–2010*. New York: Crown.

Naftulin, Julia. (2020). "3 Reasons Why People Join Cults, According to a Cult Recovery Therapist." *Insider*, September 23. Available at: https://www.insider.com /why-people-join-cults-according-to-therapist-who-treats-survivors-2020-9.

National Public Radio. (2016). "What You Need to Know About the Alt-Right." NPR, August 26. Available at: https://www.npr.org/2016/08/26/491452721/the-history -of-the-alt-right.

National World War II Museum. (n.d.). "Research Starters: Worldwide Deaths in World War II." Available at: https://www.nationalww2museum.org/students -teachers/student-resources/research-starters/research-starters-worldwide-deaths -world-war.

Naylor, Brian. (2021). "Senate Republicans Block a Plan for an Independent Commission on January 6th Capitol Riot." NPR, May 28. Available at: https://www .npr.org/2021/05/28/1000524897/senate-republicans-block-plan-for-independent -commission-on-jan-6-capitol-riot.

Neuman, Scott. (2020). "Trump Now Says He Condemns 'All White Supremacists,' After Declining to at Debate." NPR, October 1. Available at: https://www.npr .org/sections/live-updates-protests-for-racial-justice/2020/10/01/919375470/trump -now-says-he-condemns-all-white-supremacists-after-declining-to-at-debate.

Nichols, Tom. (2021). *Our Own Worst Enemy: The Assault from Within on Modern Democracy*. New York: Oxford University Press.

Oath Keepers. (n.d.). "Declaration of Orders We Will Not Obey." Available at: https: //oathkeepers.org/declaration-of-orders-we-will-not-obey/.

Olander, Olivia. (2022). "Trump: I Could Declassify Documents by Thinking About It." *Politico*, September 21. Available at: https://www.politico.com/news/2022/09/21/trump-i-could-declassify-documents-by-thinking-about-it-00058212.

Olds, Jacqueline, and Schwartz, Richard S. (2009). *The Lonely American: Drifting Apart in the Twenty-first Century*. Boston, MA: Beacon Books.

Olmstead, Kathryn. (2011). *Real Enemies: Conspiracy Theories and American Democracy, World War I to 9/11*. New York: Oxford University Press.

Orr, Gabby; Brown, Pamela; and Reid, Paula. (2022). "Archives Threatened to Go to Congress and Justice Department to Get Trump to Turn Over Records." *The Mercury News*, February 13. Available at: https://www.mercurynews.com/?returnUrl=https%3A%2F%2Fwww.mercurynews.com%2F2022%2F02%2F11%2Farchives-threatened-to-go-to-congress-over-trump-records%2F%3FclearUserState%3Dtrue.

Palmer, Ewan. (2022). "Trump Lawyers Stopped FBI Agents Checking Storage Room Boxes." *Newsweek*, August 31. Available at: https://www.newsweek.com/trump-search-documents-fbi-maralago-lawyers-june-1738370.

PBS. (n.d.). "WWI Casualty and Death Tables." Available at: https://web.archive.org/web/20150307054112/http://www.pbs.org/greatwar/resources/casdeath_pop.html.

Pengelly, Martin. (2022). "Trump Ordered Records Moved After Subpoena, Mar-a-Lago Staffer Said—Reports." *The Guardian*, October 13. Available at: https://www.theguardian.com/us-news/2022/oct/12/donald-trump-mar-a-lago-documents.

Perez, Evan; Orr, Gabby; and Brown, Pamela. (2022). "Feds Removed Documents from Mar-a-Lago in June with Grand Jury Subpoena." CNN, August 11. Available at: https://www.abc57.com/news/feds-seized-documents-from-mar-a-lago-in-june-with-grand-jury-subpoena.

Perry, Samuel; Whitehead, Andrew; and. Grubbs, Joshua B. (2020). "Culture Wars and COVID-19 Conduct: Christian Nationalism, Religiosity, and Americans' Behavior During the Coronavirus Pandemic." *Journal for the Scientific Study of Religion*, July 26. Available at: https://onlinelibrary.wiley.com/doi/full/10.1111/jssr.12677.

Pettigrew, Thomas. (2017). "Social Psychological Perspectives on Trump Supporters." *Journal of Social and Political Psychology*, 5(1): 107–16. Available at: https://doi.org/10.5964/spp.15:1.750.

Pineda, Khrysgiana. (2020). "The Boogaloo Movement Is Gaining Momentum. Who Are the Boogaloo Bois and What Do They Want?" *USA Today*, June 19. Available at: https://www.usatoday.com/story/news/nation/2020/06/19/what-is-boogaloo-movement/3204899001/.

Politico Staff. (2021). "30 Things Donald Trump Did as President You Might Have Missed." *Politico*, January 18. Available at: https://www.politico.com/news/magazine/2021/01/18/trump-presidency-administration-biggest-impact-policy-analysis-451479.

Polychroniou, C. J. (2017). "The Difference Between Fascism and Trumpism." CommonDreams, July 10. Available at: https://www.commondreams.org/views/2021/07/10/differences-between-fascism-and-trumpism.

Posner, Sarah. (2021). "How the Christian Right Embraced Voter Suppression." *Vox*, September 28. Available at: https://www.vox.com/22696286/evangelicals-texas-georgia-voting-law-trump.

Pottratz, Robert. (2021). "Donald Trump and Gaslighting." *SC Times*, January 15. Available at: https://www.sctimes.com/story/opinion/2021/01/15/donald-trump-and-gaslighting/4167553001/.

Pressman, Sarah. (2020). "COVID-19 Blew Up the Epidemic of Loneliness." *Psychology Today*, September 2.

Public Religion Research Institute. (2020). "The American Religious Landscape in 2020." Available at: https://www.prri.org/research/2020-census-of-american-religion/.

Putnam, Robert. (2001). *Bowling Alone: The Collapse and Revival of American Community*. New York: Simon & Schuster.

Quince, Annabelle, and Phillips, Keri. (2016). "The Grand Old Party." ABC.net, July 10. Available at: https://www.abc.net.au/radionational/programs/rearvision/grand-old-party/7550832.

Reuters. (2021). "Congress Demands Facebook, YouTube and Others Turn Over January 6-Related Documents." *Reuters*, August 27. Available at: https://www.reuters.com/world/us/us-house-committee-seeks-social-media-records-related-capitol-attack-2021-08-27/.

Reyes, Lorenzo, and Stanglin, Doug. (2017). "What Is Antifa and What Does the Movement Want?" *USA Today*, August 23. Available at: https://www.usatoday.com/story/news/2017/08/23/what-antifa-and-what-does-movement-want/593867001/.

Rhodes, Ben. (2020). "The Path to Autocracy." *The Atlantic*, June 15. Available at: https://www.theatlantic.com/ideas/archive/2020/06/american-orbanism/612658/.

Rhodes, Ron. (2001). *The Challenge of Cults and New Religions: The Essential Guide to Their History, Their Doctrine, and Our Response*. New York: Zondervan.

Riccardi, Nicholas. (2020). "Here's the Reality Behind Trump's Claims About Mail Voting." Associated Press, September 30. Available at: https://apnews.com/article/virus-outbreak-joe-biden-election-2020-donald-trump-elections-3e8170c3348ce3719d4bc7182146b582.

Richardson, Heather Cox. (2014). *To Make Men Free: A History of the Republican Party.* New York: Basic Books.

Riguer, Leah Wright. (2016). *The Loneliness of the Black Republican: Pragmatic Politics and the Pursuit of Power*. Princeton, NJ: Princeton University Press.

Rose, Joel. (2020). "Even if It's Bonkers, Poll Finds Many Believe QAnon and Other Conspiracy Theories." NPR, December 30. Available at: https://www.npr.org/2020/12/30/951095644/even-if-its-bonkers-poll-finds-many-believe-qanon-and-other-conspiracy-theories.

Rose, Joel. (2021). "Dangerous and More Widespread: Conspiracy Theories Spread Faster Than Ever." NPR, March 2. Available at: https://www.npr.org/2021/03/02/971289977/through-the-looking-glass-conspiracy-theories-spread-faster-and-wider-than-ever.

Rose, Matthew. (2017). "The History of the Republican Party." OurPolitics.net, October 24, Available at: http://ourpolitics.net/history-of-the-republican-party/.

Rosenfeld, Gavriel D. (2019). "An American Fuhrer? Nazi Analogies and the Struggle to Explain Donald Trump." *Cambridge Core*, December 4. Available at: https://www.cambridge.org/core/journals/central-european-history/article/an-american-fuhrer-nazi-analogies-and-the-struggle-to-explain-donald-trump/25CBE639F23D2D80870EA4D3F1E6D566.

Ross, Rick Alan. (2014). *Cults Inside and Out*. North Charleston, SC: CreateSpace Independent Publishing Platform.

Rothschild, Michael. (2021). *The Storm Is Upon Us: How QAnon Became a Movement, Cult, and Conspiracy Theory of Everything*. New York: Melville House.

Rubin, Olivia, and Mallin, Alexander. (2021). "Because President Trump Said So: Over a Dozen Capitol Rioters Say They Were Following Trump's Guidance." ABC News, February 9. Available at: https://abcnews.go.com/US/president-trump-dozen-capitol-rioters-trumps-guidance/story?id=75757601.

Rucker, Phillip, and Leonnig, Carol. (2022). *I Alone Can Fix It: Donald J. Trump's Catastrophic Final Year.* New York: Penguin Press.

Rybicki, Elizabeth, and Whitaker, L. Paige. (2020). "Counting Electoral Votes: An Overview of Procedures at the Joint Session, Including Objections by Members of Congress." Congressional Research Service. Available at: https://sgp.fas.org/crs/misc/RL32717.pdf.

Sada, Elena. (2021). "Is Trump Leading a Cult?" *CT Mirror*, January 19. Available at: https://ctmirror.org/category/ct-viewpoints/is-trump-leading-a-cult/.

Saldana, Grace. (2021). "Explained: The Ideology of Trumpism." Freedomwire.com, March 2. Available at: https://freedomwire.com/ideology-of-trumpism/.

Sandel, Michael J. (2018). "Populism, Trump, and the Future of Democracy." openDemocracy, May 9. Available at: https://www.opendemocracy.net/en/populism-trump-and-future-of-democracy/.

Sanger, David E. (2021). "Biden Bars Trump from Receiving Intelligence Briefings, Citing 'Erratic Behavior.'" *New York Times*, February 6. Available at: https://www.nytimes.com/2021/02/05/us/politics/biden-trump-intelligence-briefings.html.

Sasse, Ben. (2018). *Them: Why We Hate Each Other and How to Heal.* New York: St. Martin's Press.

Sawchuck, Stephen. (2021). "What Is Critical Race Theory and Why Is It Under Attack?" *Education Week*, May 18. Available at: https://www.edweek.org/leadership/what-is-critical-race-theory-and-why-is-it-under-attack/2021/05.

Schmidt, Michael S., and Broadwater, Luke. (2021). "Officers' Injuries, Including Concussions, Show Scope of Violence at Capitol Riot." *New York Times*, July 11. Available at: https://www.nytimes.com/2021/02/11/us/politics/capitol-riot-police-officer-injuries.html.

Schulson, Michael. (2021). "Can Cult Studies Offer Help With QAnon? The Science Is Thin." *Undark*, February 24. Available at: https://www.undark.org/2021/02/24/can-cult-studies-qanon.

Scott, Eugene. (2021). "Data About the Capitol Rioters Serves Another Blow to the White, Working-Class Trump Supporter Narrative." *Washington Post*, April 12. Available at: https://www.washingtonpost.com/politics/2021/04/12/data

-about-capitol-rioters-serves-another-blow-white-working-class-trump-supporter
-narrative/.

Serwer, Adam. (2018). "White Nationalism's Deep American Roots." *The Atlantic*,
April. Available at https://www.theatlantic.com/magazine/archive/2019/04/adam
-serwer-madison-grant-white-nationalism/583258.

Shear, Michael D., and Saul, Stephanie. (2021). "Trump, in Taped Call, Pressured
Georgia Official to 'Find' Votes to Overturn Election." *New York Times*, January 3.
Available at: https://www.nytimes.com/2021/01/03/us/politics/trump-raffensperger
-call-georgia.html.

Shelton, Shania. (2022). "Photos Show Handwritten Notes That Trump Apparently
Ripped Up and Attempted to Flush Down the Toilet." CNN, August 8. Available at:
https://www.cnn.com/2022/08/08/politics/trump-white-house-notes-toilet-photos
-cnntv.

Sherman, Mark, and Tucker, Eric. (2022). "Justice Department Asks Court to Deny
Donald Trump Plea over FBI Search." PBS, October 11. Available at: https://www
.pbs.org/newshour/politics/justice-department-asks-court-to-deny-donald-trump
-plea-over-fbi-search.

Sherman, Rhona. (2022). "What Does Woke Mean? Definition of Woke Culture
in 2021—and What Critics Mean by 'Woke Police.'" National World, January
31. Available at: https://www.nationalworld.com/whats-on/arts-and-entertainment/
what-does-woke-mean-definition-of-woke-culture-in-2021-and-what-critics-mean
-by-woke-police-3215758.

Shirer, William, L. (2010). *The Rise and Fall of the Third Reich: A History of Nazi
Germany.* New York: Blackstone.

Shivaram, Deepa, and Lucas, Ryan. (2022). "Trump Says FBI Agents Searched His
Mar-a-Lago Home in Florida." NPR, August 9. Available at: https://www.npr.org
/2022/08/08/1116427430/trump-says-fbi-agents-raided-his-mar-a-lago-home-in
-florida.

Singer, Margaret Thaler. (2003). *Cults in Our Midst: The Continuing Fight Against
the Hidden Menace*. San Francisco, CA: Jossey-Bass.

Smith, David Norman, and Hanley, Eric. (2018). "The Anger Games: Who Voted for
Donald Trump in the 2016 Election and Why." *Critical Sociology*, 44(2): 195–212.
Available at: https://doi.org/10.1177/089692051774065.

Smith, David. (2022). "Trump's 'Cult-Like Control' of Republican Party Grows
Stronger Since Insurrection." *The Guardian*, January 5. Available at: https://www
.theguardian.com/us-news/2022/jan/05/donald-trump-republican-party-capitol
-attack-insurrection.

Snyder, Timothy. (2017). *On Tyranny*. New York: Crown.

Southern Poverty Law Center. (2019). "White Nationalist." Available at: https://www
.splcenter.org/fighting-hate/extremist-files/ideology/white-nationalist.

Southern Poverty Law Center. (n.d.). "Alt-Right." Available at: https://www.splcenter
.org/fighting-hate/extremist-files/ideology/alt-right.

Southern Poverty Law Center. (n.d.). "Proud Boys." Available at: https://www
.splcenter.org/fighting-hate/extremist-files/group/proud-boys.

Spielvogel, Jackson J., and Redles, David. (2009). *Hitler and Nazi Germany* (sixth edition). New York: Pearson.

Srikantiah, Jayashri, and Sinnar, Shirin. (2019). "White Nationalism as Immigration Policy." *Stanford Law Review*, 71 (March): n.p. Available at: https://www.stanfordlawreview.org/online/white-nationalism-as-immigration-policy.

Stanley, Jason. (2020). *How Fascism Works*. New York: Random House.

Starkey, Brandon. (2017). "Why Do So Many White People Deny the Existence of White Privilege?" *The Undefeated*, March 1. Available at: https://theundefeated.com/features/why-do-so-many-white-people-deny-the-existence-of-white-privilege/.

Stein, Alexandra. (2016). *Terror, Love, and Brainwashing: Attachment in Cults and Totalitarian Systems*. New York: Routledge.

Stein, Chris. (2022). "Trump Admitted Letters to Kim Jong-un Were Secret, Audio Reveals." *The Guardian*, October 19. Available at: https://www.theguardian.com/us-news/2022/oct/19/trump-north-korea-kim-jong-un-letters-bob-woodward-audio.

Stewart, Emily. (2018). "Trump Again Says He's the Least Racist Person There Is." *Vox*, January 15. Available at https://www.vox.com/policy-and-politics/2018/1/15/16891996/trump-least-racist.

Stewart, Katherine. 2020. *The Power Worshippers: Inside the Dangerous Rise of Religious Nationalism*. London: Bloomsbury.

Stockman, Farah. (2020). "A Fact-Checked List of Trump Accomplishments." *New York Times*, September 11. Available at: https://www.nytimes.com/2020/09/11/opinion/fact-check-trump.html.

Stoltzfus, Nathan. (2016). *Hitler's Compromises: Coercion and Consensus in Nazi Germany*. New Haven, CT: Yale University Press.

Strachan, Hew. (2001). *The First World War*. Vol. 1, *To Arms*. New York: Oxford University Press.

Sumner, William G. (1940). *Folkways: A Study of the Sociological Importance of Usages, Manners, Customs, Mores and Morals*. Boston: Ginn & Company.

Sylvan, Robin. (2002). "Eyes of the World: The Grateful Dead and Deadheads." In Sylvan, Robin (ed.), *Traces of the Spirit: The Religious Dimensions of Popular Music*, pp. 83–116. New York: New York University Press.

Tan, Shelly; Shin, Youjin; and Rindler, Danielle. (2021). "How One of America's Ugliest Days Unraveled Inside and Outside the Capitol." *Washington Post*, January 9. Available at: https://www.washingtonpost.com/nation/interactive/2021/capitol-insurrection-visual-timeline/.

Taub, Amanda. (2016). "White Nationalism, Explained." *New York Times*, November 21. Available at https://www.nytimes.com/2016/11/22/world/americas/white-nationalism-explained.html.

Terry, Ruth. (2019). "The Christian Right and Left Share the Same Faith but Couldn't Be More Different." *Yes Magazine*, December 24. Available at: https://www.yesmagazine.org/social-justice/2019/12/24/political-christian-belief.

The Skimm. (2020). "The History of the GOP and How the Party Changed." February 23. Available at: https://www.theskimm.com/news/history-of-gop-4z2tVlvLHXAcnRIEDPzj9Y.

Thomas, Jake. (2022). "Judge Cannon's Ruling on Classified Documents Ripped by Legal Experts." *Newsweek*, September 29. Available at: https://www.newsweek .com/judge-cannons-ruling-classified-documents-claim-ripped-legal-experts -1747727.

Thomsen, Jacqueline. (2022). "Justice Department Asks Appeals Court to Allow Review of Classified Documents in Trump Problem." Reuters, September 17. Available at: https://www.reuters.com/legal/us-justice-department-appeals-court -ruling-seized-trump-documents-2022-09-17/.

Treene, Alayna; Solender, Andrew; and Cai, Sophia. (2022). "Jan. 6 Committee Opens a Pandora's Box of Retaliation." *Axios*, May 13. Available at: https://www .axios.com/2022/05/13/jan-6-committee-opens-a-pandoras-box-of-retaliation.

Tucker, Eric. (2022). "Veteran Judge Named Special Master in Trump Documents Search." Associated Press, September 16. Available at: https://apnews.com/article/ new-york-donald-trump-brooklyn-mar-a-lago-government-and-politics-4a6200ebc 4fe6418c25ca380a43a6338.

Turner-Cohen, Alex. (2021). "Capitol Riot Mob Wanted to Kill Mike Pence and Run Pelosi Over With a Car." News.com, January 11. Available at: https://www.news .com.au/world/north-america/us-politics/us-capitol-riot-mob-wanted-to-kill-mike -pence-run-pelosi-over-with-a-car/news-story/ab3277f484a9d04c162dc1c985aa4 edc.

Ullrich, Volker. (2016). *Hitler: Ascent:1939–1945.* New York: Knopf.

Valverde, Miriam. (2017). "Trump Claims He Got Rid of the Johnson Amendment. Is That True?" PolitiFact. July 18. Available at: https://www.politifact.com/factchecks /2017/jul/18/donald-trump/trump-claims-he-got-rid-johnson-amendment-true/.

Vogt, Adrienne. (2021). "McConnell: Trump Is Practically and Morally Responsible for Provoking Capitol Riot." CNN, February 13. Available at: https://edition.cnn .com/politics/live-news/trump-impeachment-trial-02-13-2021/index.html.

Wacker, Grant. (n.d.). "The Christian Right." National Humanities Center. Available at: http://nationalhumanitiescenter.org/tserve/twenty/tkeyinfo/chr_rght.htm.

Wade, Peter. (2021). "Dozens of Oregon Cops Have Paid Dues to the Oath Keepers Militia Group: Report." *Rolling Stone*, October 15. Available at: https:// www.rollingstone.com/politics/politics-news/oregon-cops-oath-keepers-members -1243194/.

Wagner, Meg; Mahtani, Melissa; Macaya, Melissa; and Roch, Veronica. (2021). "Donald Trump Acquitted in Second Impeachment Trial." CNN, February 13. Available at: https://edition.cnn.com/politics/live-news/trump-impeachment-trial -02-13-2021/index.html.

Walker, James. (2020). "What Donald Trump Accomplished as President." *Newsweek*, October 22. Available at: https://www.newsweek.com/what-donald -trump-accomplished-president-1541363.

Walsh, Deirdre. (2021). "4 Takeaways From the Emotional First Select Committee Hearing on the Capitol Attack." NPR, July 28. Available at: https://www.npr.org /2021/07/28/1021113538/4-takeaways-from-the-emotional-1st-select-committee -hearing-on-the-capitol-attac.

Walsh, Deirdre; Mohammad, Linah; Kenin, Justine; Campbell, Barbara; and Pfeiffer, Sacha. (2022). "Jan. 6 Committee Issues Subpoena on Trump and Wants Him to Testify Mid-November." NPR, October 21. Available at: https://www.npr.org/2022 /10/21/1130644852/jan-6-committee-issues-a-subpoena-on-trump-and-wants-him -to-testify-mid-november.

Walsh, Joan. (2022). "Kevin McCarthy Is a Terrible Liar." *The Nation*, April 22. Available at: https://www.thenation.com/article/politics/kevin-mccarthy-trump -impeachment/.

Wendling, Mike. (2020). "US Election 2020: Who Are the Proud Boys and Who Are Antifa?" BBC, September 30. Available at: https://www.bbc.com/news/election-us -2020-54352635.

Whitehead, Andrew; Perry, Samuel; and Baker, Joseph O. (2018). "Make America Christian Again: Christian Nationalism and Voting for Donald Trump in the 2016 Presidential Election." *Sociology of Religion* 79: 147–71.

Williams, Aimee, and Hopkins, Valerie. (2019). "Trump Praises Hungary's Orbán in White House Visit." *Financial Times*, May 13. Available at: https://www.ft.com/ content/06f69c6c-75a8-11e9-bbad-7c18c0ea0201.

Wise, Alana. (2021). "The Political Fight over Vaccine Mandates Deepens Despite Their Effectiveness." NPR, October 17. Available at: https://www.npr.org/2021/10 /17/1046598351/the-political-fight-over-vaccine-mandates-deepens-despite-their -effectiveness.

Wolf, Zachary B. (2022). "Analysis: The Case Against Trump is Starting to Come into Focus. Here's What We Know." CNN, August 31. Available at: https://www.cnn .com/2022/08/31/politics/doj-trump-mar-a-lago-what-matters/index.html.

Wolfe, Jan. (2022). "Trump Likely Committed Crime with Plan to Obstruct Congress, US Judge Rules." Reuters, March 28. Available at: https://www.yahoo.com/news/ trump-likely-committed-felony-obstructing-160842714.html.

Wolfson, Aaron. (2021). "Actor Profile: Proud Boys." The Armed Conflict Location and Event Data Project (ACLED), April 22. Available at: http://acleddata.com /2021/04/22/actor-profile-proud-boys/.

Woodruff Swan, Betsy; Cheney, Kyle; and Wu, Nicholas. (2022). "FBI Search Warrant Shows Trump Under Investigation for Potential Obstruction of Justice, Espionage Act Violations." *Politico*, August 12. Available at: https://www.politico .com/news/2022/08/12/search-warrant-shows-trump-under-investigation-for -potential-obstruction-of-justice-espionage-act-violations-00051507.

Woodward, Alan. 2020. "'A Phantom Plague': America's Bible Belt Played Down the Pandemic and Even Cashed In. Now Dozens of Pastors Are Dead." *The Independent*, April 24. Available at: https://www.independent.co.uk/news/world/ americas/bible-belt-us-coronavirus-pandemic-pastors-church-a9481226.html.

Yen, Hope; Swenson, Ali; and Seitz, Amanda. (2020). "AP Fact Check: Trump's Claims of Voter Rigging Are All Wrong." Associated Press, December 3. Available at: https://apnews.com/article/election-2020-ap-fact-check-joe-biden-donald -trump-technology-49a24edd6d10888dbad61689c24b05a5.

Yudkin, Daniel; Hawkins, Stephen; and Dixon, Tim. (2019). "The Perception Gap: How False Impressions Are Pulling Americans Apart." More in Common. Download of the report available at: https://perceptiongap.us/.

Zanotti, Emily. (2021). "House Dems Plot Own Investigation of Capitol Riot After Senate Votes Down January 6th Commission." *The Daily Wire*, May 30. Available at: https://www.dailywire.com/news/house-dems-plot-own-investigation-of-capitol-riot-after-senate-votes-down-january-6-commission.

Zeitz, Joshua. (2017). "The Real History of American Immigration." *Politico Magazine*, August 6. Available at: https://www.politico.com/magazine/story/2017/08/06/trump-history-of-american-immigration-215464.

Zengerle, Patricia. (2021). "US House Jan. 6 Committee Demands Trump White House Records." Reuters, August 26. Available at: https://www.reuters.com/world/us/us-house-committee-demands-records-over-jan-6-attack-us-capitol-2021-08-25/.

Index

Page numbers in italics refer to tables.

critical race theory (CRT), 36, 37;
anger and fear misdirected, 148–50;
bill proposed or passed related to,
149–50; CR and, 105–8; defined,
105–6; Noem on, 149; Stop WOKE
Act and, 148–49; tenets, 106–7;
Trump on, 149
Cruz, Ted, 15
cuckold conservatives, 79
cults: BITE model and, 54; conclusions,
71–72; defined, 51–52; double
standard and, 53–54; examples,
48–49; features of, 52–54; groups
that are not, 57–58; narcissism
and, 61–64; overview of, 51–54;
QAnon and, 64–67, 71–72; rationale
for joining, 59–61; secrecy and,
53; Trump as leader of, 61–64;
Trumpsters and, 48–50, 67–71; types
of, 54–58; violence and, 49–50. *See
also specific cults*
cultural arrogance, 116–17
culture: alt-right and, 78; white
supremacy and, 75–76; woke, 151–
53. *See also* social life

DACA. *See* Deferred Action for
Childhood Arrivals
*The Dangerous Case of Donald
Trump* (Lee), 61
Deadheads, 48–49
dead voters, 6
Dearie, Raymond, 163, 164
deep state, 65
Deferred Action for Childhood Arrivals
(DACA), 80–81
dehumanization, 35, 92
democracy, free elections critical to, 1–2
Democrat Party: civil rights era, 30;
Civil War era, 28; elite versus
working class and, 172–73; Great
Depression and, 29–30; Hidden
Tribes project and, 146–47;
inaccurate labeling and, 146;
Reconstruction era, 28–29; 20th

century turn and, 29. *See also*
German Social Democrat Party
Department of Homeland Security,
US (DHS), 4
Department of Justice, US (DOJ), 4;
Garland and, 167; Mar-a-Lago case
and, 160–64; Trump prosecution
considerations, 165–67
DeSantis, Ron, 148
DeVos, Betsy, 113
DHS. *See* Department of Homeland
Security, US
Dobson, James, 99, 100
DOJ. *See* Department of Justice, US
double highs authoritarians, 48
doxing, 89
Drexler, Anton, 123
drops, 65–66
Duda, Andrzej, 69

Eastern religion cults, 54–55
Eastman, John, 156, 167
education, 36; CR and, 105–8;
culturally relevant teaching and,
107; perception gap and, 147; Stop
WOKE Act and, 148–49. *See also*
critical race theory
election, 2016, popular vote, 42
election, 2020: intimidation of officials
following, 10–11; lawsuits filed
by Trump, 9–10; popular vote, 42;
trends shifting during, 5–6
election certification: majority
requirement for, 3; process of, 1–3;
Safe Harbor provision and, 2; tellers
and counting of votes, 2–3
election fraud: ballot dumping and,
5–6; conspiracy theories and, 46–47;
dead voters and, 6; evidence against,
11; founding fathers concerns over,
1–2; lies continue, 167–68; mail-in
ballots and, 7; Nevada and, 8–9;
poll watchers and, 5; significance
of, 21–23; summarized, 4; Supreme
Court and, 9, 10; Trump and, 3–9,

www.ingramcontent.com/pod-product-compliance
Lightning Source LLC
Chambersburg PA
CBHW031127270326
41929CB00011B/1536